SECOND SIGHT

*An Editor's Talks on
Writing, Revising, and Publishing
Books for Children and Young Adults*

Cheryl B. Klein

Asterisk Books
Brooklyn, New York

Book design by Whitney Lyle
Text type set in Adobe Jenson. Display type set in Nicolas Cochin.

10 9 8 7 6 5 4   15 16 17

In memory of my grandmother, Carol Jean Devers Sadler,
and my grandfather, Philip Anthony Sadler

TABLE OF CONTENTS

AN EXPLANATION
OF THIS BOOK

Some people are music nerds: They can identify every variation of "A-Tisket, A-Tasket" and the genesis of every song on the White Album. Some people are science nerds: They like nothing better than reading about the workings of the heart or the possible composition of dark matter. Some people are sports nerds, and they can spend hours and hours debating Ruth vs. Musial, Kobe vs. Michael, Billie Jean King vs. Venus Williams.

I am a narrative nerd. I love reading stories, taking them apart and seeing how they work, then putting them back together with each piece polished and gleaming. I love thinking about how a character grows through action and talking with a writer about how to sharpen or open up a plot. I love the process of line-editing, considering every word's contribution to the whole. And I am incredibly fortunate to have a job in which I get to do all those things every day, the better to make great books that children, teenagers, and discerning adults will love.

This book, *Second Sight*, is a collection of much of my thinking on these narrative and writing topics between 2003 and 2010, as expressed in talks delivered at writers' conferences and posts on my blog and website. The title refers to the service I try to provide my authors — a second, independent look at their work — and to what I hope this book might teach in turn: some methods or principles through which writers can get a "second sight" of their work, to help evaluate and revise their manuscripts and develop their craft as a whole.

The talks themselves are arranged in the order I wrote and delivered them, culminating in four interconnected lectures on point, character, plot, and voice, and the practical "Twenty-Five Revision Techniques," which draws from all the preceding material. Because the talks were written to be delivered orally, their texts sometimes come off a little choppy, as I made automatic transitions when speaking by ad-libbing or varying my tone of voice. Moreover, because each talk was delivered to a different group of people in a different far-flung section of the country, I borrowed liberally from myself in writing each new speech, and thus, for instance, examples from "The Art of Detection" show up again in "Quartet: Voice," and the endings of several talks are more or less identical. And while I think the core principles remain the same throughout, you can see my thoughts on all these subjects developing over time, so ideas in some later talks may repeat or modify ideas from earlier talks. I trust readers will forgive these foibles in print form.

The blog posts and manifests have been placed to try to complement the themes of the talks they precede or follow. I'm using the term "manifest" for the practical-application worksheets here because of the neat double meaning in the word: They will ideally help you create a physical manifest of your book — that is, a list or invoice of its plot or character cargo, so you can see the dimensions and weight of the choices that have been made. And then they should assist in making manifest places where you might forge new connections or round out those that already exist. I hope that these tools, and the other ideas throughout this book, will be of use or interest to you in your own writing. Questions, comments, and conversation are welcome via e-mail: asterisk.bks@gmail.com.

Thank you very much for your kind attention and support.

With best wishes,

Cheryl Klein
January 2011

MANIFESTO:
What Makes a Good Book?

December 10, 2005

Earlier this week, the child_lit listserv was discussing how we define good books, who gets to decide what makes a good book (especially a good children's book, considering the critics and the intended audience are often completely different), the qualities of a good book, etc. This was obviously too tempting for me to resist, so I wrote a message that articulated a lot of things I'd been thinking about vaguely for a while. There is more to say on it, but this is my beginning:

I'd like to say a word here, since I think about this problem daily in the manuscripts I consider for publication and the books I edit. I've mostly set aside my concerns about being an adult judging materials for children — I just start from this perspective, every day:

I think good fiction books (good art in general) create a deliberate emotion in the person experiencing it — "deliberate" meaning it's the emotion the author of the book set out to create, so well as that intention can be discerned by the reader. The emotion is achieved authentically through immersing us in the character's lived experience, not through cheap manipulation. This is most often accomplished through well-crafted prose: prose where every word has been considered carefully by the author and belongs in the work; prose that communicates clearly what the author wants us to see and know, so that we can see it too and (again) be immersed in the character's experience or the narrator's perspective. Think of *Lolita*, where against one's will one is seduced by Humbert's genius, his creativity, his fever for Dolores, so that one understands his passion intellectually and possibly even sympathizes with it emotionally.... It's a morally horrifying but artistically incredible feat.

And while every reader's interaction with a text is different, in great books, the emotion the author intends — what I think of as the emotional point — is experienced by the vast majority of the people who come in meaningful contact with the work. Otherwise the author isn't achieving what he or she set out to do.

In good children's books, the emotional point of the book will speak to or expand the child's own emotional experience — usually at least partly through their identification with the main character — and will be appropriate for a child. The Newbery winners usually excel at creating emotion, especially sad ones; I well remember my grief reading *Bridge to Terabithia*, *A Single Shard*, *Out of the Dust*, even *Because of Winn-Dixie*, and how transported and elevated I felt by that emotion. It's the classical (Aristotelian) model, where great sadness equals moral elevation equals great art.

But kids don't always WANT to experience great sadness — and who can blame them? And so they love *Captain Underpants* and *Goosebumps* and *Artemis Fowl* and *The Sisterhood of the Traveling Pants* and all those books that make them feel more pleasureable emotions, humor or warmth or excitement or "safe" (controllable) fear.

I think Harry Potter is such a tremendous success because it succeeds at creating emotion in readers almost instantly; its characters are all realistic (I know Rons and Harrys, I occasionally AM Hermione) in an unrealistic but fascinating setting; and it provides a wide range of emotions that echo the wide range of emotions in real life. . . . You grieve over the loss of a friend, but you also laugh at Fred and George, you crush on Ginny Weasley, you squabble with your best friend, you struggle with homework — and that range is much more realistic than being in a constant haze of misery (a la more than one Newbery I can think of).

On a wider scale, I think we can make critically-agreed-upon lists of Great Books because we all experience the same emotions in reading a certain book; we then agree that those emotions are good for other people to have, and we recommend said book. Things get interesting when we can't agree on the emotions that should be experienced, especially by children (cf. Newbery winners vs. *Goosebumps* above) or teenagers (cf. people who want to ban *The Catcher in the Rye*, no matter how beautifully it speaks to the teenage search for meaning). . . .

And the discussion goes on from there.

DEFINING GOOD WRITING
(POSSIBLY *SENTENTIOUS*)

September 17, 2009

Child_lit was having one of its periodic discussions about the definition of "good writing" this past week, so I wrote the bulk of the message below offering my perspective. Reposting it here, edited somewhat for blog form and further thoughts:

If you'll forgive some possible sententiousness on this question of judging good writing, there are five qualities I think about a lot when considering whether I want to acquire a manuscript:

1. Good prose. The sheen of the writing — its quality on a sentence-by-sentence level. Sometimes this beauty is lyricism, sometimes it's personality (especially with a first-person voice, though that introduces questions about the character-building as well as the prose), sometimes it's just plain cleanliness (no redundancies, lack of awkwardness — cleanliness is a great virtue). And also the movement of the writing, its sense of timing and pacing and flow in connecting those sentences together, turning them into paragraphs, and moving the narrative forward.

2. Character richness. Are they interesting people with some dimension to them? Do they show that depth and change as the book progresses? Do I care about them?

3. Plot construction. Do things happen? Why? How? Do the events make logical sense or do they grow out of coincidences and implausibilities? Are they surprising or utterly predictable? What's at stake?

4. Thematic depth. Is the writer interested in more than just telling a story — is s/he trying to make that story mean or say something

about being in the world (without hitting me over the head with it)? Is what he or she has to say original, or at the least a new take on an old thought?

5. Emotion. Can the writer catch me (and most readers) up in what the characters are feeling, particularly the viewpoint character? Or, if we're meant to have some distance from that character, get us readers feeling whatever emotion the writer intends us to feel? The emotion intended can vary widely, from sadness to terror to hilarity to peaceful quiet, depending on the story and characters; and it usually (but somehow not always) grows out of #1-4.

To be a literary success, a finished book has to be really strong in at least four of those categories, most importantly (to me) #2 and #5. It doesn't have to have equal strength in all of those; I read and reread Hilary McKay's Casson series more because I love the characters so much than because of their plot construction (although they ARE tremendously well-put-together in retrospect). Different readers will value #1-4 in different quantities depending on personal taste and at different times — sometimes I love a good plotty mystery and sometimes I like something with gorgeously lyrical writing. And having all five equals, I would say, masterpieces: the Harry Potter series and *The Golden Compass* and *Because of Winn-Dixie* and *Holes*.

But a book can work solely as an entertainment, a page-turner, as long as it has #5; and if that emotion is strong enough and exciting enough, the reader will keep reading even if they recognize and care about the lack of everything else. (Which, I have to say, lots of readers don't seem to.) This is especially true if that emotion is a temperature-raising one, like violence (*The Hunger Games*) or deception/betrayal (*The Da Vinci Code*) or sex (*Twilight*). *Not* that I think *The Hunger Games* is solely a page-turner or succeeds only at #5 — it's terrific at everything else as well. But that compulsion to keep reading grows out of the way the characters and the plot and even the very structure of the sentences are all built for speed and conflict. And at the other end of the scale, as I've said before, I think *Twilight* gets a D+ at best in #1-4, and yet it somehow gets an A for emotion, in the way it's able to grab even readers like me, who are rolling our eyes at the flatness of the prose, characters, and plot construction, and yet we just keep reading on.

However it happens, the stronger that successful emotional reaction, the more likely the reader is to think that book good; the stronger the word-of-mouth from the editor onward, and the more likely it is that that book will become a bestseller.

FINDING A PUBLISHER
AND FALLING IN LOVE:
A Convivial Comparison

———⟡———

*I gave this talk at the Iowa and Arizona SCBWI Fall Conferences in 2004, and
the Missouri Writers Guild spring conference in 2006. It's one of my favorite
things I've ever written because it combines so many of my favorite things to think
and talk about: books, writing, publishing, the psychology and processes of love
and relationships. . . . I had a wonderful time writing it, and I hope you like it too.*

I'm Cheryl Klein, an associate editor at Arthur A. Levine Books, an
imprint of Scholastic Inc. The title of my talk today is "Finding a
Publisher and Falling in Love: a Convivial Comparison." This grew
out of something I was thinking about a couple of years ago: Writers
can sometimes feel like they're battling against the publishers, that
publishing companies are this huge faceless mass out to reject everyone
but the Madonnas of the world.

But in fact we editors are just people, readers, like you, looking to
make connections just like you. And that led me to the comparison
I'm going to make today: The submissions process is like dating — an
intensely personal endeavor where everyone is looking for the right
match. Editors are looking to find books they love. Writers are looking
to find editors who can help their books be their best. There is a giant
pool of all of us out there. And when it doesn't work out, it can be the
most depressing thing in the world.

But while not everyone is right for each other, that doesn't mean there
will never be anyone who's right for you. And almost nothing is better
on both sides than making that connection and finding that match.

Thus I'm going to point out some of the ways these two processes
are alike, and I think, hope, it can be a useful way for you to think about

the business of writing and publishing. After all, how many of you have published books? (Not so many.) How many of you have been in love? (More.) So see, you've been through all this before!

So let's suppose you've just written a new manuscript, and it's time to step back and think about it not as a literary work, but as a book that's going out into the world. The dating analogy here — you know you're ready to find a new significant other. What kind of person are you? What kind of person do you want to meet? If you love books and classical music and Persian cats, you probably shouldn't try to meet someone in a sports bar.

It's the same way with your book. So you might ask yourself: Is your manuscript commercial? Literary? Somewhere in between? That is, if it were a book, would you expect to see it sold mostly in Wal-Mart or in Barnes & Noble? What are the manuscript's strengths? What audiences might it appeal to? What was your vision for the book, your goal in writing it? What response did you want to evoke in the reader? What did you hope to accomplish?

Once you've identified these things, you want to find a publisher — or more specifically, an editor — who reaches those audiences and wants their books to accomplish the same goals. That means you have to research publishers.

First you have to get the basic facts about whether they're right for your book. What size publisher do you want? Which editors there do the kind of manuscript you've written? In dating, this is like checking off the list: male, in my age bracket, financially independent, breathing. There are lots of ways to find out this information about publishers: the *Literary Market Place*, SCBWI, publishers' catalogs and websites.

Then the nuances: What kind of books does this editor like? Do their tastes and interests in writing — their style and personality as a publisher — coincide with yours? By far the best way of finding this out is to look at the books themselves. Editors tend to publish books they're passionate about in some way. So if you love a book too, chances are you might have a similar outlook to that editor.

A true story: A writer named Neil Connelly had just completed his first YA novel, *St. Michael's Scales*. He didn't know who he wanted to send it to, though, so he went to a bookstore, sat down in the YA section, and read the flap copy and first chapters of about twenty books. One of his favorites was *When She Was Good*, by Norma Fox Mazer — the very first book our imprint published. He sent us a query letter mentioning it, we asked to see the manuscript, and three years later, we published *St. Michael's Scales* as well.

Writers often ask how they can find out which editors edited what books. SCBWI provides a list of editors and books on its website, under Publications → SCBWI Publications → Members "Click here for a complete list of publications" → Edited by.

Incidentally, I encourage you all to read as many new children's/YA books as you can. It's good for you as a writer to read good books; it keeps you au courant with what's being published — you're seeing what's out there and not out there, and who publishes what kind of books. And if you can buy the books, that's even better, because when publishers make money from established authors, we can buy manuscripts from new ones.

So, once you've done your research, you should have a list of four to eight publishers to whom you'd like to send query letters, with perhaps one or two favorites. In most cases — pretty much in all cases with unpublished writers — you are the pursuer and the publisher is the pursued. So it's your job to introduce yourself and your book in a way that will be attractive to the pursued. In the dating world, this is known as a pick-up line. In publishing, it's called the query letter.

What sets a yes apart from a no, in dating and in publishing? This is what your query letter should show:

- Personality — I want to see that your ms. has something interesting to say, that we haven't heard five hundred times before, or that it's saying it in a fresh way.

- Expression — said well. Basically, the description of your plot should sound like jacket or catalog copy for your book.
- Interest in the other person — in your introduction or conclusion, it's very useful if you can point to reasons why the listener (the editor) is right for the speaker (the book).
- And — it has to be said — a nice, clean outward appearance, with no copyediting errors, and a self-addressed stamped envelope.

Do NOT emphasize numbers like word count. That's the equivalent of taking your date out and reciting your ACT and IQ scores: interesting, maybe, but only relevant if the rest of it works out.

It's often helpful if you can compare your book to another book the editor might know — especially one of the editor's books. It allows us to get a handle on it, and it shows you've done your research. Last year the first novel I co-edited came out, *Millicent Min, Girl Genius* by Lisa Yee — the very funny story of an eleven-year-old child prodigy who has trouble making friends. In January I received a query letter from someone who said she loved *Millicent*, and because we'd published it she knew someone at our imprint had a sense of humor, and she'd written a funny picture book, and would we take a look at it? You bet I would.

Now, queries don't have to be exclusive — you can send out more than one at a time. But you should try to tailor each one to the editor to whom you're sending it. There's nothing more off-putting than when I get a query letter addressed to another editor: It's sloppy on the writer's part, and it's not personal to me. If you send queries simultaneously, though, do note that in your letter. Just like in relationships, you need to be honest with everyone involved.

When I talk to writers, they are often very nervous about the apparent *rules* of queries. How many pages? Should it include a synopsis? Can I send it to more than one editor in a house? The truth is, there are no rules, in love or in publishing. There are certainly time-honored forms you can follow that you are probably wise to follow, because they've mostly been proven to be useful and right. But just like I'm not going to reject a really great guy because he has a little mustard on his shirt, I'm not going to throw out a fantastic query letter because it spills onto two pages. Don't worry about the rules. Worry about writing the best description of your book that you can.

I'm going to digress for a moment upon agents. Agents serve as matchmakers in this dating scenario: people who know a wide range of authors and a wide range of editors and do their best to bring the two together. And if they make a successful match, they often assist in the formal details of contracting the marriage—negotiating the contract, checking royalties, etc.

Lots of people ask — Do I need an agent? This is a personal decision, not a universal one. It depends on the amount of time and energy you have to invest in looking for an editorial match and (hopefully) managing the business details of your publishing. If you decide "yes," then you approach an agent in much the same way as you approach an editor.

So you write a query, you send it, and the agent or editor will respond with a yes or a no. If it's a no, it hurts a bit, but you've only invested a little time, so you get right back out there and try again. If it's a yes, congratulations! You are now dating. So you send in your manuscript and wait for a response.

While waiting for the phone to ring, use the time well. Especially: Write something else. This keeps you from obsessing over the submissions already out there, and you'll have something else to send if they ask to see more.

Here's a dirty secret: Editors and agents are often having at least twenty relationships at the same time. Books under contract, requested revisions, other manuscripts — we'd like to be exclusive, really, but we're cheating on you right and left. So I'm afraid sometimes we get behind on our responses. You deserve to be treated well, though — you wouldn't want to date someone who never calls you back. Many houses or agencies post their average response time with their submissions guidelines. If that amount of time has passed and you haven't heard a thing, write and check in.

Some writers tell us in their cover letters, "If you haven't responded by this date, I'm withdrawing the manuscript and taking it to someone else." In dating, this would be known as trying to make your significant other jealous, and just as in dating, that can work both ways. Some editors will try to get back to you sooner because they *are* jealous. And some editors think "Fine, take it somewhere else," and will not respond. So use this strategy carefully. The good thing about it is, if you don't get an answer by your date, you're absolutely free to move on.

So what's going on at my end of the relationship? That is, what do editors want?

This is something authors ask us all the time, and I'm afraid we editors usually come up with frustrating generalities. This is partly because we love a lot of things. I like picture books, fantasies, mysteries, historical fiction, realistic fiction, nonfiction . . . just about everything you can name, and I'm always looking for all of it.

And it's also partly because we editors don't want to close any doors. You never know what you might love: All you can do is look. Ursula Nordstrom, the legendary editor at Harper Children's Books, once said, "I never want to forget that if Lewis Carroll had asked me whether or not he should bother writing about a little girl named Alice who fell asleep and dreamed that she had a lot of adventures down a rabbit hole, it would not have sounded awfully tempting to any editor." Or to sound the dating theme again: If someone asked you before you met your significant other, "What kind of person are you looking for?", would you have described the exact person you're with now? For instance, if you asked me that question, I would not have said "A Chinese-American corporate lawyer from Queens who really likes Dungeons and Dragons," which pretty much describes my last boyfriend. And if you pitched that guy to me as a possible date, I might have been, "Ehhh, not so much." But if you said, "I know a really sweet, funny, smart guy who likes to read and is taller than you are" — well, we'd be in business!

And that just goes to show: While we editors often can't describe exactly what we're looking for, we can tell you about the qualities of the books we love — the things they all share. So when I read your manuscript, I am looking for three things.

• **The first is Truth, particularly emotional truth.** Real people, real situations, real emotions. "Real" meaning "It's believable that these characters would act and speak in these ways according to the setting and relationships within the novel." "Real" also means "recognizable" — even if it's not a situation I as a reader have ever been in personally, I recognize the feelings and actions as something that happens within the range of human experience.

I'm going to read you a brief excerpt from *The Slightly True Story of Cedar B. Hartley* by Martine Murray. Cedar is a twelve-year-old girl who's training to be an acrobat, and Kite is a boy who's training with her. Caramella is her best friend.

> When I got home from training with Kite at his house, Caramella wanted to hear everything. I know Caramella is my friend, because when we talk it makes me feel that what I saw and felt and said in any kind of situation means something.
>
> "Was Kite pleased that you wanted to keep training?"
>
> "I dunno. He didn't say. You know what he's like, he doesn't say how he feels."
>
> "Well, couldn't you tell?" (It becomes a girl's job to read

a boy's unexpressed feelings in other ways. Girls get good at looking for signs.)

"No. Maybe."

"Did you get that funny feeling?" (The funny feeling is when you like someone and your tummy goes all empty and pounding and words bury down blunt inside and suddenly erupt out your mouth all wrong, like a spew, so you go red in the face, because it matters a great deal that you make a good impression.)

"At first I did, but after a while I felt normal."

"So, you've got a crush on him, haven't you?"

"He put his hand on my shoulder," I said, faintly sidestepping the question, because I wanted to draw it out, make it last, like eating an ice cream slowly.

"You have got a crush. I can tell." She folded her arms triumphantly, as if she'd just won a game of Fish.

Now, I am not a twelve-year-old acrobat in Australia, but this sounds exactly like the conversations my girlfriends and I have about the guys we're interested in — we go into every little detail of our interaction with the guy, we have this code language for specific emotions, we know everyone's past romantic histories, the whole thing. Thus I can recognize and empathize with Cedar's emotions. My favorite line from that excerpt is probably "when we talk it makes me feel that what I saw and felt and said in any kind of situation means something," because that's the way my friends make me feel, and I was enthralled when I read that because Martine Murray put words to that feeling.

The excerpt also demonstrates the second thing I'm looking for:

• **Good writing.** It shows, not tells. Editors harp on the show-not-tell thing because as readers we want to have the same emotional experience as the characters, to see what they see and feel what they feel through the whole journey of the novel or picture book. I am extremely wary of the word "feel" in a manuscript, as in "Cheryl felt extremely wary." If you're having to tell me what your character is feeling, that makes me suspicious that I'm not feeling it too.

Something that sounds obvious, but actually comes up a lot: Good writing doesn't use generalizations, but rather very specific words and phrases to create a voice or evoke the effect the author intends. Look back at that description of the funny feeling: How would the passage be different if Martine had used the phrase "words can't come out" instead of "words bury down blunt inside"? Or "go out of your mouth" instead of "erupt out of your mouth"? Or if she'd left out the similes like "like a spew," or later, "like eating an ice cream slowly"? It's those specific choices Martine made that give Cedar such an interesting and lively voice.

Speaking of which . . . good writing also means the voice of the book is interesting and appropriate for the character, if it's first person, or for the situation and audience, if it's third person or nonfiction. From *Millicent Min, Girl Genius*:

> I have been accused of being anal retentive, an overachiever, and a compulsive perfectionist, like those are bad things. My disposition probably has a lot to do with the fact that I am technically a genius. Unfortunately, this label seems to precede me wherever I go. . . . As I emptied the contents of my locker into my briefcase earlier in the day, I had been optimistic that someone might ask me to sign their yearbook. In anticipation of this, I had drafted a truly original inscription — one that would showcase my sense of humor, something I have had little chance to share with my fellow students. I would start with *Quantum materiae materietur marmota monax si marmota monax materiam posit materiari?* Which, translated from Latin, means "How much wood would a woodchuck chuck if a woodchuck

could chuck wood?" And then, here's the really funny part, I'd close with *Vah! Denuone Latine loquebar? Me ineptum; Interdum modo elabitur.* In English, that's "Oh! Was I speaking Latin again? Silly me. Sometimes it just sort of slips out." I would then finish with a flourish, "Signed, Millicent L. Min."

Arthur met Lisa Yee at an SCBWI conference in Florida in 1997, and he and I worked with her for five years on this book before it was published. It was her first novel, with no agent attached, and we did a lot of work on the plot and pacing. But what stayed the same that whole time was this wonderful voice. Listen to Millicent's vocabulary and diction: big words; long, complex sentences; formal tone. Millicent the character isn't being pretentious; she genuinely thinks that Latin inscription is funny. You get her whole character from those two paragraphs, and even though Millicent tells us she's a genius, the way she tells us actually shows us it's true. And the book won the 2003 Sid Fleischman Award for Humor from the SCBWI.

The third thing I'm looking for: **What is new, or feels new. The thing I haven't seen before.** *The Hickory Chair* by Lisa Rowe Fraustino, illustrated by Benny Andrews, is the story of a young boy whose grandmother dies, and he inherits her beloved hickory chair — the kind of story you've heard before. But the boy is blind, so the story is told entirely through details only a blind person could perceive — sounds, smells, the feel of surfaces; even the illustrations themselves are textured. And rather than just passing on the chair in her will or something boring like that, the grandmother hides little notes in the objects she wants each family member to inherit, so her legacies become a treasure hunt.

The blindness and the treasure hunt are what I call *hooks* — things that set this book apart from every other grandmother-dies story on the market. The hooks make it fresh, and the truth of the love between the boy and his grandmother makes it real. I usually write flap copy by making a list of all the hooks in the book, then weaving those into a readable and interesting whole. This is a good strategy for query letters too.

A digression on art for a moment: We look for artists whose work looks like nobody else's. There are a lot of artists who seem to be working "in the style of" Mary GrandPré or "in the style of" Tiphanie Beeke, but we love artists who, when you look at their work, you think "That's Benny Andrews, because nobody else has that style and artistic personality." Artists can submit their work to editors the same way writers do.

If a manuscript works for me, it is actually very much like falling in love, where I just want to spend all my time with this book and ignore all my responsibilities and everything else going on in my life because I'm so enthralled by it. Last year I had a mad passionate affair with an adult novel called *The Time Traveler's Wife* by Audrey Niffenegger — I read it on my lunch breaks, I rushed home from work to be with it, and once we stayed in bed together *all weekend*. I love finding books like that.

So suppose I have your manuscript and we've been dating for a while — a few weeks or months. I've read your work. Now comes the crucial time — will we make a commitment? Of course there are a number of factors involved, but it all starts with whether I've had the experience I just described: Do I love this? If it's a yes, we'll go on and get married: That is, we'll sign a contract for the manuscript, edit it and publish it, and hopefully have lots of beautiful books together.

But when I'm looking at a manuscript, far more often than not, I don't love it. And then it is time to break up. You will likely hear one of two things at this point: "It's not you, it's me," or in editorspeak, "not right for our list at this time." This means the manuscript could be fine, but it may not be the editor's taste. Or it may be a bad time for the editor to publish that particular kind of book — she's just published another book with similar subject matter, for example. In this case, you just need to go on and find an editor it *is* right for. Do not ask the editor who's rejecting the book to recommend someone. The editor's job is only to know his or her own taste, not everyone else's. You would not ask your ex-boyfriend to recommend a friend you might date after you break up.

However, a rejection can also mean: "It's not working" — that in the editor's opinion, there's something wrong with the manuscript. Sometimes the editor will tell you why. Listen carefully to what he or she says. Does the editor seem to "get" your manuscript — that is, does s/he understand what you were trying to do in your story? If so, and if the criticism is useful in better accomplishing that, then you should follow it and revise the manuscript. If not, then you should still take a hard look at the manuscript, because obviously the editor wasn't understanding your book the way you expected your readers to understand it. How might this have happened? Did anyone in your writing group have the same reaction as the editor? That might mean it's not an isolated problem. What can you do to better shape the reader's approach to your book?

Often the editor will not tell you what isn't working, and then you can go crazy trying to figure it out. Just as in a real breakup, try not to obsess over it. Grieve a little, talk to your friends about it, eat chocolate, but then move on. There are other publishers in the sea.

And remember that both dating and getting published take time. It's not something you can expect to happen instantaneously, and if it does, if it's too easy, it's sometimes not a relationship that's good for the long term.

Speaking of time, if you're getting response letters, that means it's probably been at least a month since you focused on the manuscript . . . which equals a great opportunity to reread it with as critical an eye as you can and make any revisions you think necessary. Use that emotion you're feeling from the reject to make your manuscript stronger — the grief, the pain, the anger, whatever it is. Give that to your characters when something goes wrong for them, and see what happens.

There's a line in Emily Dickinson: "I like a look of agony / because I know it's true." Another way to put it is "Everyone's pain is real." Nobody fakes unhappiness. So when I see honest pain in a manuscript — or, in a relationship, when someone I love trusts me enough not to pretend everything is okay all the time, but tells me what they're feeling, and I do the same for them — then I know we're at the truth. And that's terrifying and hard, but it's also wonderful.

So you use your pain. You revise the manuscript. And then you send it out again, and keep the faith.

I've been talking here about the methods of getting published and getting married — the *how*. But after a breakup, particularly, it's a good time to step back and ask *why* — why we want to be published, why we want to fall in love. Of course there are many reasons, most of them excellent ones. (Though I have to say, if you're looking for financial security in love or in children's books, you need to rethink your strategy.)

But there's also a dangerous trap that you have to watch out for. I think many people seek to get published for recognition and affirmation: Out of all the people or manuscripts in the whole world, someone has chosen *me*, my thoughts, my self. And that provides affirmation that I am good, whole, and worthy.

If I may be permitted a brief social digression, I think this can also be why people (particularly women my age) can be so desperate to get married, and why so many marriages end in divorce. The entire meaning of one's life is focused upon getting that recognition, not the actual rewards of the relationship: the pleasures of getting to know someone and being known the same way; the companionship, the small things, building a life together.

And it can be the same way with publishing. Writers can sometimes focus so much on getting published, on those rules I mentioned earlier, "what the market wants," or what the latest "trends" are that they get distracted from the truly important thing.

And that is the writing. Telling your truth. Telling yourself the story you've always wanted to hear, the story you've never read anywhere else, the one that scares you with the pleasure of writing it. Being as honest as you can — creating a reality, the artist's highest aim — except you have the pleasure of a reality you create from the ground up.

Treasure the joy of the work, because it is hard work, but when you can find that just-right word, that perfect plot twist: There are very few greater pleasures.

Now, that does not mean what you write will be *good*.

That does not mean what you write will be published.

But you will have the story you always wanted. You will have preserved a little bit of yourself forever in the world. You will have a true thing. And then you look for people who respond to that truth: the truth of what you've written in publishing; the truth of who you are in love.

E. B. White, the author of *Charlotte's Web*, once wrote, "All I hope to say in books, all that I ever hope to say, is that I love the world."

And I think that's truly what it's all about: the way writing, or love, or a good book can open you to know and experience and indeed love more of the world. I'm in this business to bring books that offer that opening to readers. You're in this business to create them. And if we're right for each other, I hope we have the chance to do that together.

Thank you.

THE ANNOTATED
QUERY LETTER FROM HELL

During the first year I was an editorial assistant, my friend Katy had to listen to me complain a *lot* about some of the painful query letters we received at work. She took all of my comments and wrote a letter from the immortal "Missy Snodgrass," which still makes me twitch every time I read it. Most of these mistakes are very, very basic — the SCBWI, any book on publishing, or common sense should teach you not to make them. But for your reading pleasure, here's the annotated Query Letter from Hell:

> Sheryl Cline (1)
> Wendy Lamb Books (2)
> 557 Broadway
> New York, NY 10012
>
> Dear Sheryl (3),
> Thanx (4) for talking with me on the phone. When Art (5) said at that conference (6) that he would love to publish my book (7), I was very pleased (8). He said "Wizard Magick High" (9) would be great for you and earn lots of money (10). It's sort of like that book, "Harry Potter", written by a woman from England. Have you heard of her? (11) I want you to know that I would very happy to make any changes to my book, if you find anything you want to change. (12) I also have lots of ideas for toys and games and posters and things, and have plans for a whole series — a "Sweet Valley High with Wands" sort of thing. I'm currently working on the screenplay. (13) I'm sending along my book as an e-mail

attachment (14), and I would be happy if you could get to it quickly. (15)

Thanx again,

Missy Snodgrass

P.S. Alot of other publishers are also reading it now (16), and if we could get the book published by my birthday next April, that would be magical. ;-) (17)

(1) She misspelled my name. This isn't terminally damning if the proposal is good, but it's evidence of extreme sloppiness — like showing up for a date in a mustard-stained shirt. Do your research.

(2) She misidentified my publishing house. This happens often when writers have just come back from a conference and decide to mail-bomb all the presenters with the same manuscript or query letter. Like (1), not terminally damning, but it is *deeply* annoying because it tells me you're mail-bombing and you haven't really thought through whether this manuscript is right for me.

(3) She calls me by my first name (again misspelled). I am not a stuffy person, really, and I have absolutely no objection to someone calling me "Cheryl" when we meet in person. But this is a professional letter — business correspondence — and in professional correspondence, you show someone the respect of calling them by their last name until you become better acquainted.

(4) "Thanks" spelled "Thanx." Again, this is business correspondence and not the place for cutesy colloquialisms.

(5) *No one* not related to Arthur calls him "Art." No one. So this writer obviously doesn't know him as well as she thinks she's showing me she knows him. And again with the overfamiliarity.

(6) "At that conference." Query letters aren't just professional letters — they're also friendly introductions of the writer and the work; or, if you've met an editor at a conference, a chance to reestablish the acquaintance in order to move it forward. Editors can attend several conferences

in a year, so it's thus very helpful if you can identify specifically where we met before or where you found my name.

(7) "He would love to publish my book" — again, this person thinks she's establishing her authority and familiarity with Arthur over me, the lowly editorial assistant. But as the lowly editorial assistant, I know Arthur would never say such a thing to a person he met for two minutes at a conference.

(8) "I was very pleased." What annoys me about this is that a query letter should not be about you and how you feel as an author about your work. Of course you would be pleased if you received an offer to publish your book, and of course you should be proud of your work. But as of this point in the letter, I have no reason to care about you or your manuscript, and you should be working on making me care, not wasting my time telling me the obvious.

(9) "Wizard Magick High" — oh lord. Another failure of research: If an editor already has a book on their list set, say, in a school for wizards, s/he will be extremely unlikely to take on another one with the same basic plot, *unless* the voice or point or magic or overall story is easily and demonstrably different from the first book (all the students in the school were dragons, for example, or they only practiced romantic magic, or it was written entirely in first-person plural voice because the story is really about the dangers of mass conformity, etc.). If you want to pitch your book to an editor who already has a book with the same basic plot, as here, then it's good to spend the time and space explaining how yours is different, with specific reference to the previous book if needs be.

(10) "and earn lots of money" — Of course we want our books to earn lots of money; that's how we keep our jobs, after all, and how the author earns a living. But this is not the way we at Arthur A. Levine Books talk about a manuscript, especially when we're first acquiring it; we talk about how much we love it and why we love it, and what in the manuscript makes us willing to read it at least five times in order to publish it (five times being the minimum number of times an editor will read

a book before it's published). So again I suspect this person hasn't met Arthur at all, because that's not the way he talks about our books; and then I'm annoyed because this person is valuing the money she's going to make off the book (not at all guaranteed, even for a "Wizard Magick High") over the joy and quality of the book itself, and those values don't match mine. The lesson to take away here is to talk about your book and what you value in it in the terms that the editor will or the editor thinks in, so much as you can discern them.

(11) "written by a woman from England" — an actual line from an actual query letter, I kid you not.

I would also like to pause here and identify all the things the writer has NOT done in the query letter thus far:

+ established the book's setting
+ provided a description of the plot
+ conveyed any sense of the characters and why I should care about them
+ demonstrated her writing ability (except to annoy me)
+ revealed how her book differs from the nine hundred and ninety-nine other fantasy novels on bookstore shelves at this moment, and more specifically,
+ told us how her book differs from the fantasies already on our list, though this isn't a surprise as
+ she hasn't shown any specific interest in or familiarity with our imprint at all.

(Apologies to my readers — I can hear myself getting a little cranky as I type the annotations here. This letter *really* annoys me.)

(12) "I would be very willing to make any changes" — Something so obvious it doesn't really need to be said, unless you're *not* willing to make changes, in which case I don't want to work with you. I am not an autocratic editor, and I will never force changes on a writer; but maybe

one manuscript in ten thousand arrives on my desk already absolutely perfect, and if you're not open to constructive feedback, I don't want to waste my time.

(13) tie-ins/series/screenplay — Again, all signs that the writer is thinking about money and the future more than the quality of this book, which is really the only thing she can control.

(14) an e-mail attachment — You should always send manuscripts according to the publisher's guidelines, which in our case specify hard copy.

(15) "I would be happy if you could get to it quickly" — Honey, I'd be happy about that too, but you have given me no reason to make you a high priority, so your odds are not good.

(16) "Alot of other publishers are reading it now" — Here she actually does a good thing and informs me that this is a simultaneous submission—an act I appreciate, because, if I *did* find this query really exciting, I could then move this manuscript up and make it a reading priority. In cases like this, where I'm not excited about the manuscript, knowing this is a simultaneous submission makes it easier for me to reject it, because I know (a) the author hasn't thought specifically of me for this project and (b) if I don't like it, there is still the chance that someone else might. Also, "a lot" is two words.

(17) "published by . . . next April" — I once received a manuscript (handwritten on paper torn from a yellow legal pad) from a grandfather who asked to have his book fully illustrated and published for his grandchild before Christmas. This was in October. It did not happen. (For the record, it takes a year from when we receive the final art for a picture book to be published and arrive in stores; and it's usually at least several months from the time we acquire a picture book manuscript to the time the illustrator starts work on it.)

So that is the Query Letter from Hell. If you have committed these errors, do not be embarrassed; just go forth and sin no more. And in the meantime, thanx for reading! :-)

AN ANNOTATED QUERY LETTER
THAT DOES IT RIGHT

In May of 2006, a writer named Olugbemisola Rhuday-Perkovich sent me a query letter for a novel then called *Long Time No Me*. After several reads and a noncontractual revision, I acquired the book in December of 2007; and two years and a month later, that novel was published as *Eighth Grade Superzero* — praised by *Publishers Weekly* as a "masterful debut" in a starred review.

Gbemi has kindly allowed me to reprint her original letter here and annotate it as a companion to the Annotated Query Letter from Hell; I think of this as the Annotated Query Letter That Does It Right. Much of what it Does Right is that it speaks so specifically to me and my tastes, as you'll see — my interest in writers of color and in racial, religious, and other moral questions — and clearly those tastes would not be applicable to all acquisitions editors. But if you can divine from an editor's books, blog posts, talks at conferences, or other material what his or her tastes are, then this might provide some sort of guide for shaping your description of your book to fit those tastes. And if you have no idea about an editor's tastes, this is still a useful example for its professionalism, efficiency, thoroughness, and overall grace.

May 31, 2006

(1) Cheryl Klein
Arthur A. Levine Books
557 Broadway
New York, NY 10012

(2) Dear Ms. Klein:

(3) We met at the Rutgers University Council on Children's Literature (RUCCL) One-on-One Plus Conference last October, and (4) I've since enjoyed your words on moral dilemmas and character values, as well as some of the books you've worked on. (5) I loved Lisa Yee's painfully funny *Millicent Min, Girl Genius*, and Saxton Freymann's *Food for Thought* has been a crafting inspiration as well as a teaching aid.

(6) In my middle-grade novel *Long Time No Me*, (7) Reginald "Pukey" McKnight created a superhero character in kindergarten; (8) now secretly dreams of being a real-life hero. (9) The Guy who's got game and gets the Girl. Instead, he threw up on the first day of school. In the middle of the cafeteria. In front of everyone. 8th grade has gone downhill ever since.

(10) Now Reggie can't even look The Girl in the eye, and his former best friend is bent on shredding his already tattered reputation. Sometimes he thinks it would be best to just exist between the lines and slide under the school's social radar. (11) That won't be easy when Reggie's current best friend is white, a fact that seems to matter more and more, and his oldest friend is bent on "speaking truth to power" to anyone and everyone. (12) Reggie wonders why things are so bad if God is so good; his faith at all levels is challenged by (13) his father's unemployment, his encounters with a homeless man, and his role as a "Big Buddy" to a younger version of himself. (14) When he finally decides to "be the change he wants to see" and run for school President, Reggie learns that sometimes winning big means living small.

(15) I've been published in national teen publications such as *Rap Masters*, *Word Up*, and *Right On*, and developed teen-oriented projects for clients including Queen Latifah, Girls, Inc., and Sunburst Communications. (16) I focused on my

writing for children in workshops with Madeleine L'Engle and Paula Danziger, and was a three-time mentee at the RUCCL One-on-One Plus Conference. The Echoing Green Foundation twice awarded me a public service fellowship for my work with adolescent girls. I received my M.A. from New York University in Educational Communication and Technology with a concentration in Adolescent Literacy, and my B.Sc. from Cornell University in Print Communication. (17) I am a member of the Society of Children's Book Writers and Illustrators (SCBWI).

(18) Would you like to see sample chapters of *Long Time No Me?* An SASE is enclosed. I can be contacted at [phone number redacted] and by email at [email address redacted]. Thank you for your time and consideration.

Sincerely,
Olugbemisola Rhuday-Perkovich

(1) & (2) In the spirit of contrasting this with the Query Letter from Hell, it's worth pointing out: She spells my name and gets my publishing house right, and refers to me as "Ms. Klein," as is proper in business correspondence. I would call her "Ms. Rhuday-Perkovich" in turn.

(3) She identifies where we met, at the One-on-One Conference seven months previously. Even if I don't remember an attendee specifically (which I often don't, I confess, given that I attend four to six conferences a year), a line like this is useful in establishing that this isn't a query out of the blue: The writer has heard me speak and knows something about me, my editorial values, and likely what I'm looking for, which increases the odds that this is a thoughtful query I will like, as opposed to a query-bomb directed to ten editors plucked at random from the *Children's Writer's and Illustrator's Market.*

(4) She mentions material posted on my website or blog. I always appreciate small compliments like these, particularly when they show that the writer values the same things I value — in this case, moral dilemmas and characters with depth. At the risk of sounding egotistical, though, I would caution writers not to place too much emphasis or spend too much time on these sorts of personal compliments to editors with blogs or websites or what have you: We judge a query on the description of the book and the strength of your writing, not how nice you are to us.

(5) She brings up two of the books I've edited, which again indicates that she knows something about me and what I like; and she adds comments that show she has read and really "got" the books, not just picked them out of my list of books I edited. I especially love her description of *Millicent Min* as "painfully funny," because that's exactly what that book is — a perfect little fugue of awkwardness and hilarity — and the fact that Ms. Rhuday-Perkovich (as I thought of her then) recognized and praised the pain in it, not just the funny, made me sit up and take notice of her own work.

(6) She identifies upfront what genre her novel is. This is extremely useful as queries for picture books have to be judged by a different standard than those for middle-grade novels, and ditto for middle-grade vs. YA, or all of them vs. nonfiction or poetry; and an early-in-the-letter identification of the genre helps me move my brain into the standards of that particular form.

(7) The name "Reginald McKnight" would have signaled to me that this was likely a novel about a young African-American man (as that first name and surname are most common in the African-American community), and this also would have been a point in the manuscript's favor, as I'd like to publish more books about and by people of color.

(8) Yes, there is a subject missing here after the semicolon, and I point this out only to say that I requested the manuscript anyway — that

the writer and character and book all sounded interesting enough to outweigh the "mustard on the shirt" (in Query Letter from Hell terms) of a minor grammatical error.

(9) "The Guy who's got game and gets the Girl. . . . In the middle of the cafeteria. In front of everyone." Coming out of this description, I sympathized with Reggie not just because of the grossness of the event — puking in the cafeteria in front of everyone! Ugh, poor guy — but because I got a glimpse of him in the language. Those little details of capitalization and rhythm hint at the manuscript's voice, and that it's a distinctive voice, not a voice I've seen in many other query letters and manuscripts.

(10) This, the major plot and theme paragraph of the query, says to me that this is a fairly domestic novel, concerned with local relationships among family and friends rather than any large-scale external plot to be confronted — which was and is fine with me; my favorite novelist in life is Jane Austen, after all. However, that also means that the characters have to be really well-drawn and well-rounded in order to make readers care as much about the stakes of the characters' everyday lives as they would about how to defeat the Evil Overlord, say. Here, I've already noted that the voice is distinctive, which is a good start, and the rest of this paragraph will bear out the characters' and relationships' complexity and depth.

(11) The fact that Reggie's best friend is White, and that this is remarked upon, confirms my earlier guess that this protagonist is a person of color, and the earlier points in the manuscript's favor. This next sentence also would have told me that the manuscript delved into racial and political issues, which I find fascinating — all the more so as they often aren't discussed in middle-grade novels for children; and thus this revealed that Ms. Rhuday-Perkovich wasn't afraid to tackle big and complex topics in the context of her characters' lives.

(12) I also love religious questions . . .

(13) ... and economic issues, so clearly this query is just pushing all my little readerly pleasure buttons. The reason I love racial, political, religious, and economic questions in books (among many other things, of course) is because we all, even kids, live in a world filled with such questions in real life; and if part of the greatness of art is its fidelity to life, great art, by its realness, must raise such questions. This query letter is saying to me that Reggie and his world and the people in it are all very real.

(14) A very humble, and therefore highly unusual, conclusion to draw; and unusualness + quality realism + ambitious questions + good writing = my interest is piqued.

(15) A biography paragraph in which every fact can be directly connected to (a) Gbemi's knowledge/experience in working with children or teenagers, (b) her experience in print communication (which translates as marketing and publicity), or (c) her experience in writing for children. If an author has experiences or expertise related to the subject of her novel — if the book deals with a young girl in the world of professional horse racing, say, and the author had been a jockey at Del Mar for two years — then she could also have added (d), her personal knowledge of the subject; that would have indicated that she was writing from a position of some authority, which is good to know for both editing and publicity purposes. In general with queries, any biographical fact that does not fit in categories (a)-(d) should be omitted.

(16) I was especially impressed by the reference to Madeleine L'Engle and Paula Danziger, both of whose fiction I love; and my knowledge of their books and styles told me that most likely *Eighth Grade Superzero* would have elements of religious inquiry (as the query already demonstrated) and humor, which I would appreciate.

(17) If a writer belongs to SCBWI, that tells me that he or she should be at least somewhat familiar with the submission and publication processes for children's books, which is very useful in setting

expectations on all sides. . . . I can rest assured that the writer won't be expecting a manuscript submitted in October to be published in book form by April, as in the Query Letter from Hell.

(18) Having made her excellent pitch, Ms. Rhuday-Perkovich exits gracefully, with a recap of the letter's implied question—*Would you like to see this?*—and all relevant information should my answer be yes—which it was! (These days I ask writers to submit two chapters and a synopsis of their novel along with their query letter; this letter was submitted before those guidelines were in place.)

For another great query-letter formula, see Nathaniel Bransford's blog post at http://blog.nathanbransford.com/2008/03/query-letter-mad-lib.html, and the other posts beneath "The Essentials" in his sidebar.

My thanks again to Gbemi for letting me share this letter, and I hope you all enjoy the book!

THE RULES OF ENGAGEMENT:
How to Get (and Keep!) A Reader
Involved in Your Novel

———◆◇◆———

I gave this talk at the Rocky Mountain SCBWI conference in the fall of 2005. The ending and many thoughts throughout are adapted from "Finding a Publisher and Falling in Love."

One of my favorite analogies for the submissions process is that it's like dating: Query letters are like pick-up lines; if an editor agrees to read your manuscript, you're going out; if the editor sends it back to you, it's like a break-up, and so on. That analogy was inspired by the fact that when I talk about a wonderful reading experience, I often talk about falling in love. You're intrigued by this person you've seen — that's the cover. You find out a little more about them — that's the flap copy. You spend some time with them — that's the first chapter. And then you're in love and this person is your *life*; you read the whole book, and it's a magical experience.

So: How do you make a reader fall in love with your book?

Well, as always with love, there are all kinds of theories here. And in lots of ways it isn't explainable: The magic just happens. But there are a few tried-and-true techniques, and we're going to look at how they work. Then we'll go through my Top Ten Turnoffs in Novel Submissions — or, "How to Disengage Your Reader in Ten Easy Steps." And after that, if we have time, we'll look at our case study: *Harry Potter and the Sorcerer's Stone.*

The first and most important technique for getting a reader hooked on your novel is its voice. The voice is the soul of the book. You know how you have that friend who will always find the silver lining in everything, or the friend who will always drag the conversation back to *his* problems? A narrative voice has that same type of personality in the type of jokes it might tell, the kind of details it will offer, what it talks about, what it doesn't say.

And the first Rule of Engagement is that the narrative voice is that of a person the reader is interested in. Note I'm not saying necessarily that it's a person the reader likes, or a morally admirable person. Have any of you read *Lolita*? Humbert Humbert is reprehensible, but he has possibly the most brilliant narrative voice ever, because he seduces us into reading about his pedophilia. What I'm saying is that the narrative voice should belong to someone the reader is intrigued by and enjoys listening to. Let's look at some notable first lines or first paragraphs here.

> *I have been accused of being anal retentive, an over-achiever, and a compulsive perfectionist, like those are bad things. My disposition probably has a lot to do with the fact that I am technically a genius. Unfortunately, this label seems to precede me wherever I go.*
>
> — *Millicent Min, Girl Genius* by Lisa Yee

Listen to Millicent's vocabulary and diction: big words; long, complex sentences; formal tone. Millicent the character isn't being pretentious; that is actually the way she thinks and speaks. You get her whole character from those three sentences, and even though Millicent *tells* us she's a genius, the *way* she tells us actually *shows* us it's true. I love this voice because it has that truth and because it makes me laugh — I want to keep reading.

> *Claudia knew that she could never pull off the old-fashioned kind of running away. That is, running away in the heat of anger with a knapsack on her back. She didn't like discomfort; even picnics were untidy and inconvenient: all those insects and the sun melting the icing on the cupcakes. Therefore, she decided that her leaving home would not be just*

running from somewhere but running to somewhere.
> — *From the Mixed-Up Files of Mrs. Basil E. Frankweiler*
> by E. L. Konigsburg

This is in third-person, but again note how well the details establish character: "all those insects, and the sun melting the icing on the cupcakes." You know from that that Claudia is a very fastidious girl, and that the novel is going to follow her point of view. I love the economy of that and I sympathize with her distaste for discomfort, so I want to keep reading.

This next one I'm throwing in just for fun:

> *You are about to begin reading Italo Calvino's new novel,* If on a winter's night a traveler. *Relax. Concentrate. Dispel every other thought. Let the world around you fade. Best to close the door; the TV is always on in the next room. Tell the others right away, "No, I don't want to watch TV!" Raise your voice — they won't hear you otherwise — "I'm reading! I don't want to be disturbed!" Maybe they haven't heard you, with all that racket; speak louder, yell: "I'm beginning to read Italo Calvino's new novel!" Or if you prefer, don't say anything; just hope they'll leave you alone.*
> — *If on a winter's night a traveler* by Italo Calvino

Are any of you familiar with this novel? It's a story of a Reader, the "you" here, who buys a book, starts to read it, and discovers he has only the first chapter. So he returns it to the bookstore, gets a replacement, discovers it's a completely different book from the first book he bought — but then there's only the first chapter in that one too. So it alternates second-person "you" chapters with the first chapters of ten different novels. It's a wonderful book if you love reading and thinking about reading.

The key quality these three voices share is Authority: a sense that the writer knows where he is going and what she is doing; the feeling that the reader is in good hands. Authority comes from:

Specificity of language: Look at how E. L. Konigsburg characterized picnics:"all those insects, and the sun melting the icing on the cupcakes." Suppose she just said "bugs and sticky food"— it wouldn't be nearly as effective.

Not wasting the reader's time: The voices tell you the information you need to know and move on; they don't include detail that isn't relevant at this point in the novel.

Recognizability: The reader believes in this voice because the things it says or the way in which it speaks chimes with real human experience. In the Calvino, those details about how to deal with the noisy TV in the next room felt spot-on to me.

And because of that, the thing these voices *do* is establish a believable, authoritative, interesting character and world.

So the voice is the foundation on which your whole novel is built — or again, the soul with which you fall in love. But we all know that love does not survive on soul alone. There has to be some sort of development, some action, some deepening of what begins with that connection. As we look at a few more first lines here, I hope you'll consider how the techniques they demonstrate are applicable to your novel as a whole — they're all qualities of good writing, not just great first lines. So:

> *When Mary Lennox was sent to Misselthwaite Manor to live with her uncle everybody said she was the most disagreeable-looking child ever seen. It was true, too. She had a little thin face and a little thin body, thin light hair and a sour expression.*
>
> — *The Secret Garden* by Frances Hodgson Burnett

This is what I think of as a description beginning, where the writer describes the main character or the setting as an introduction to the action. (If you're using a description beginning, be careful that the description is relevant and intriguing, and that it doesn't go on too long before it gets to some action.) In this beginning I love that "It was true, too" — the narrative voice insinuating itself in there to say, "Yup, she really is that awful. I am somebody you can trust because I'm giving you the straight and terrible truth about this girl." But what really captures me here is the fact that there *is* a straight and terrible truth — Mary Lennox is "disagreeable-looking" with a "sour expression." This book is called *The Secret Garden*, for goodness's sakes, it ought to be about bunnies and kittens and happiness and flowers. The fact that it doesn't start out like that, that Mary is actually a bad-tempered brat, is so different and refreshing that of course I want to read more.

The Rule of Engagement here: **Be surprising.** If you feel yourself writing something that's been written before — the plucky fantasy heroine battling the evil overlord, the kid grieving for her dead grand-mother — think of all the ways you can reverse that, and try something else instead. Maybe the heroine is shy. Maybe the overlord is her father (though that's *Star Wars*). Maybe the grandmother was really mean, but she left the child a huge amount of money that got her out of poverty, so the child's relief is mixed with guilt. Invert the clichés.

> *My name is India Opal Buloni, and last summer my daddy, the preacher, sent me to the store for a box of macaroni-and-cheese, some white rice, and two tomatoes and I came back with a dog.*
> — *Because of Winn-Dixie* by Kate DiCamillo

This is a situation beginning, where she just lays the opening situation right out for you, then backtracks to explain in detail how she got into this situation and what happened next. Note the specificity of it all: "My name is India Opal Buloni." What an intriguing name, and where would she get a name like that? I want to know. "My daddy, the preacher": Huh. I don't read a lot of novels with preachers as characters. That's different and surprising. "A box of macaroni-and-cheese, white rice, and two tomatoes": I love what this tells you about their lives: plain but good. But the thing I love the most about this line is the lack of a comma after "tomatoes." You just tumble right forward into "I came back with a dog," and how can you not read the rest of the book after that?

The Rule of Engagement here: **Be real.** Even if your novel is fantasy or historical fiction, or even if it's an animal story and the characters aren't human, the characters' behavior must be anchored in real human psychology and behavior. This sounds obvious, but those little recognizable gestures — like going to the store to get macaroni-and-cheese — establish the humanity of your characters. And if they do something that's contrary to the established reality — like, say, if India with her plainspoken voice and preacher father said she was going to the store to get foie gras and Evian — the reader would notice, and you better be able to explain the disjunction that creates pretty darn quickly and believably.

> It is a truth universally acknowledged, that a single man in possession of a good fortune must be in want of a wife.
> — *Pride and Prejudice* by Jane Austen (of course)

This is an insight beginning: It offers a truth that makes the reader laugh or nod in recognition, and boom, they're hooked.

The Rule of Engagement: **Tell emotional truths,** either right out like this or through the action. (This is sort of the emotional corollary to "be real" above.) I love it when a writer articulates an emotion for me, so I have the pleasure of seeing my experience put into words — it's one of the most comforting and connecting things in the world, because it means someone else has had that experience too (even if they're only fictional). Though of course sometimes the pleasure is having experiences you've never had before:

> *Lyra and her daemon moved through the darkening hall, taking care to keep to one side, out of sight of the kitchen.*
> — *The Golden Compass* by Philip Pullman

This is an action beginning, where from the very first line you're in the middle of what's going on. The action beginning is a little dangerous because the reader doesn't necessarily care about the characters or know what the world is like, so you have to establish these things quickly and well — which Philip Pullman indeed goes on to do in the chapter that follows.

The Rule of Engagement: **Take action.** Your main character must do things, either in response to the circumstances thrust upon him or to drive the action himself. That's why he deserves to be your main character. Are any of you familiar with *Artemis Fowl?* Even though Artemis behaves badly, stealing fairy gold, among other things, he's undeniably attractive because he goes after what he wants, even if it's illegal — and he's proud of it.

Coming back to the *Golden Compass* example: This demonstrates another Rule of Engagement: **Have mysteries.** Lyra and her daemon don't want to be seen — why? They're someplace grand enough that it has a whole hall — where? And most especially: What's a daemon? You can bet I'm going to read until I find out. (To be honest, these questions don't exactly count as mysteries within the larger book, since the reader learns the answer to all of them within the first chapter. But they *function* as mysteries right here, since they leave a space that makes the reader want to read more and fill it up.)

I want to think about mystery a little more, because it's probably the single most effective plot technique for hooking a reader: Have a secret, let the reader know there's a secret, and then *don't tell them what it is* until it absolutely serves your purpose to do so. It's a classic childhood strategy, the equivalent of dancing around your reader saying "neener-neener-neener." Or if we were indeed talking about falling in love, this would be playing hard to get. It could be a secret the narrator knows and is keeping from the reader, like Lemony Snicket did in his series of books. Or it could be a secret the characters have to find out — for instance, who is the murderer in a mystery novel. Mysteries in novels tend to fall into two categories:

> *One hundred and thirty-six days before*
> — *Looking for Alaska* by John Green

This is a plot mystery, as the question that instantly pops into our minds is "One hundred thirty-six days before *what?*" Every entry in the book has a section title like this, until you come to the big event, the what. Then the section titles change to "One day after," "Five days after," "Ninety days after," etc. (For the record, publishers and booksellers *love* gimmicks like this because they set a novel apart and make it easy to handsell. But they only work if they're necessary and organic to the story.)

A good plot mystery *develops* — it has clues that lead you to the answer. It has stakes that matter to the reader (most often, what will happen to the main character given the answer or the situation). And it has to pay off: The answer has to have a significance equal to the effort the reader has invested in it. Note that word "effort": Mysteries are a terrific tool because they make readers active participants in the novel — they make 'em work, because they have to figure out what's going on in this world and in the characters' heads. What are these people trying not to reveal? What's their real goal? You the writer should know all these things. And when you do and you deploy that knowlege well, readers love it. This basically explains the Harry Potter series.

The other kind of mystery is emotional mystery.

It is the first day of high school. I have seven new notebooks, a skirt I hate, and a stomachache. The school bus wheezes to my corner. The door opens and I step up. I am the first pickup of the day. The driver pulls away from the curb while I stand in the aisle. Where to sit? I've never been a backseat wastecase. If I sit in the middle, a stranger could sit next to me. If I sit in the front, it will make me look like a little kid, but I figure it's the best chance I have to make eye contact with one of my friends, if any of them have decided to talk to me yet.

— *Speak* by Laurie Halse Anderson

Our main character here, a girl (readers will surmise from the skirt), has a stomachache. Okay, it's the first day of school. But "if any of them have decided to talk to me yet" — why wouldn't her friends talk to her? Why is she in such a bad mood? That is the secret that drives the whole book. One of the many great things about this novel is that the emotional mystery is also the plot mystery — that is, the secret of why her friends hate her is deeply tied to the secret of why she's depressed; and her first step out of that depression is her admitting the secret to herself and the reader, which she can't do at the beginning. And it is devastating.

And that experience demonstrates a Rule of Engagement that's been proven again and again and again: **In the end, what will hook and keep a reader most is caring about the characters.** You have probably noticed that all of these examples demonstrate more than one Rule of Engagement — and that's because all of those other Rules serve this one: Through the reality of the characters' insights, their voices, the pleasure we take when they surprise us, we come to care for and identify with them; we fall in love with them, you could say. And because of that, everything else in the novel has meaning. The ultimate engagement is when readers care so much for the characters that they feel everything the characters feel in the action of the novel: their triumph, their love, their excitement, their pain.

So now we come to "How to Disengage Your Reader in Ten Easy

Steps." Here I'm going to use negative examples — things you should *not* do. I have made all of these examples up, but they demonstrate things I've seen happen in actual manuscripts. The first four, you'll see, are all things that knock me out of the main character's head and remind me I'm reading, not actually there in the action.

1. Switching brains; changing point of view. Sometimes the voice is established and believable, but then the writer keeps flipping out of that perspective:

> I dropped my backpack on the floor. Wow, it had been a tough day. As I entered the kitchen, I was so glad to be home that I even hugged Thomasina.
> "How was school today, honey?" said Mom, thinking about the Anderson file.

Problem: How does the speaker know that Mom is thinking about the Anderson file? In that one point we switch out of the narrator's head and into Mom's head, which is none of our business. It's jarring.

Fix: Ninety-eight percent of the time, these switches are unnecessary. Either stay with your narrator, or rework the scene so that the character's thought would be evident to an outside observer.

Better:

> I dropped my backpack on the floor. Wow, it had been a tough day. As I entered the kitchen, I was so glad to be home that I even hugged Thomasina.
> "How was school today, honey?" said Mom as she picked up a big folder labeled ANDERSON.

Another thing that keeps me from identifying with the characters is if I'm not experiencing their emotions for myself.

2. Telling emotion outright.

> After my dachshund, the Pipster, died, I felt so sad.

Well, *duh.*

Problem: This is the most common show-not-tell problem. I think it happens usually because writers are thinking so much about their characters and so much in their emotional states themselves that they offer just confirmation of the emotion for the reader, rather than building the feeling organically.

Fix: There are lots of possibilities for different revision directions here, depending upon the context and the needs of the story. Sometimes you just cut. Other times you can show the emotion through action.

Better:

> After the Pipster died, I curled up on my bed with my other dachshunds, the Squeakster, the Yapster, and Long John Silver, who licked the tears from my face with their tiny tongues.

This example is an improvement because it does show the emotion (the narrator's sadness) through action (the curling up on the bed, the tears). On the other hand, it also demonstrates *another* Rule of Disengagement, which is the writer's being so pleased with her own cleverness that she doesn't actually serve her point. I came up with the names the Pipster, the Squeakster, etc. for dachshunds and I liked them so much I was determined to use them — even though they actually distracted from the point I was trying to make about telling emotion. Don't do this.

3. Overactive dialogue tags

> "I'm going to be late for school," I whined. "Can't you pack my lunch more quickly?"
>
> "If you'd just gotten up on time, this wouldn't be a problem,"

Julianne snapped.

"Stop it, you two!" Mom ordered.

"Honey, have you seen my tie?" Dad bellowed from upstairs.

Rationale: Hey, all those different speech verbs show emotion, right? They also vary the use of "said."

Problem: Yes, but they push the emotion on the reader with almost physical force, and as "whining," "snapping," "ordering," and "bellowing" all imply strong emotions, the conversation is exhausting. Also, what each person is feeling is perfectly evident from what they say — you don't need the strong dialogue word to reinforce that.

Fix: Use dialogue tags only when justified by the extremity of the emotion. Otherwise, use "said" or other neutrally emotional tags, and let the content and the punctuation carry the emotion.

> "I'm going to be late for school," I said. "Can't you pack my lunch more quickly?"
>
> "If you'd just gotten up on time, this wouldn't be a problem," Julianne snapped.
>
> "Stop it, you two!" Mom said.
>
> "Honey, have you seen my tie?" Dad bellowed from upstairs.

4. Adverbial dialogue tags

> "Get in that submarine right now," Rosellen said bossily.

Problem: Again, you don't need the tag, because the emotion is perfectly evident from the statement.

Fix: Delete the adverb.

So these have all been cases where we're knocked out of the protagonist's head, but sometimes, frankly, we never get there at all.

5. Unbelievable first-person voices

> Suddenly my grandmother Barbara Wallace Finkelman appeared at the top of the stairs, wearing a mauve muumuu, neon-pink Jimmy Choo kitten heels, a white cashmere turban fastened with a gigantic marcasite brooch, and delicate frangipani perfume. As she tottered down the steps of her Cherry Creek mansion and swept me up in her fleshy, bangled arms, she cooed, "Well, aren't you the cutest little six-year-old boy I've ever seen!"

Problem: The authorial need to tell or describe or set up gets in the way of who this character is and how he or she would actually speak. I am never going to believe in a six-year-old who talks like this unless you show me the really extraordinary circumstances that make him so.

Fix: Rewrite from this character's perspective or switch into third person.

This example also demonstrates:

6. Too much information! The narrator tells us way more than we need to know, violating the "efficiency" principle we established earlier. Situations like this always make me think of one of my favorite quotes about writing:

> *The author makes a tacit deal with the reader. You hand them a backpack. You ask them to place certain things in it — to remember, to keep in mind — as they make their way up the hill. . . . If you hand them a yellow Volkswagen and they have to haul this to the top of the mountain — to the end of the story — and they find that this Volkswagen has nothing whatsoever to do with your story, you're going to have a very irritated reader on your hands.*
>
> — *Frank Conroy*

You always want to be sure that every piece of information in that backpack is important and relevant to the action at hand.

Problem: The writer is working too hard and not pacing the information properly or making it appropriate for the audience.

Fix: Cut!

Better:

> Suddenly Davey's grandmother appeared at the top of the stairs. She wore a mauve muumuu, neon-pink low-heeled shoes, and a white cashmere turban fastened with a gigantic black-and-silver brooch. As she tottered down the steps and swept Davey up in her fleshy arms, she cooed, "Well, aren't you the cutest little boy I've ever seen!"

As you can see, I not only put this in third person, which went some way to solving the unbelievable first-person voice problem by making this *not* a first-person voice; I also removed a lot of adjectives, particularly the proper-noun ones. Child readers would not know or care who Jimmy Choo is; the "six-year-old" and "Cherry Creek mansion" revealed things that the reader could probably figure out from context (Davey is young, the grandmother is rich); and "marcasite," like "kitten heels," is a signifier adults might recognize, but kids would likely have no clue about, so it's better just to give a physical description of the object they name.

Sometimes the voice and the information is fine, but heck, you just don't like the character. This leads to:

7. Whiny protagonists without charm or truth. Suppose this is the first line of a middle-grade novel.

> *My life is so boring*, Jenny thought as she stared out the window of her new room. *I hate it here. Why did we have to leave Cleveland to come to this little town in the middle of nowhere?*

So she's whiny and she's not doing anything. Do you want to spend time with this character? Neither do I. Note also that that example is more or less the standard beginning of any manuscript that involves a character moving to a new place in the first chapter: The protagonist contemplates how much he or she hates his/her life and parents right now. This is understandable but boring, and runs the risk of alienating your reader at the very beginning of the book.

Fix: Go deeper into the character or the situation to show something attractive, intriguing, or interesting about them or their situation, until the reader gets more firmly hooked in. Compare the beginning of *Speak* quoted on p. 42 to the above. Melinda can get away with being negative because her voice (what she finds awful) is so specific and strong and the beginning sets up mysteries, as we discussed earlier.

Under this same heading, you should also watch for:

8. Negative dialogue tags for positive characters.

> "I'm going to be late for school," I whined. "Can't you pack my lunch more quickly?"

Problem: I don't like whiners. Therefore I dislike this kid. And that dislike is a problem if she's going to be my protagonist.

Better 1:

> "I'm going to be late for school," I said. "Can't you pack my lunch more quickly?"

Better 2:

> "I'm going to be late for school," I said. "Can I help you with my lunch?"

The character is taking positive action, which gives us more reason to like her. (In this example she also sounds a little bit like a goody-two-shoes, which is off-putting, but you get the idea.)

And then sometimes you like the characters, you're in their heads — you just don't experience in their lives.

9. Narration vs. dramatization

This is narration:

> After Billy and Laurel talked a little bit about the basketball game and her plans for the next day, he kissed her. Laurel felt really happy. After that, they were boyfriend and girlfriend.

This is almost certainly a big moment in the book, a turning point in the characters' relationship, and we readers aren't seeing any of it, which we'd need to do to feel fully invested in the relationship and involved with their lives. So here's the dramatization:

> "That was a great last shot you made," Billy said as they entered the restaurant.
>
> Laurel felt as if everyone instantly turned to look at them — the ostrich and the kiwi bird, they must be thinking. She ducked her head. "Thanks."
>
> "I guess you have practice again tomorrow."
>
> "Yeah."
>
> "Will it be easier since you won?"
>
> "Maybe. I don't know."
>
> "Hey." He stopped and she looked at him inquisitively. "Here." And he leaned up on his toes and kissed her. "There. That's out of the way. Will you talk to me now, O Tall One?"
>
> She smiled down at him. "Yeah, Shorty. Let's have dinner."

For the record, after I wrote the narration here and knew I needed to dramatize it, I thought, "All right, he has to lean down for the kiss" — and then it occurred to me how much more interesting it would be if *she* leaned down to kiss *him*. And that actually created their whole characters for me, because a guy who would ask out a girl who's taller than he is probably possesses a lot of confidence and energy, but the girl might be a little more self-conscious about it.

10. Lack of subplot OR too many subplots. As charming as Billy and Laurel are, and as intrigued as I am by the possibilities of their romance — if the only story in this novel was about their romance, it would be boring and unrealistic. Real life is multistranded, even when you're a kid: You have parents, you have friends, you have a best friend, you have an enemy, you have the project you're working on, you have the crush you think is cute. Books that have action in only one of these relationships feel flat. Writers can also go to the other extreme and crowd the novel with so many characters and subplots that the reader feels bewildered and overloaded with information.

Fix: Think through all the relationships in the novel and what each one is doing for your main character — what each one teaches him, how they force him or her to change and grow. Do any of the functions the relationships serve duplicate each other — e.g., the main character's best friend teaches her to look beyond surfaces, and so does her art teacher? Maybe you don't need both of those characters.

Consider counterpoint. Is the character's relationship with his mother filled with conflict? Perhaps he needs a girlfriend who gives him peace and steadiness. If Billy ends up teaching Laurel to have more confidence in herself, then perhaps she needs to pass that lesson on to a kid she's tutoring, with whom she already has confidence.

And once you've figured all of these things out, you can add or cut characters, relationships, or plots as necessary. (. . . The editor who doesn't have to do the work writes breezily!)

So we've been through the Rules of Engagement and the Demons of Disengagement. Now we're going on to our case study: the first two chapters of *Harry Potter and the Sorcerer's Stone* by J. K. Rowling. (If you have never read the book, please go find a copy at this point and read the first two chapters. Besides the sheer pleasure of it, if you don't do that, the rest of this essay will not make very much sense.)

I've heard Harvard students and alumni talk about sometimes having to conceal where they went to school, poor babies. They know that as soon as they say they attended Harvard, their listeners will make certain judgments about their brains and financial status, so they call that moment when they have to say where they went to school "dropping the H-Bomb." I feel like that sometimes when people ask me what I work on, and I say "Harry Potter" — it's my personal H-Bomb (and oh, poor me whining about it!).

But the truth is, no matter how much madness there is about how many million copies sold, how many tickets the movies sell, how many midnight parties there are, a *theme park*, for goodness's sakes — this all happens because J. K. Rowling is so *good*. And these first two chapters are one of my favorite examples of that in all the books.

The first line: "Mr. and Mrs. Dursley of number four, Privet Drive, were proud to say that they were perfectly normal, thank you very much." This is a terrific first line for many of the reasons we identified earlier: It has specificity of language, with the "number four, Privet Drive"; a demonstration of strong voice/character with "thank you very much," which has the self-satisfied tone that the Dursleys themselves take; and finally, it even promises a mystery in "They were perfectly normal." If I've ever heard an invitation to have abnormal things happen, this is it.

The next paragraph is a description of the Dursleys. Mr. Dursley makes drills. Mrs. Dursley spies on her neighbors. They have a son named Dudley, "and in their opinion there was no finer boy anywhere." How do you feel about the Dursleys now?

The third paragraph: "They didn't think they could bear it if anyone found out about the Potters. . . . [Mrs. Dursley's] sister and her good-for-nothing husband were as unDursleyish as it was possible to be. . . .

This boy was another good reason for keeping the Potters away; they didn't want Dudley mixing with a child like that."

Now, how do you feel about the Potters? What do you know about them? Nothing, really. But you already loathe the Dursleys a little and so you're inclined to like the Potters — if you were having a barbecue, they're definitely the family to invite. This is the main characterization strategy Ms. Rowling uses throughout these first two chapters: The Dursleys are so, so awful that you feel sympathy for and an interest in Harry without him having to do a thing. I call this technique "reverse characterization": The enemy of any character the reader dislikes is automatically the reader's friend.

The fourth paragraph: "When Mr. and Mrs. Dursley woke up on the dull, grey Tuesday our story starts, there was nothing about the cloudy sky outside to suggest that strange and mysterious things would soon be happening all over the country." This introduces the main narrative strategy of pretty much the next six pages, alternating an account of Mr. Dursley's day with the "strange and mysterious things" like people in cloaks and lots of flying owls. These things sound really cool, and the Dursleys disapprove of them, so obviously they are to be encouraged.

This is one of the other ways the book gives pleasure: The reader feels superior to the Dursleys because they're so small-minded and unimaginative. Note that this happens entirely without J. K. Rowling saying "Look what small-minded people we have here." She just tells you about them, describes what they do and how they think, and lets their actions speak for themselves. *That* is good writing. And once we readers know the pattern of their behavior, we get pleasure from the Dursleys because they live up to our expectations. "Dudley had learned a new word ('Won't!')." That's exactly the kind of contrary, spoiled behavior I expect out of some kid named Dudley Dursley.

Finally, we can't forget the mystery element here. Who are these people in cloaks? What's with the cat on the wall? What does all this have to do with the Dursleys? The reader wants to read on and find out.

And on page 8, we do, when Dumbledore appears. Again, Ms. Rowling starts with a description:

> Nothing like this man had ever been seen on Privet Drive. [CK note: I like him already!] He was tall, thin, and very old, judging by the silver of his hair and beard, which were both long enough to tuck into his belt. He was wearing long robes, a purple cloak that swept the ground, and high-heeled, buckled boots. His blue eyes were light, bright, and sparkling behind half-moon spectacles, and his nose was very long and crooked, as though it had been broken at least twice. This man's name was Albus Dumbledore.

I will say, different writers have different theories about description. Some people feel it cramps the reader's imagination if you get too much description upfront — and this is one of the things the Harry Potter series has been criticized for, as those people say it hits the reader over the head with description or emotion, so you don't get to decide for yourself how you feel. But I think it's also possibly part of what makes the books work for so many readers, because everyone has the exact same experience unfolding before their eyes. In this case, I'm already intrigued by a man with a history of having his nose broken and a name like "Albus Dumbledore."

So moving on with the action: Dumbledore magically turns off all the streetlights. The cat becomes Professor McGonagall. They discuss owls, shooting stars, this whole magical world. Intrigued yet? We now have two communities opposed — the world of Number Four, Privet Drive versus the wizarding world. Which one do you want to be a part of?

And then — Lord Voldemort and Harry Potter. McGonagall says, "After all he's done . . . all the people he's killed . . . he couldn't kill a little boy? How in the name of heaven did Harry survive?" "We can only guess," said Dumbledore. "We may never know." And BOOM — THE BIG MYSTERY. If you read on through the rest of the series, you'll find out that this is one of the central questions through all seven books, and J. K. Rowling sets that up right here on page 12 of Book One.

After that, Hagrid shows up on a flying motorcycle. "Young Sirius Black lent it to me." Sirius Black, as many readers know, is the prisoner of Azkaban who shows up in Book Three. That's another reason people love these books: The small details matter.

Finally it comes time for the magical characters to say goodbye to Harry. "For a full minute the three of them stood and looked at the little bundle; Hagrid's shoulders shook, Professor McGonagall blinked furiously, and the twinkling light that usually shone from Dumbledore's eyes seemed to have gone out." Before we saw the negative characters loathing the Potters; now we see the positive characters feeling sorry for Harry. I think, at this point, you would have to have a heart of adamantine not to feel at least warm toward and interested in Harry and what might happen to him next. The chapter ends thus:

> Harry Potter rolled over inside his blankets without waking up. One small hand closed on the letter beside him and he slept on, not knowing he was special, not knowing he was famous, not knowing he would be woken in a few hours' time by Mrs. Dursley's scream . . . He couldn't know that at this very moment, people meeting in secret all over the country were holding up their glasses and saying in hushed voices: "To Harry Potter — the boy who lived!"

Note the emphasis upon Harry being special, famous, worthy of a toast. That says events will gather around this person; he has a destiny to fulfill.

Chapter two repeats a lot of these strategies, particularly the ones that build sympathy for Harry: The Dursleys are awful, he lives in a cupboard filled with spiders, he's small and scrawny and made to wear baggy clothes and broken glasses. But he hasn't been made bitter or cruel by the experience — he's an optimistic, kind boy. And we're told that strange, interesting things happen around him, so he's not merely the victim of his circumstances; he's making things happen, whether he knows it or not. I just want to look at one scene in detail here:

> Dudley stood with his nose pressed against the glass, staring at the glistening brown coils.
>
> "Make it move," he whined at his father. Uncle Vernon tapped on the glass, but the snake didn't budge.
>
> "Do it again," Dudley ordered. Uncle Vernon rapped the glass smartly with his knuckles, but the snake just snoozed on.
>
> "This is boring," Dudley moaned. He shuffled away.
>
> Harry moved in front of the tank and looked intently at the snake. He wouldn't have been surprised if it had died of boredom itself — no company except stupid people drumming their fingers on the glass trying to disturb it all day long. It was worse than having a cupboard as a bedroom, where the only visitor was Aunt Petunia hammering on the door to wake you up; at least he got to visit the rest of the house.

Harry goes on to have a conversation with the snake, where he empathizes further with it and finally sets it free. Instead of reverse characterization, this is simple positive characterization: He is kind to a snake, of all creatures, and puts himself inside of its head rather than being self-centered like Dudley and demanding things of it. He even explicitly compares its situation to his situation and decides the snake has it harder — all the more kind and unusual given how much the reader has been made to pity Harry! Then he lets it go, showing his good heart is inclined to action (however inadvertent). And of course, our final reason to like him is that he can talk to snakes, period, which is *trés* cool.

So if all this worked, then you should want to read on from here. And I hope you do.

I started out talking about falling in love with a book, and the pleasure that can give. And while I've laid out a lot of rules here, I truly believe that pleasure has to start with you the writer.

So here's Rule of Engagement #11. **When you're writing that first draft, don't worry about following the rules.** Instead, tell yourself the story you've always wanted to hear, the story you've never read anywhere else, the one that scares you with the pleasure of writing it. Treasure the joy of the work, because it is hard work, but when you can find that just-right word, that perfect plot twist — there are very few greater pleasures.

Now that does not mean what you write will be good — especially in the first draft. And that does not mean what you write will be published. But you will have the story you always wanted. You will have preserved a little bit of yourself forever in the world. You will have a true thing.

E. B. White, the author of *Charlotte's Web*, once wrote, "All I hope to say in books, all that I ever hope to say, is that I love the world." And that's truly what it's all about: the way writing, or love, or a good book can open you to know and experience and indeed love more of the world. I'm in this business to bring books that offer that opening to readers. You're in this business to create them. And I hope we have the chance to do that together.

Thank you.

MUDDLES, MORALS,
AND MAKING IT THROUGH;
or, Plots and Popularity

I gave this talk at the Eastern Pennsylvania SCBWI conference in the Pocono Mountains in April 2006. It was inspired by my fascination and frustration with "Be Yourself" books; a Zadie Smith lecture called "Love, Actually," available online at <u>http://www.guardian.co.uk/books/2003/nov/01/classics.zadiesmith</u>; and thinking about "electric-fence emotions" and turning points in my own life as well as the fiction I read. The section on plot was adapted from two plot talks available online at <u>http://www.cherylklein.com/talks.html</u> — "The Essentials of Plot" and "Aristotle, Austen, Plot and Pleasure."

I'm going to begin by telling you a story. In fact, you can think of it as the opening of a middle-grade novel. Once upon a time (or rather, in 1988), there were three girls named Alyssa, Nicole, and Cheryl, who lived in a small town in Missouri. Alyssa was the tallest and wisest, the one most likely to come up with a smart solution for any problem. Nicole was the prettiest and funniest, the one most likely to chat up the boys, and Cheryl was the most solitary and bookish, the one most likely to come up with obscure facts or information on any given subject.

All through third grade with Mrs. Schenck and fourth grade with Mrs. Walton, these girls were best friends. They swung on the monkey bars at recess. Alyssa and Cheryl held a joint birthday party. And when Cheryl wrote a story for the local young writers' festival, it was about three girls named Suzanne, Lynn, and Beth — the friends' middle names — who went on fantastic adventures together.

But in fifth grade, things changed. Cheryl was assigned to Mrs. Downs's class; Nicole and Alyssa to Mr. Cline's. And suddenly Nicole and Alyssa weren't interested in swinging on the monkey bars. They wanted to play foursquare and tetherball with the boys, or sit at the edge of the blacktop and talk to Stacey Smith and Jenny Proctor. When the girls got together outside of school, Alyssa and Nicole scorned the whole concept of "playing." They read magazines like *Teen* and *Seventeen*, and talked about who was cuter, Doug Ford or Jeff Adams. They found things laugh-out-loud funny that Cheryl could only smile at. They whispered together at lunch and didn't fill her in, till eventually she sat at a different table altogether. Once, Cheryl thought, they looked at her and laughed, and she immediately worried: Was it her glasses? Her shirt? Her jeans? Something she said? And thus it went for all of Cheryl's fifth-grade year.

So that's our opening situation — and I admit, it is a true story. But let's pretend it's a middle-grade novel-in-progress. I've set up my characters; I've established a conflict of Cheryl vs. Nicole and Alyssa. What do you think is going to happen next? Any ideas?

This is, you will have seen by now, the time-honored story of the outsider who doesn't fit in. Outsider stories usually follow one of two plot structures. The first plot structure is "Rudolph the Red-Nosed Reindeer." Someone who is different from the community is scorned, reviled, made an outsider: "They wouldn't let poor Rudolph join in any reindeer games." But the outsider sticks to whatever it is that makes him different — sometimes out of love, often because he has no choice — and eventually that difference ends up saving the entire community. "Then how the reindeer loved him, / and they shouted out with glee / 'Rudolph the Red-Nosed Reindeer, / you'll go down in history!'" This is also a Christ story, you'll notice, someone suffering at the hands of the community and coming back to redeem them all. And at the same time, it's a story about Darwinistic evolution: the community at first resisting an odd mutation and then adapting to and benefiting from it.

The other outsider plot structure is the Ugly Duckling, the reverse of Rudolph. Here the outsider is again scorned, reviled, tormented inside and out. But rather than saving his community, he leaves it, to find another group where he truly belongs, where they understand him and appreciate his talents. This is also the Cinderella story, where inner worth is rewarded despite an unattractive outward appearance — and then that inner worth gets revealed in exterior beauty as well, as happens in "The Ugly Duckling" too.

Now, there are other directions an outsider tale could go. The outsider could make direct and declared war on the community — the beat'em path. The outsider could give up what makes him different and become part of the community once and for all — the join'em route.

But these latter two stories are not the ones we tell children again and again and again. We tell the Ugly Duckling and Rudolph. And what fascinates me about these two story structures is that they do not offer the option of change. The Ugly Duckling never tries to pluck its feathers out to be like the other ducks in the yard. In the animated version of "Rudolph" that I grew up with, Rudolph paints his nose black to be like all the others, but the paint washes off again in a snowstorm. These stories say, You can only be who you are. You can change outwardly, you can hide that glowing red nose of yours, you can pretend to be interested in clothes and boys, but the nose is still a nose and clothes are still boring.

When I said the conflict in this novel was Cheryl the Outsider versus Nicole and Alyssa the Popular Girls, I wasn't being quite accurate. I wasn't *against* Nicole and Alyssa; I still really wanted to be their friend. Rather the conflict was within me: the parts of me that wanted to keep my connection with them, and perhaps even be popular myself, versus the parts of me that really didn't give a damn about the same things they did — that wanted just to read and play and keep on being a kid. I wasn't sure what I wanted or what was the right thing to do; how to behave, or even who I was.

In other words, I was in a muddle. A muddle is a concept I'm borrowing from the writer E. M. Forster, who wrote *Howards End* and *A Room with a View* among many other lovely novels. And it's the point at which your vision of yourself and your purpose in the world is clouded by other things — by other people's opinions, by the fact that you don't know who you are or if you *have* a purpose in the world. It's an identity crisis, essentially. Forster's characters are all grown-ups, but they spend a lot of time in muddles, trying to figure out how they should live and who they really love. One can enter a muddle at any age.

But I would say the prime time for muddle, the world capital, the Mount Everest of muddles, happens in middle school. Your body is changing. Your view of the world is changing — you're becoming self-conscious for the first time, really aware of other people perceiving you. And you really care how these people perceive you, because you can figure out who you are and who you should be based on their reactions. And everyone else your age is going through these changes too, so there's very little respite from them.

Writers can spend a lot of time in muddles as well, when we don't know which direction to turn next, what our story should be, whether we should listen to our writing group or editor about that plot development or whether it's perfect just as we envisioned it. And as we become more and more aware of the morass, we sink further and further into it.

Muddles are pretty much hell. And I rarely meet people who enjoyed middle school.

But if we're defining a muddle as not knowing what you want or how to get it — the paralysis caused by infinite self-consciousness, or infinite choices — there's only one solution. And that's action. Making a choice. Right choice, wrong choice, whatever — it's going to be *a* choice, and that gets things started. For a writer, an artist, making a choice gives you something to work with. You make a choice, get the words on the page, see if it feels right. If it doesn't, you edit it or go back and make a different decision. The hardest thing is getting past the fear of making a choice at all.

For middle schoolers, it's testing out an identity — am I a Goth? A jock? An art kid? You try something and see if it connects with you, or you connect with someone; and if something happens, you go from there.

In a book, when a character takes action, that not only moves the plot forward, it demonstrates to readers who that character actually is. You don't have to tell us about your character's fine and upstanding qualities; rather, their actions and choices show us every step of the way. And if they back away from making a choice, why, that's a choice right there.

John Gardner says, "Real suspense comes with moral dilemma and the courage to make and act upon choices. False suspense comes from the accidental and meaningless occurrence of one damned thing after another." I love this quote, and this concept of moral dilemma: where a character has to choose between two people he loves; or between two values (honesty vs. loyalty); or between what is right and what is easy, to quote Harry Potter; or between who s/he is and fitting in with the group. And once that choice is made, it has consequences that lead to the next choice, so the story is more than just "one damned thing after another."

My moral dilemma in the Nicole, Alyssa, and Cheryl story I set up: I could choose to keep being who I was, unpretty, uncertain, loving books and school, not really that interested in boys and clothes as yet; or I could choose to try to be part of the popular crowd, pretend to care about New Kids on the Block, attempt to sculpt my bangs into that perfect early-nineties puff.

Before I reveal what choice I made, I'd like to talk a little more about moral dilemmas, and particularly that word "moral." When most of us think of "moral," we think of rightness or virtue, yes? The Moral Majority, moral values. But the first definition of "moral" in Webster's is "of or relating to principles of right and wrong in behavior: ethical." And ethics is "the principles of conduct governing an individual or a group; a guiding philosophy." And that's the sense in which you should hear the phrase "moral dilemma" here: as an ethical dilemma, a choice between two competing philosophies or priorities — what will be the right one.

All authors put forth an ethical philosophy through the way they treat their characters, from how much "screen time" they get in the plot, to the author's attitude toward the characters while they're on the page, up to of course the fates they all receive in the end. In less skilled children's books, the author's ethical philosophy gets said outright. And that brings us back to another common definition of "moral": "a passage pointing out the lesson to be drawn from a story."

If you study the history of children's literature, it begins with morality tales. There's a set of German children's stories called *Struwwelpeter* about little Peter, who wouldn't cut his fingernails or his hair, and Pauline, who burnt herself up by playing with matches. But as children's fiction has evolved through the last hundred and fifty years or so, it's taken on the literary and psychological complexity that adult fiction has had for centuries, away from the moral and heavy-handed, toward the complex, the nuanced, the *real*.

And now we're at a point where most editors and reviewers dislike stories with clearly defined morals, or at least stories that were written to put forth a moral. When I see the line "_____ learns a lesson about _____" in a query letter, it's almost always a mark against it, because it sounds so flat and didactic.

This is not to say I'm opposed to characters learning lessons — in fact, learning is at the heart of most good fiction. In *Millicent Min, Girl Genius*, by Lisa Yee, Millicent Min is a child prodigy who lies to a new friend about her intelligence. This eventually backfires, of course, and Millicent learns a lesson about the value of brains without heart and the true nature of friendship. But lesson is effective *not* because Lisa set out to educate her readers about not lying to their friends. Rather, it works because we're interested in Millicent, we care about her, we suffer with her through her mistakes and regrets. So when she recognizes those mistakes and learns and grows from her experiences, we learn and grow right along with her. The most effective morality in fiction is that which is dramatized in the lives of your characters.

I saw a worksheet in a writing book recently that was headlined "Create a Character!" And then it listed a number of categories you could fill in for your character — some factual categories, like name, physical description, family; some taste categories, like their hobbies and favorite foods; and then some values categories: what the person loves, hates, dreams, and fears.

Now, it's definitely good to have all this information about a character — what he'd carry in his pockets and all that. But I think it's the values categories that really give a character personality and psychology and *life*, because they most directly reveal who he is, what he wants, and how he will behave in the novel. Aristotle said, "Character is that which reveals moral purpose," and values are character, essentially. And if I were making up a character worksheet, I'd try this:

+ LOVES
+ HATES
+ NEEDS
+ WANTS
+ FEARS

And then under each of those categories — WHY?

What these things add up to is your character's morality — her ethical philosophy, her worldview; what she wants most in life; what she will or won't do to get it, or what can tempt or scare her into doing something. The "why" question should bring forth how she developed that philosophy, those loves, hates, needs, wants, etc. And that's a plot right there: motivation, action, and backstory.

We're going to pause for a little digression on plot now. Aristotle defined plot as the "change from good fortune to bad, or bad fortune to good." And that means simply that things are different at the end than they are at the beginning. These changes can be big and external: The characters have moved to a new home, they've gained a new group of friends, they've defeated the evil Dark Lord and saved the world forever. Or they can be subtle and internal: They've come to understand why their mother ran away, they've developed the courage to talk to their crush.

But there must be some change. If your character isn't going anywhere, if all the circumstances are the same at the end of the book, you've just wasted the reader's time.

Now there are adult books where nothing really changes — often that's the author's point. But narrative children's books, I'm going to say, *have to* show change, have to show growth, to be at all worthwhile. The child audience is experiencing nothing but change and growth, and our books provide models — both good and bad — for how those changes happen. There is a lovely quote from Richard Peck: "A young adult novel ends not with happily ever after, but at a new beginning, with the sense of a lot of life left to be lived." At the end of your book, your main character should be better equipped to live the rest of that life, because of the change and journey they've gone through in the course of the novel.

So the changes could be big and external, or subtle and internal. And these types of changes are the two main kinds of plot in your book.

The Action Plot is the external change — what physically changes for your characters in the course of the book. In "The Ugly Duckling", the duckling's travels from the farmyard to the cottage to the peasant's house to the pond are the Action Plot. Action Plots usually follow one of three formulae:

- Conflict — one character versus another character, or one character versus herself.
- Lack — a character needs something to be complete, to live a full life.
- And Mystery — a form of Lack where what the character needs is a piece of information.

Most Action Plots will end up interweaving these three elements. The Harry Potter series is a masterful combination of Conflict and Mystery: The overarching plot of the series is a Conflict, Harry vs. Voldemort, but the driving plot of each book is a piece of information

Harry must discover: Who wants the Sorcerer's Stone? Who put his name in the Goblet of Fire? Plus Harry Lacks a home and friends until he goes to Hogwarts — and then his desire to keep them safe is what makes the Conflict matter.

The Emotional Plot is the internal change, the moral and emotional development of your characters as a result of the external action. In "The Ugly Duckling," the duckling's suffering leads him to a point where he just wants to give up. And that's the moment he recognizes himself as a swan. Emotional Plots always involve suffering, in the teeth of an moral dilemma, the quicksand of a muddle, or the slings and arrows of everyday life and conflicts. That's what gives the happy ending its value — you've come at last out of the pain.

Going back to that Character worksheet, your Action Plot will usually be driven by the character's WANTS, and your Emotional Plot will usually be driven by the character's NEEDS. And when those two things have been fulfilled, the story's over.

(A warning here: Your character will usually not be aware of what she truly needs emotionally, and you should avoid at all costs saying outright in the text what she truly needs emotionally. Being obvious is the quickest way to be dull.)

Books with lots of Action Plot but no Emotional Plots, or obvious or familiar Emotional Plots, often get called "flat" or "noisy" — sure, stuff is happening, and the explosions are cool, but it doesn't really mean anything to anyone. Think any Jerry Bruckheimer movie. Books with lots of Emotional Plot but little Action Plot often get called "quiet" or "subtle" — for instance *Criss Cross* by Lynn Rae Perkins, which just won the Newbery. There are readers and editors for both kinds of books.

So coming back to the Nicole-and-Alyssa novel. I'm still in that moral dilemma about trying to be popular. I have Coke-bottle glasses, terrible hair, no fashion sense, and a body encased in a back brace for scoliosis. You don't believe me? Take a look at my fifth-grade picture.

I would like to say, if some grown-up had entered the novel at this point — my mom or a librarian or a gym coach or someone — and fed me a moral, told me to "Be myself," I would have stabbed that person with a spork. There wasn't anyone I wanted to be *less* than I wanted to be myself. And this was pretty much the case from fifth grade up until the very end of eighth grade. My moral philosophy at this point was really this:

- LOVES reading, drawing, riding my bicycle.
- HATES team sports, spiders, math, loneliness.
- NEEDS . . . better glasses, to start with. I don't know, this is hard to say about oneself. I guess I needed a group of friends who shared my interests and values. I had some individual friends like that, certainly. But I wanted a whole group the way the popular kids had a whole group, so I'd have some sense of identity . . . someone to define myself *as*, instead of just *against*.
- WANTS to be pretty, to be accepted.
- FEARS tornadoes, spiders again, being made fun of.

So out of all this . . . I left off at a point in our Action Plot where I was in a muddle, and I said I needed to make a choice, right? Did I want to be popular, or did I want to be myself? Because I obviously couldn't be both.

Well, the choice I made was not to make a choice. (This is not a story with a great deal of Action Plot.) As said above, I feared being made fun of. So I tried to be Rudolph, and paint my nose. I asked for "Guess?" sweatshirts. I learned to curl my bangs. And I developed an opinion about which of the New Kids on the Block was the cutest — Jonathan — so I could talk about it if it came up.

But I never gave up my essential self of being one of the top ten students in my class, of going to gifted classes, of reading every chance I got. As the stories say: I could not be anyone other than who I was. I was teased — not too badly, but a little. I grew further and further away from Nicole and Alyssa; we still hung out sometimes, but that gap always hurt. I read lots and lots of books about outsiders who are redeemed; particularly I loved *Buffalo Brenda* by Jill Pinkwater and *A Little Princess* by Frances Hodgson Burnett.

And then I made it through middle school to high school and college, where I found the friends I needed and accepted my identity as a smart reader. I joined the quiz bowl team and the theatre kids in high school. I went to Carleton College in Minnesota, full of intellectual book-loving weirdos like myself; and then I moved to New York City, also full of intellectual book-loving weirdos like myself.

(And I have to say, I got contacts and better hair.)

So the plot changed to the Ugly Duckling. And this is the route I think most outsider kids take — the popular group doesn't fit, so they join the theatre geeks. Or the theatre geeks don't fit, so they join the stoners. If there's a moral to it, it's that there are communities out there for everyone. When you're a kid, the hardest thing is just being patient and enduring long enough to find yours. But if you can . . .

> But what did he see in the clear stream below? His own image;
> no longer a dark, gray bird, ugly and disagreeable to look at,
> but a graceful and beautiful swan. . . . He now felt glad at
> having suffered sorrow and trouble, because it enabled him to

enjoy so much better all the pleasure and happiness around him; for the great swans swam round the newcomer, and stroked his neck with their beaks, as a welcome.

The happy ending. Or, as Richard Peck said, a new beginning.

As an epilogue, Nicole is now a pharmacist in Houston, Texas. Alyssa lives in Kansas City and manages a construction company, I think. They visited New York together a couple years ago, and we had dinner and I showed them around. We aren't best friends; we never were best friends again after that fifth-grade year. But we stayed cordial acquaintances, social friends, all through middle school and high school. And I'm glad they've had happy endings too.

Three more points, and then I'll be done. One, stories should always start with and be driven by character. You may not be able to fill the values chart out from the very beginning — usually you will discover those things about your characters as you're writing along. But once you have a first draft, you might use the chart to better define who your character is and where you want him/her to go.

And once you have those values set up, see what happens when you bring different characters together. The woman who needs relentless affirmation with the boy who's never spoken a kind word in his life. The Southerner with bone-deep languor and charm versus the Virgo who only wants to be efficient and get stuff accomplished. In both of those situations, you'll have instant Conflict in your Action Plot because they're operating so thoroughly at cross-purposes. Or mix up those qualities within *one* character — suppose you have a Southerner who's also a Virgo. How's that going to work? (No offense meant to Southerners or Virgos, of course.)

Writers say sometimes, "Oh, I have these great characters, but I don't know how to develop a plot." As you might see from that, a character *is* a plot. You just have to find the other characters, and the moral dilemmas, that will force the character to change and grow ... creating the muddles, essentially, that make him question who he is and who he ought to be.

In early drafts of *Millicent Min, Girl Genius* — another outsider story — there was a character named Frederick, who, like Millicent, was an eleven-year-old child prodigy. My boss Arthur and I were editing the manuscript together, and I said to him, "Oh, wouldn't it be great if Frederick and Millicent became friends?" Arthur said, "No, that would be boring, because it wouldn't challenge Millicent."

And he was *so right*. Frederick had the same values and the same interests as Millicent; he reinforced everything she already was. He and Millicent would get along great, but there was nothing there to make her change or create dramatic tension or action. The real challenge for Millicent came from Emily Ebers, the new non-genius girl in town, and Stanford Wong, the very non-genius boy Millicent tutored. So Lisa dropped Frederick and focused the plot around Stanford and Emily. And that's partly how it became the book it is today.

Another take on character as plot: The science-fiction novelist Lois McMaster Bujold, whose books are *huge* fun, says she thinks of the absolute worst possible thing she can do to her characters, and does it to them. The same for the wonderful Patrick O'Brian. Again, this comes back to that character worksheet — what the character LOVES, HATES, NEEDS, WANTS, and FEARS. If you've developed the LOVES, HATES, and FEARS, but you're still not sure about NEEDS or WANTS, take one of the LOVES away. Have the HATE or the FEAR move in next door. See how your character reacts, and go from there.

But your story shouldn't just deal with what your character loves and hates — you as the author need to be excited about it too. So, point number two: Put those characters in situations that fascinate or trouble you personally — problems you want to write about, conflicts that move you in some way. What were the things you struggled with most as a child? What scared you then? What thrilled you? As an adult — what's hurt you? Delighted you? Is there some way you can use that situation, that emotion, in your character's life?

When I look back, the Nicole and Alyssa situation stands out as pretty much the single most painful experience of my childhood. It hurt with what I think of as an "electric-fence hurt," where I couldn't touch my feelings with words. And it ended up being one of the great turning points of my life, really shaping who I became as I grew up. I lost a lot of confidence in myself and my ability to connect with people, particularly "cool" people. I spent many, many years huddling in the kitchen at parties, where it's still my instinct to retreat sometimes. And I've never had much faith in my fashion sense.

But that disconnect also freed me from needing to be cool, which was a great blessing in the end: I just accepted that I wasn't popular, or ever going to be popular, so I went on and did the things I loved instead — being an intellectual book-loving weirdo, etc. And that's what's given me the generally happy life I have now.

All these years later, you can see, I'm still thinking about what happened then, because it raises some of the Big Questions that fascinate me most: the way two or three people can make a connection, or lose a connection; the relationship between self-consciousness and growing up; how we define coolness and happiness.

The writer David Lodge said, "A novel is a long answer to the question 'What is it about?'" Think about the things you want your book to be about, a question you want to answer (*not* a question you already have the answer to), the electric-fence emotion you want to touch at last; and then build the characters and the Action Plot that would address those things.

And for the third point, remember: Art is about emotional connection and emotional response. Aristotle said that the point of all drama was to effect catharsis in the audience. "Catharsis" is a Greek term that means "purgation or purification of the emotions through art," and it was meant to lead to renewal and restoration: You'd identify so closely with the main character, all the terror she was experiencing in her situation, all the pity you had for him, that when the drama was over, those feelings were purged right out of you, leading to a renewed sense of appreciation for living and for the possibilities of the world.

And this is exactly what great writing does, whether it's a novel or picture book, an essay or play. Your job is to create that emotion, through fascinating characters, involving action, questions that excite you and the reader, and always showing not telling.

We need books — and I want to publish books — that reflect the whole range of a child or teenager's emotional experiences, and take us through those experiences with them. So the stories come through a child's heart, and speak to a child's heart; so they have the bravery and honesty to look at a muddle and acknowledge its pain, and *not* to be moralistic or easy; and, in the end, to help us all make it through.

Thank you.

POSTSCRIPT: When I gave this talk in the Poconos, I distributed my own version of a character chart, including Facts, Values, and Tastes. Afterward, writer Joelle McClure suggested that I add "FLAWS" to the chart, and indeed flaws are an essential part of an interesting and realistic character. But I think flaws are more a function of *behavior* than they are of *values* or philosophy, which is what my chart was originally meant to ponder.

So I revised the chart and dropped the "Tastes" section completely, because while it's nice to know what your character's favorite color and food is, that usually doesn't have much effect on the plot of the novel. Instead, I added a "Behavior" section with the following categories:

• VIRTUES.
• FLAWS. As with Needs in the Values Chart, you *must* resist at all costs the temptation to tell us readers your character's flaws.

Instead let us discover them as they unfold in her actions and come to influence her choices.

- INTERESTS. Hobbies, favorite pastimes, common activities.
- QUIRKS / PATTERNS OF BEHAVIOR. Example: I never leave my apartment without wearing my watch and ring. The watch is a silver Fossil with a blue metallic face, always worn on my left wrist. The ring is sterling silver engraved with the words "In my beginning is my end," which has multiple meanings for me: It's a Christian religious reference; it's the first line of T. S. Eliot's "East Coker," which is part of his "Four Quartets," probably my favorite poetic cycle ever; and it's quietly clever and postmodern ("In my beginning is my end," and it's a ring — get it?). The watch and ring are the last things I put on before leaving the apartment in the morning, marking each day's debut of Public Cheryl, and the first things I take off when I return at night, marking my return to Private Cheryl. A very few details like this can go a very long way. Choose them carefully, to illuminate important or hidden parts of your character, and use them sparingly so they don't obscure the actual action of the book.
- KEY PHRASES, VOCABULARY, OR SPEECH PATTERNS. Example: I started saying "Damn and blast" while reading Dorothy Sayers in college, and I still use the phrase "Bloody hell" a lot. I also say "Y'all" thanks to a church trip to Arkansas in seventh grade, and because it's fun to watch New Yorkers do a double take when I drop it into a conversation.

And I'm adding two more categories under "Values":

- RELIGIOUS OUTLOOK. This is certainly not something that needs to be explicitly discussed in the novel, but if your character believes in a Higher Being That Judges Us All, he will act one way; if he believes in a Higher Being That Neither Judges in Heaven Nor Interferes on Earth, he will act another

way; if he does not believe in a Higher Being or believes in
multiple Higher Beings, he will act in third and fourth ways;
and if he believes he IS the Higher Being, that's something else
altogether. So religious outlook is worth thinking about as an
indicator of or influence on your character's morality.

+ THE MOST IMPORTANT THING IN LIFE FOR THIS
CHARACTER IS . . . Honor; fame; being a good person;
doing good acts; money; love; sex; taking care of her family;
taking care of his friends; having a laugh; being respected, etc. If
you ever doubt what the character should do next, take a look
at this and write forth accordingly.

And ask the "WHY?" question in every single category to see what it
might turn up about the character's personality and history. For example,
my name is Cheryl Beth Klein. WHY? My mother's best friend was
named Cheryl; "Beth" sounded good with it; the family surname. Note
what these choices reveal about my parents: honoring a best friend;
aesthetic effect; my mother chose *not* to keep her maiden name and *not*
to hyphenate mine, so she wasn't that kind of late-1970s feminist, if she
was a feminist at all. (If I hadn't been named Cheryl, I would have been
named Jennifer. Would my life have turned out completely differently?
It's interesting to think about.)

I LOVE: reading. WHY? My entire family reads all the time; my
grandfather was a children's literature professor; books are friends that
are never too busy and will never abandon you; exploring new worlds
and having new experiences while sitting in the comfort of my own
home, etc. I WANT: To own my own apartment in New York City.
WHY? To earn equity rather than paying rent; to have a place that's
truly mine; to be able to paint the walls hot pink (not really). And all of
those things say something about my values and history, and would help
make me more real as a character within a book.

The complete revised character chart as it stands follows.

INFORMATION   WHY?

Facts

Name

Age at beginning of action

Current place of residence

Father's name

Mother's name

Names and ages of any brother and sisters

Other significant relatives

Friends

Enemies

Behavior

Virtues

Flaws

Interests

Quirks/Patterns of Behavior

Key Phrases, Vocabulary, or Speech Patterns

INFORMATION   WHY?

Values

Loves

Hates

Fears

Wants

Needs

Religious outlook

The most important thing in life for this character is:

This is the change that takes place in the character over the course of the novel:

THEORY:
A Definition of Young Adult Literature

June 5, 2009

So I've been thinking off and on about a practical definition of YA literature — something I could look at to help me decide whether a manuscript is an adult novel or a middle-grade novel or, indeed, a YA. Such delineations don't matter to me as a reader — a good book is a good book — but they do matter to me as an editor and publisher, because I want every book I publish to find the audience that is right for it, and sometimes, despite a child or teenage protagonist, a manuscript is meant for an adult audience. Hence I have written the definition below to help me think through these situations as they come up. This is very much a WORKING theory; I hope you all will offer challenges, counterexamples, additions or arguments to help me improve what I'm saying here. But here's what I have right now — the definition broken into five parts for easier parsing:

1. A YA novel is centrally interested in the experience and growth of
2. its teenage protagonist(s),
3. whose dramatized choices, actions, and concerns drive the
4. story,
5. and it is narrated with relative immediacy to that teenage perspective.

Some definition of terms here:

1) "centrally interested": The book's central storyline focuses upon the emotional, intellectual, and all other forms of experience and growth of its main character. It may be interested in other things as well — dragons, the definition of justice, life in 1908 Russia — but all

of those interests are secondary to the experience of the main character, and usually filtered only through him/her.

This is often where I find adult books separating themselves out here, because while they may have a younger protagonist, the adult books aren't interested in that protagonist's life per se — they're interested in showing the world the protagonist will encounter in all its ugliness or glory, and a younger character often provides a useful "innocent" or "naive" viewpoint, or at the very least a figure of instant sympathy to adults. As an example, it's been years since I read *Paddy Clarke Ha Ha Ha* by Roddy Doyle, but I remember it as a wonderful book that avoided the "innocent/naive" pitfall by making Paddy a fully-rounded and rather foulmouthed boy. Still, I felt it was rightly classified as an adult book because to me it read as much like a work of anthropology — *A Report on the Mindset and Behavior of a Representative Ten-Year-Old Male in 1968 Ireland* — as it did a work of fiction; that is, it felt as much like a *study* of a childhood in Ireland at a time of social unrest Paddy didn't fully understand, as the *story* of a child there. (See also note below on "story" in #4.)

"growth": the character is different at the beginning than he is at the end, and usually for the better. I always think of Richard Peck's wise dictum that a YA novel ends "ends not with happily ever after, but at a new beginning, with the sense of a lot of life yet to be lived"; and that the events of the book have left the character better prepared for that.

2) "teenage protagonist(s)": Yeah, I'm going to posit that YA novels require a protagonist at an adolescent stage of life, between childhood and the full rights and privileges of adulthood. I do not think this is true of children's books, particularly picture books (that is, that they must have a child main character); but I think it's true of teen books, because life between the ages of thirteen and eighteen is such a unique time, full of so much intensity and so many firsts, that only a very sheltered adult or a very advanced child could have those same sorts of experiences and changes.

3) "dramatized": shown, not told; dialogue, not narration; the primary action happening before our eyes, not offpage.

"choices, actions, and concerns": the protagonist does things; s/he makes choices, takes action, and has interests in and/or connections to the world outside his/her head.

"drive": the protagonist is expected (by the reader at least) to make a difference in this fictional world, and by the end of the book is empowered to take some action to do so.

4) "story": a sequence of events linked by cause and effect, generally with a recognizable beginning and end. When people ask me why I went into children's books editing, I have often said just this, story: that things were required to *happen* in children's/YA books, that they had to have a forward action beyond the events of everyday life, as it often feels they don't in adult books. Maybe what I really mean here is that the events of the book have to have shape and meaning, while in adult books things can just happen because that's what happens in life: things happen.

5) "narrated with relative immediacy to that teenage perspective": The book does not have to be in first person (though goodness knows a good eighty-five percent of YA fiction seems to be these days; I wonder what the actual statistics are on this), but it stays close to the viewpoint of that teenage protagonist, without the distance of, say, an adult looking back at his teenage years. The exception that proves the rule here might be *The Disreputable History of Frankie Landau-Banks*, whose detached, almost academic third-person narrator is nonetheless sympathetic to Frankie and describes her emotions as well as her excellent plotting.

There is one more assumption running through everything I'm saying here that I'm hesitating to codify into part of the definition — but perhaps I should. And that is that a YA novel should end with hope, that there must be some thread of a ghost of a promise of a happy ending or more growth, that there is indeed meaning to the events enclosed. Not necessarily a moral, certainly not an explicit one; but no existentialist despair, either, or random horrors that do not cohere other than aesthetically (I am thinking of Thomas Pynchon's *V.* here, but I may just be a bad reader of Pynchon). In terms of the Richard Peck quote above, if a YA novel leaves its reader with the sense of a lot of the protagonist's life left to be lived, perhaps it should also leave the reader with the sense that that life (and the reader's life) is worth living. But do we limit the art of the genre if we say it can't go fully into the darkness?

To see the many useful and thought-provoking comments on this theory, visit the original post at http://chavelaque.blogspot.com/2009/06/theory-definition-of-ya-literature.html

THE ART OF DETECTION:
One Editor's Techniques for Analyzing and Revising Your Novel

I wrote this talk for the Michigan SCBWI conference in October 2007. (The conference was themed around "Mystery," hence my choice of Holmes quotes as a unifying element.) The subtitle, "One Editor's Techniques," was chosen to be deliberately low-key — that this is nothing like the final word on all editors' techniques or on revision, just some techniques that I personally use in thinking through a novel as I edit it. You will want to have one particular work-in-progress in mind during the exercises. My very great thanks to Lisa Yee for allowing me to share materials from the editing process of her So Totally Emily Ebers.

As the Sherlock Holmesians among you will know, "The Art of Detection" is the title of his as-yet-unpublished multivolume opus on the work of a detective. Editing and detective work actually pull in opposite directions: Detectives work backward from the evidence to find out the truth, while editors work forward from the manuscript to make its truth all it can be. But in the end, they both come down to paying attention to details that add up to an overall result. As Holmes says, "It has long been an axiom of mine that the little things are infinitely the most important."

So just as a detective evaluates a crime scene and decides what action to take from there, I'm going to take you through my process as I evaluate and respond to a manuscript — *So Totally Emily Ebers* by Lisa Yee — which I co-edited with Arthur Levine, alongside some useful illustrative quotes from Master Holmes.

Before I get into the analysis, I want to offer four caveats:

1. **These are critical techniques you should apply only after you've finished your first draft and put it away for at least two weeks.**

The goal of these techniques is to defamiliarize your novel so you can see it with objective eyes, as an editor would on first reading. Though of course editors aren't wholly objective in our responding either, as we approach a manuscript with certain standards to which we want it to conform. I think a good novel is defined as one with:

+ Characters in whom the reader takes an interest. Usually the reader will identify with the protagonist — but not always.
+ A story in which things happen and change.
+ Good prose.
+ A point to its telling.

We will discuss all these in more detail as we go along.

2. **And when I edit a book, this is what I will edit it towards, and what all of the techniques I discuss below will point towards.**

The standards of literary fiction — which may or may not apply to your novel.

3. **But not all techniques are needed for or should be used on all books. Every single book is different and needs different things.**

4. **The editor's motto, like the doctor's: If it ain't broke, don't fix it.**

To start off the defamiliarization process, I'm going to quote Holmes: "We approached the case, you remember, with an absolutely blank mind, which is always an advantage. We had formed no theories. We were simply there to observe and to draw inferences from our observations." This is Step One in any editorial process: Read the book. I read through the manuscript and make notes of my impressions every step of the way: "I'm bored." "Love this." "Where is this going?" "Hmm." It's incredibly advanced and sophisticated editorial thinking, as you can tell. But this is a really important step, as this is the *only* time in the process when I'll approach the book as the first-time reader would: "with an absolutely blank mind . . . there to observe and to draw inferences from our observations."

The goal of this reading is to find answers to two questions:

1. What is the story?
2. What is the point?

The answers to these two questions will be my guidelines for the rest of the editorial process, so I'm going to discuss them in more depth now. I feel a little odd putting these questions in a specific order because they are both essential, and so deeply entwined I consider them both at once. But since I can't talk about them both at once . . .

• **Question Number One: What is the story?**

You might have already heard me go on about Action Plots and Emotional Plots. The Action Plot of a book is simply the external action or conflict that the characters experience. A great detective solves the case of a supposedly haunted house on a lonely moor. A ragtag team of heroes journeys to Mordor to get rid of a ring. A boy goes to wizard school, where he makes friends, flies a broomstick, and discovers a whole lot of backstory. If you break it down to its most basic elements, this plot usually fits into one of three categories: Conflict, Mystery, or Lack.

The Emotional Plot of a book is the internal action, or to be more specific, the moral and emotional development of your characters as a result of the external action.

Both Action Plots and Emotional Plots revolve around change: a conflict being settled; a mystery being solved; a need getting fulfilled. Things are different at the end than they are at the beginning. So we might restate Question Number One as "What changes, and how does that change happen?"

You remember I told you to think about your current Work in Progress. Quickly here — I'll give you thirty seconds, no more — I want you to write down the central Action Plot of your book, in two lines at most. Go.

How many of you found that easy? How many found it really, really hard? It's hard for most writers, but if you can get that down, it's going to prove useful to you in so many ways — to help you clarify the action of your plot; in query letters; at family reunions when people ask you, "So, whatcha writing?" Sherlock Holmes says, "Nothing clears up a case so much as stating it to another person," and the same pretty much goes for a story. So right now we're going to concentrate on clearing up the action of your plot. Look at what you just wrote. It ought to be a sentence where your protagonist is the subject and the action regarding his problem is the verb. Do all of the developments of your story ultimately serve that plot?

You have just completed the first TRUCK exercise. TRUCK is an extremely silly acronym that stands for Techniques of Revision Used by Cheryl Klein. I want to emphasize that I did not make all of these up — editors have been using many of these for years. But I use them too, so....

That was **TRUCK #1: Write out the story of your book in one sentence.**
Most of the TRUCKs we will discuss are basically expansions of this two-line story summary at greater levels of detail.

Before we delve further into plot, though, I want to think quickly about character:

TRUCK #2: List the first ten meaningful things your protagonist says or does.
Viewed objectively, out of the context of the action, who does that character seem to be? Would you like him or her? Or at least be interested in what he's going to do next? That is who that character is to the reader. If, in your first ten actions, your character flops down on his bed and says, "I hate Smallville. There's nothing to do in this town!" then that character is a whiner. And while we might ultimately sympathize with him, he's not that easy to like from the beginning. On the other hand, if he is first seen building a raft out of driftwood to float downstream out of Smallville, then he's creative and resourceful and will probably be someone the reader wants to follow.

Your protagonist doesn't have to be morally good. But he has to be interesting enough to justify the time we're going to spend with him. If he's not living up to that, based on this list of the first ten meaningful things, then consider bringing out more of his positive qualities upfront:

humor, creativity, kindness, a can-do spirit, his unique take on the world. Positive energy, in general.

Now we're going back to expanding on that one-line summary of the story:

TRUCK #3: Write the flap copy — a summary in 250 words.

Flap copy, as you know, is a two- or three-paragraph summary of a book's events. When I actually write flap copy for books, I try to make it sound as interesting and mysterious and suspenseful as possible, so the reader feels he or she *has* to buy this book to find out the end of the story. And I try to be all fresh and creative as well to get the reader's attention.

Well, no one besides you will ever see it what you're about to write. So don't try to be mysterious and don't pretty it up. Write not what you think should happen, but what actually does happen, in about 250 words. Generally this includes the opening situation; the inciting event of the action — the thing that gets the story started; at least one action your protagonist takes to follow that up, setting up the conflict or mystery; and the stakes — what your protagonist could gain or lose in the course of the action. Flap copy generally does *not* give away the ending, but for the purposes of what you're doing here, I'd include that too.

And when you've done it, congrats! — you have the core of your first query letter.

Here's one of my flap drafts — I call them "flapdoodles" — for *So Totally Emily Ebers.*

Emily Ebers is having a bad summer. Her parents just got a divorce. Her rock-star dad can't be reached on tour (perhaps you know his hit "Heartless Empty-Hearted Heartbreaker"?), and her mom just moved Emily across the country — all the way to California. Emily misses her friends, but she really, really misses her father: He gave her a credit card for "emergencies," but that doesn't make up for his absence.

Then Emily meets Millicent Min, who's funnier — and stranger — than anyone else she knows. And then there's Stanford Wong, the smartest, hottest boy in Rancho Rosetta. Thanks to them, Emily's life may finally be getting back on track. But there are a few more surprises coming her way — though the biggest one may lie with Emily herself.

Funny? Angry? Emotional? Sweet? That's so totally Emily Ebers.

What should you notice here?

- The opening situation: Emily Ebers is having a bad summer. Her parents just got a divorce.
- The inciting event: Then Emily meets Millicent Min.
- The action of the protagonist: . . . "Life getting back on track"
- The stakes: Emily's life and happiness, implicitly.

Once you've gone through this exercise for your own book, look at what's missing or what feels weak. You might even give the copy to an honest friend or writing partner and have them tell you what sounds great and what isn't quite working.

In this case, what was missing was the action of the protagonist. This is a very domestic book, built around its characters' relationships much more than significant action. For the first half of the book, which is more or less what flap copy covers, Emily is a victim of her parents' whims. She takes what action she can — writing letters, shopping — but it's only in the second half that those actions pay off. Moreover, because this book covered the same time period and action as Lisa's two previous books from other perspectives (*Millient Min, Girl Genius* and *Stanford Wong Flunks Big-Time*), Lisa *couldn't* introduce any new major action on Emily's part, as that would contradict the earlier books. To deal with this problem in the flap copy, we rejiggered it to focus on another strength — Emily's voice:

Emily Ebers on cross-country travel:
How did the pioneers do it?
Did they have to ride with their mothers?

Emily Ebers on divorce:
Alice has a bunch of books about divorce and how it affects kids.
It affects kids in a bad way, okay? Does she really need a book
to figure that out?

Emily Ebers on friends:
I guess good can come out of volleyball.

Emily Ebers on romance:
I think the only real way to tell if a boy like-likes you is to be direct.
Even though it might be scary, the thing to do is just march right up
and ask one of your friends to ask someone else
to ask one of his friends what he thinks about you.

Journeys. Parents. Shopping. Love.
Beginnings. Changes. Lies. The truth.
Funny. Angry. Smart. Sweet.
So Totally Emily Ebers.

Once you have identified the central story of your novel (TRUCK #1), and you have a sense of what's missing or what feels weak (TRUCK #3), then you need to zoom in on where those weaknesses happen. And this brings us to:

TRUCK #4: Make a bookmap of your novel.

Sit down with your book, go through it chapter by chapter, and write out a one-line to one-paragraph summary of each chapter's events. Try to include the key plot information that appears in each chapter — for instance, if the antagonist reveals an important clue to the protagonist, then both that fact and what the protagonist learns should be listed. What this lets you see is the overall development of your story, separate from the language in which it is told. And then you can ask yourself:

+ Do the plot events follow each other in a logical physical and emotional order?
+ Is all the information there? Is it where it needs to be?
+ Do any thoughts or events repeat themselves?
+ Where are the turning points of the action, where everything changes?
+ What is your main character doing all this time? Is it significant action or mostly talk?
+ Look at each plotline or subplot individually. How does each one develop? Do some plots disappear for a long time? (I often highlight each plotline in its own color to get a visual representation of this.)

Here's my outline for a portion of the second draft of *So Totally Emily Ebers*. (I didn't do one for the first draft.) This book is in epistolary form, so the dates are the dates of the letters Emily is writing. EE = Emily Ebers; MM = Millicent Min; SW = Stanford Wong.

June 7 – last day of school
June 8 – Saying goodbye to Dad; Emily and Alice leave New Jersey
June 9 – explanation of the letter journal
June 10 – Johnny Appleseed Museum
June 12 – More museums
June 14 – the Grand Canyon; Alice wants to be called "Alice"
June 15 – description of the new house; Rancho Rosetta has a volleyball league; Stout's
June 17 – the new house; many boxes; Alice's computer obsession
June 18 – Alice has signed EE up for volleyball; fight with Alice about volleyball

June 20 – Emily's birthday; Dad gives EE a credit card; Alice and EE go out for dinner; EE has Dad's aftershave

June 22 – first day of volleyball; fight with Alice after she asks about volleyball

June 24 – Alice in the bathroom crying

June 25 – postcard from Dad; EE feels bad when she talks to Nicole and AJ; lonely

June 26 — first conversation with Millicent, including fat attacks from Julie and brief discussion of homeschooling

June 29 – EE wants to have MM over, so Alice and EE work on the house and get a lot of things unpacked, set up Emily's room

June 30 – EE asks MM to come for a sleepover

July 2 – Alice shows up in hippie gear; the sleepover

July 3 – EE calls MM as soon as she gets home from the sleepover

July 4 – fireworks; EE reminisces

July 5 – EE and MM go to the Rialto and the recycling plant

July 7 – EE sleeps over at MM's

July 9 – Dad sends a postcard

July 10 – EE meets Maddie

July 11 – EE and MM take pictures at the mall; MM alludes to homeschooling; EE sees Stanford in Rite-Aid

July 13 – Another postcard from Dad; ranking boys at the mall and other fun with MM and family

July 14 – MM and EE talk about calling boys

July 16 – Maddie is moving to England; MM and EE are best friends; Neighborhood Watch meeting

July 18 – NJ house sold; EE talks to MM about it; EE puts quarters in parking meters

July 19 – Dad sends a postcard; MM and EE argue over what makes a guy attractive and romance in general; EE tells MM the Alice-meets-Dad story; MM talks to Alice

July 21 – MM talks to Alice, EE reminisces about Dad and the Talky Boys

July 23 – MM and EE discuss fashion; MM talks to Alice

July 24 – volleyball not as bad as it was; pillow fight

July 25 – postcard from Dad; EE meets Stretch

July 26 – MM taking a summer school class, since English isn't her dad's best subject; EE has to read a Shakespeare play; EE thinks about her relationship with Alice, stonewalls her on problems, receives the same treatment when she inquires about Office Ramsey

A few things to notice here:

On June 9, the format of the novel — a letter journal — is explained to Dad and to the reader. But by that point Emily would have already made three entries in the journal, so the explanation is coming a bit late! I suggested moving it up to the first or second entry so the terms of the book get established immediately.

July 19, July 21 and July 23 are all dates marked "MM talks to Alice." That indicates that probably Lisa, the author, was trying to establish how well Alice and Millicent were getting along. The problem was, I got this point very quickly, which means I felt bored by the time we got to July 23, and I wanted to vary the action a bit. I asked Lisa to cut July 23 in her revision.

Another example: What happens June 22? EE starts volleyball. When's the next time we hear about what happens at volleyball? July 24. So I suggested that Lisa add a few more brief scenes or updates about what's going on at volleyball throughout. This gives the volleyball plot continuity and makes it feel more like Emily's real life.

Finally, look at July 26. Just in that one day, there's five events or actions, so as a reader, I found it really hard to figure out what was most important in that chapter. What was I supposed to focus on there? What should I take away? I asked Lisa to simplify it.

Here was the suggested revised outline that went to Lisa, with notes:

BOLD = Suggested insertion or cut (if an insertion from another place

in the manuscript, I put the date of the place it originated in front
of it)

Italic = suggested new scene

[brackets] = editorial note

EE = Emily Ebers; MM = Millicent Min; AE = Alice Ebers (Emily's
mom); DE = David Ebers (Emily's dad); SW = Stanford Wong

June 7 – last day of school; (**June 9**) **the letter journal**

June 8 – Saying goodbye to Dad; Emily and Alice leave New Jersey

June 9 – ~~the letter journal~~ (June 12) traveling with Alice; (June 10)
Johnny Appleseed Museum;

~~June 10 – Johnny Appleseed Museum~~

June 12 – More museums

June 14 – the Grand Canyon; Alice wants to be called "Alice"

June 15 – description of the new house; Rancho Rosetta has a volleyball
league; Stout's

June 17 – the new house; many boxes; Alice's computer obsession

June 18 – Alice has signed EE up for volleyball; fight with Alice about
volleyball

June 19 – Dad calls? [I suggested adding this here and in July 6 and 15 so it
seems like Dad really does want to be involved in EE's life — which
she slowly discovers is not 100% true.]

June 20 – Emily's birthday; Dad gives EE a credit card; Alice and EE go
out for dinner; EE has Dad's aftershave

June 21 – EE thinks about volleyball the next day?

June 22 – first day of volleyball; fight with Alice after she asks about
volleyball

June 24 – Alice in the bathroom crying

June 25 – postcard from Dad; EE feels bad when she talks to Nicole and
AJ; lonely

June 26 – first conversation with Millicent, including fat attacks from Julie
and brief discussion of homeschooling

June 29 – EE wants to have MM over, so Alice and EE work on the house and get a lot of things unpacked, set up Emily's room

June 30 – EE asks MM to come for a sleepover

July 1 – (July 25) EE sees Stretch

July 2 – Alice shows up in hippie gear; the sleepover

July 3 – EE calls MM as soon as she gets home from the sleepover

July 4 – fireworks; EE reminisces

July 5 – EE and MM go to the Rialto and the recycling plant

July 6 – volleyball? Alice? Dad calls? Full discussion of homeschooling with MM? the August 4 letter from Nicole and AJ? (All of these things could occur on any blank date in EE's calendar . . .)

July 7 – EE sleeps over at MM's

July 9 – Dad sends a postcard

July 10 – EE meets Maddie

July 11 – EE and MM take pictures at the mall; MM alludes to homeschooling; EE sees Stanford in Rite-Aid

July 12 – Volleyball? Alice? Maybe introduce Neighborhood Watch?

July 13 – Another postcard from Dad; ranking boys at the mall and other fun with MM and family

July 14 – MM and EE talk about calling boys [**consider cutting or moving?**]

July 15 – Volleyball? Dad calls? Alice? (or Neighborhood Watch?)

July 16 – Maddie is moving to England; MM and EE are best friends; Neighborhood Watch meeting

July 18 – NJ house sold; EE talks to MM about it; EE puts quarters in parking meters

July 19 – Dad sends a postcard; MM and EE argue over what makes a guy attractive and romance in general; ~~EE tells MM the Alice-meets-Dad story;~~ [**I suggest cutting this because AE talks about it on August 6, and it's much more interesting and relevant to hear it from her . . . OK?**] MM talks to Alice

July 21 – MM talks to Alice, EE reminisces about Dad and the Talky Boys

~~July 23 – MM and EE discuss fashion, MM talks to Alice~~ [suggested cut for speed]

July 24 –volleyball not as bad as it was; pillow fight

July 25 – postcard from Dad; ~~EE meets Stretch~~

July 26 – MM taking a summer school class, since English isn't her dad's best subject; EE has to read a Shakespeare play; EE thinks about her relationship with Alice, stonewalls her on problems, receives the same treatment when she inquires about Office Ramsey [an all-over-the-place entry; focus/tighten?]

Once you have an outline of this draft of your book — a short visual representation of everything that happens in this draft, a map of where the novel is right now — then you might try:

TRUCK #5: The Plot Checklist (Figure A)

This is something I developed for a talk I gave in the spring of 2006 on plotting, and basically it asks explicitly all the questions we've been broaching implicitly here:

+ Is the action driven by the characters, particularly the main character?
+ How does that action develop?
+ What are the stakes?
+ Do things change?

(For an updated, downloadable version of this checklist, visit http://www.cherylklein.com/plotchecklist.html.) I didn't run this on *So Totally Emily Ebers* while editing it, because I hadn't invented it yet. But I did it as an exercise for this talk, and it was *hard*. The checklist is based on Aristotle's *Poetics*, and designed more for novels with a single straightforward movement than the web of relationships this book features. But it helped me because it made me identify the kind of plot I had — a Lack, where Emily Lacked a true understanding of her relationship with her

FIGURE A

⑤ Cheryl's Plot Checklist

PLOT CHECKLIST
(for use only after you've finished your first draft!)

The overall change my character experiences is:

From neediness to wholeness, or dependence to self-confidence

My central Action Plot is (*circle all that apply*)**:**

Conflict   (Lack)   Mystery

And that Conflict/Lack/Mystery is: Emily misses her adored father

The stakes are: Emily's happiness

My subplots are: relationships with Mom, Millicent, Stanford

My central Emotional Plot is: Coming to terms with Father's absence

The stakes are: Emily's happiness

This change happens because:

She recognizes his weakness + her own strength

Exposition: The situation at the beginning: Emily loves her dad, hates her mom, has had to leave her friends

Rising Action: The action starts when:

EE arrives in Rancho Rosetta

Then this event happens: Alice signs EE up for volleyball

Because of whose action?:   Alice

(*Keep answering those two questions for all the major events of the novel until you've arrived at:*)

Climax: Everything comes together when: A series of betrayals discovered; EE calls her dad to leave him a message + gets

Falling Action: And then?   placemats at MM's house

Betrayers + EE reconciles — by speaking honestly with one another

Resolution: The reader can tell things have changed because:

All the relationships are happy (except Dad)

The point is:

When people hurt you, you can choose how to react

father. And the story of the novel is of her getting that understanding and coming to terms with it.

You'll see it ends with our second major question here: "What is the point?" "The point" of a book, as I use the term, is its guiding idea or theme: the truth you want to communicate to readers; the emotion you want them to feel; the concept you want to explore in your story; the question you want to answer; and also the answer to the question "What is it about?"

Points fall into two related categories. The first is what, if you're being incredibly reductive, you would call the message or moral of the book — what we'll call the thematic point. The second kind of point is the emotional effect the book has on the reader — or more simply, the emotional point.

If you had just read the manuscript of *Pride and Prejudice* and you asked Jane Austen, "What is it about?", she might say "It's about pride and prejudice and the stupid mistakes smart people make when they allow those emotions to get in the way of seeing rightly." That's a thematic point — something the characters or reader discover in the course of the action. But if you asked the same question of Dav Pilkey about the Captain Underpants series, he might say, "It's about giant flying toilets that attack the earth and using the word 'poop' as often as possible." Why? To make kids (and the author) laugh. That's an emotional point — something your readers feel in response to the action.

And both of those answers are *just fine* for the books they're writing and the audiences they serve. I can't make *this* point enough. While all books must fulfill the qualities we laid out earlier, with interesting characters and story, good writing, and a point to its telling (whether emotional or moral) . . . not every book has to be deep. Not every book has to be funny. Not every book has to make you cry. Not every book has to be Harry Potter.

In fact, I don't *want* to see Harry Potter again in a submission. Yes, certainly, I want my books to give as much delight and sell as well. But the point of that book has now been said. And the book itself has been written and published and is done. I want to see the thing *you* want to think about, how *you* would tell the story of a young boy coming of age in a time of magical war.

Every book must do just two things: One, fulfill the reader's expectations for it given its provenance and genre. A literary novel has to have beautiful writing. A mystery has to have a crime, clues, and a satisfying answer. A romance has to have a romantic relationship. A Dav Pilkey book has to have giant flying toilets.

And two: Give pleasure to a reader. Besides the writer. (And the writer's mother.) But that pleasure usually starts with the writer. So don't stress yourself out about depth. Find the point of the material you're working with and the story you're telling, and go on from there.

Once you identify what your book is about or for — sheer entertainment, self-gratification, spiritual contemplation, whatever — you have an idea both to work towards and to judge the content of your story against.

In terms of an idea to work towards: As the action in your story unfolds, the main character should discover the point you've identified. For example, every plot development in the first half of *Pride and Prejudice* serves to establish Elizabeth's pride and prejudice toward Darcy. So when Elizabeth learns that he's actually a good guy, she recognizes the point: how she hasn't seen rightly and that's she just made a big mistake. Thus, when the main character gets the point about pride and prejudice, so does the reader. (Good work, Jane.)

In terms of something to judge your story against: At the other end of the scale, suppose Dav Pilkey interrupted the latest Captain Underpants book with a serious interlude where Harold and George met a Holocaust survivor. The Holocaust is an important topic, indeed, an essential one. But it is not what the Captain Underpants series is about, and its utter seriousness does not belong alongside the tale of giant flying toilets from Mars. So I would advise Dav to edit that.

Knowing your point is just as important as knowing your story, so: You have your pencils at the ready, your WIP in mind, and the question "What is the point of your book?" One minute — go!

TRUCK #6: Answer the question "What is it about?" with a one-sentence thesis statement for your book.

If you're struggling to take your plot to the next level, come back to this point — or more exactly, the thesis statement you wrote above. Do all the developments of the Action Plot inevitably lead your main character to discover the point you have in mind? Or do the developments add up to something else? If the answer is "something else," you can change the plot to get to the point you originally intended, or you can change the point to suit the plot you've written. That's a decision you have to make.

As an example, I was working with a very talented writer earlier this year on a novel that had great characters, a strong story, original magic—but something wasn't connecting. And finally I returned it to her and I just said, "I'm sorry, but this seems flat to me. I'm not getting the point you're trying to make." She told me that point — her thesis statement — and we put it together: The problem was that her main character knew that truth from the beginning. So the novel wasn't about her *discovering* the truth, but just a constant reinforcement of that truth, which wasn't as interesting since it wasn't a change. The author went back and changed her point to fit the story, I think. And she's revising the book along those lines.

And as a more practical example, this thesis statement is a really useful way to judge subplots. Which ones support or offer variations on the point? Which ones have nothing to do with that point? Are any of them redundant with each other?

Now if you can't create this thesis statement right off, if you didn't have a vision for the book particularly when you started it or you can't say what it's about now — well, sit down and sort that out. What ideas in the book get you most excited? Which conflicts thrill you most? Or which characters interest you most? What inspired the book in the first place? Come back to that, and see if you can use that to help you winnow down your material and find yourself a point. After all, as Sherlock Holmes says, "It is of the highest importance in the art of detection to be able to recognize out of a number of facts which are incidental and which vital. Otherwise your energy and attention must be dissipated instead of being concentrated."

That's really the point of the point exercise — to figure out what's the most vital thing you need to communicate to your readers, so you can concentrate on building your story around that.

With *So Totally Emily Ebers*, Arthur and I felt strongly that the book was about trust — or to quote from our first editorial letter for the book, "how you can trust others, and then what happens when they prove untrustworthy; and trust in yourself and who you are, no matter how others fail you or make fun of you." So we used that word as our guide in checking over the plot — first making sure that Emily's level of trust in each character was firmly established for the reader, then knocking those relationships down one by one, which ended with the confident Emily losing trust in herself. Then we readers can see how she acts when that trust is gone, and how she rebuilds her relationships after that. Arthur and I found out later that Lisa's guiding word for the book was "abandonment," which is the betrayal of trust, so we seemed to have gotten it right.

You remember, way back before I started discussing the story and the point, that I was talking about my editorial process, which began with reading the manuscript. Then I told you my reasons for doing so based on theory — the story and the point. Coming back to practice here: Once I'm done with that reading, I sit down and immediately write out my first impressions: what stuck out most in my mind, what was terrific, what needed work. Here's a paragraph from my freewriting on *So Totally Emily Ebers*:

Need more of the friendship between Millie and Emily earlier — hard to get a sense of Millicent herself. Understandable — if Emily looks too hard at Millicent she'll see the cracks and the lies — but we need to hear more about the places where they *are* connecting then, the things they are talking about. Have Millicent make an intentional joke, maybe, or tell one from 1001 Jokes? How about that spontaneous laugh? Need more conversations like that great one about Alice. Also the new things Millie exposed Emily to, like the Rialto et al. Set up better why Emily would miss Millie when she's gone. Millie gets funny, acerbic, only after her secret's out — bring that aspect of her in earlier. Perhaps have her tell EE about Digger.

Once that's done, I take these notes and the analysis I did of the story and the point, and I keep thinking about and writing about and refining those things until I have a coherent list of items to address in the manuscript. At this point, I often try to call or have lunch with the author to talk over these issues now that I've thought them through. Then I get to hear their answers to the story and point questions and thier intentions on the issues I raise, which strongly influences my own thinking, because my goal is to help my authors achieve what *they* want to achieve, not to impose my will upon them.

And then I turn my notes and their responses into an editorial letter. The goal of an editorial letter is to confirm and refine the Big Things: what this story is about, who the major characters are, how the central Action Plot works. I try to identify the issues clearly and sometimes offer solutions, though sometimes I leave the author to work it out for herself. I believe the great detective has a word for us here: "In solving a problem of this sort, the grand thing is to be able to reason backwards. That is a very useful accomplishment, and a very easy one, but people do not practise it much. In the everyday affairs of life it is more useful to reason forward, and so the other comes to be neglected."

One of the key problems I identified in my first notes on *Emily Ebers* was that Millicent and Emily didn't seem to be connecting. But because this is a book about trust, Emily and Millicent *have* to connect for the plot to work. So reasoning backward from that . . . how do we make them connect? This is what Arthur and I put in our editorial letter:

Arthur: Good stuff. Let's move on to Millicent now, OK?

Cheryl: OK. This was actually the relationship I believed the *least* for the first two-thirds of the book, basically because we didn't get a good sense of who Millicent was and what's likeable about her until after the girls' big fight. We can understand why it might be difficult for you to draw her character here — if Emily looks too hard at Millicent, she'll see the cracks in the "homeschooled" persona; but even if she never really examines Millicent factually, we readers need a better sense of what's connecting them emotionally, starting with their very first conversation at volleyball on June 26. Could you dramatize this scene in more detail? Even if it's old news for readers of *MMGG*, it's brand-new and exciting to Emily (her first friend!).

Arthur: . . . and I guess you don't have to repeat the conversations wholesale from the first book, but perhaps we could hear how Emily sees awkward, vulnerable Millie at that first practice. How she identifies with her, etc.

Cheryl: Yes. Emily is such a wonderfully emotional character, we would expect to see her demonstrate all of her enthusiasm and sensitivity toward this important new person in her life. (On the factual level, perhaps it could be more of a big deal upfront that Millicent is homeschooled? Emily might accept that as an explanation of why she doesn't know kid things like "nine at two o'clock" and why she's so weird in general.)

Once their connection is established, it would be great to see it developed in more depth through emotional revelations to one another as well as their general activities together — building the trust Emily has in Millicent. Even if Millicent isn't telling the whole truth about herself to Emily, Emily might still confide in her and Millicent could listen — which Emily would always appreciate! Millicent might tell Emily about the Digger experience at some point in the book (though she would never call him by name), which would be a "confession" on her part and better set up the scene at the Fiesta. Or perhaps Julie and her group might tease/bully Millicent more consistently? This is something Millicent naturally wouldn't have recorded in her journal, given her tendency to ignore unpleasant emotional facts; but we imagine it would rouse Emily's fiercest protective instincts, binding the two girls even more tightly. Emily might mistakenly admire Millicent's fashion-forwardness (the briefcase, the stark bedroom), as well as her bravery, patience (in "putting up" with Alice), and of course honesty (per p. 137 — what sort of revelations from Millicent have led Emily to think she's honest?). And then Millicent might expose Emily to new Rancho Rosetta things she would come to love, like movies at the Rialto or yoga with Maddie.

What all of these emotional connections would do is establish the emotional stakes of their relationship, so we readers feel the depth of Emily's desperation and depression when Millicent's betrayal is revealed. Right now that desperation feels a little more told than felt, frankly, partly because Emily has seemed to like Millicent's family more than Millicent herself for most of the book.

Luckily for us, Lisa agreed with most of this! So she went away to revise the book. An author's revision can take anywhere from one month to five or six, depending upon the amount of work to be done, the book's schedule, and the author's personal schedule. Then the manuscript comes back to me, and I repeat the whole reading-thinking-writing process all over again.

In the first draft, we editors try to resolve the overall story, character, and point issues to make sure everything is solid for the book's overall arc. In the second draft, we'll focus more on individual scenes — making sure they add up and round off, that everything in them is necessary, that the pacing is right, all that. And on the second and third drafts, I'll do in-depth line-edits — the line-by-line, or even word-by-word, review of a manuscript.

The same way we discussed the most basic qualities of a good novel above, we can come up with basic standards for good prose, where our goal is the perfect match of style and content. I define "style" as "A strategy for communication that reflects the point of the novel." It is different from "voice," which is not the strategy of communication itself, but rather the persona in which that strategy is embodied. Style encompasses voice, tone, vocabulary, rhythm, point of view; and most crucially, all of those elements are used in service to the point of the novel. Compare these two paragraphs:

> The evil of the actual disparity in their ages (and Mr. Woodhouse had not married early) was much increased by his constitution and habits; for having been a valetudinarian all his life, without activity of mind or body, he was a much older man in ways than in years; and though everywhere beloved for the friendliness of his heart and his amiable temper, his talents could not have recommended him at any time.

> "Give me bacon and eggs," said the other man. He was about the same size as Al. Their faces were different, but they

were dressed like twins. Both wore overcoats too tight for them. They sat leaning forward, their elbows on the counter.

The first is Jane Austen, from *Emma;* the second Ernest Hemingway, from his short story "The Killers." The Austen rolls on and on, with beautiful balance and long words — appropriate for a novel about bringing things out of balance into peace and harmony. Meanwhile, the Hemingway is staccato, uneasy, quick — appropriate for a story about sudden violence disturbing the rhythm of everyday life. If they traded styles, even if they kept all the other elements, both stories would be thrown off completely.

And this demonstrates the key thought here: Your style should serve the points of your book. If your main point is to entertain, you want to be easy to follow. To thrill, you want to be tight and fast. To tell the story of a simple country girl, you may want simple country language. (Unless your emotional point is humor, in one direction or another, and then perhaps you want fancy high-falutin' language to point up the disjunction between your style and her life.) Once you know what your point is, think about how you can shape your sentences to fit that.

Style has four key qualities, which I'll work through one at a time:

Voice. I defined "voice" above as the persona in which the style is embodied — the *intelligence* the reader senses behind the prose, choosing the words, arranging the incidents. In first-person books, this intelligence is meant to be that of the character speaking; in third person, it's the intelligence of the narrative voice.

Rhythm. The rhythm is the way the sentence sounds when it's read aloud — like meter in poetry. That Jane Austen sentence is seventy-three words long, but because she breaks it up with commas, you have places to breathe while reading it.

Variance in rhythm and language. If every sentence in a paragraph has the same length and rhythm, the effect is a bit stultifying. Suppose we edited the Hemingway example like this:

> The other man ordered bacon and eggs. He was about the same size as Al. They had different faces but wore the same clothes. Both wore overcoats too tight for them. They sat leaning forward with their elbows on the counter.

I took out the commas in the first, third, and fifth sentences, so it feels even tenser still — but also more repetitive, deadened, in the way every line is alike. I also changed the line "they were dressed like twins" to "wore the same clothes," so you could hear how the "wore" jangles in the next line. Good prose repeats words in close proximity to each other only by strategy or design, not by accident or sloppiness.

Flow. I think of flow as the connection of content and emotion between clauses in prose. The narrative voice doesn't jump from subject to subject without any connection or transition, but rather it has a natural forward motion of ideas and action, so the reader never says, "Wait, stop, where did that idea or feeling come from?" and gets broken out of the story. (For an example of flow in action, see the analysis of the Jane Austen paragraph above on p. 267.)

Originality. I'm always listening for a voice I haven't heard before — one that uses fresh and original imagery and phrasing. I recently read *Wide Awake* by David Levithan, which is a fascinating YA novel about civic responsibility (as much as that sounds like a contradiction in terms), and the main character loves American history and the Boston Tea Party. So when it's time to protest something he thinks is wrong, he says, "Let's throw some tea overboard." I love that.

One mark of a bad voice is clichés. "Trembling like a leaf," "as luck would have it," "bored to tears": These bore *me* to tears. Sometimes characters will speak in clichés, and that's fine as long as it's intentional — that is, the writer is deliberately having the character speak in clichés to show us something about that character, most likely that they're pretty shallow and not that interesting.

The best way to test the style of your work altogether is:

TRUCK #7: **Read it aloud — or better still, have someone read it aloud to you.**

You'll be able to hear the rhythms and variance — or lack of variance, which might require revision. If you find yourself editing what you're reading as you go along, write in what you're saying, because your prose will sound best when it reflects your natural voice. And watch your own emotional reactions as you read — are you excited in the action parts? Emotional in the sad parts? Do you get tired or bored in any particular scenes? If you're not having the reactions you intended, maybe that's a sign you should revise.

So that addresses the style of good prose; now it's time to go into the content of it. These are more of the things I'm thinking of when I line-edit a novel. Good prose:

Is written in voice. That is, it is within the boundaries of what your narrator could potentially say or the reader would expect to hear from him or her.

Makes steady forward progress. In other words, every thought takes the story forward or deeper in some way; it doesn't repeat information unless it's really necessary to make an important point. For example: "Joey was speechless. Not a word came out. He couldn't even open his mouth." . . . I think I got the picture after the first one, thanks.

Shows, not tells. The overall goal of this common writing adage is that the events of the story unfold in such a way that the emotion the writer intends the reader to feel is generated through those events alone. It should not just outright tell the reader what that emotion is ("I felt so sad").

But at the same time, good prose **chooses dramatization wisely.** Telling is putting something in narration, for instance: "We talked about the concert next week, and agreed it would be awesome." Showing is dramatizing it for the reader so it's as if it happens before our eyes: "Hey, are you excited about the MetroCards concert next week?" "Yeah, I can't wait!"

Showing has more weight than telling because it takes up more time and lays the situation out so readers can see it with their own eyes. As Holmes has it, "There is nothing like first-hand evidence." But you don't need to prove every single point to the reader, and if you do dramatize every point for the reader, your book will be very long and you'll probably waste some of their time. Dramatize the things that matter most to your overall story and point.

Gets the details right. When I'm line-editing, I'm also fact-checking things both within the manuscript and in the real world. If Emily Ebers says she lives at 1350 Willow Tree Lane at one point, then gives her address as 1480 Willow Tree Circle at another, I'll ask Lisa to confirm which one is correct and make the two consistent. Or if Emily suddenly decided to do a chemistry experiment and gave the boiling point of water as 160 degrees Fahrenheit, I'd say to Lisa, "You know, it's actually 212 degrees. Would you like to revise this, or were you trying to emphasize how little Emily knows about science?" As Sherlock Holmes says: "Have you tried to drive a harpoon through a body? No? Tut, tut, my dear sir, you must really pay attention to these details."

When I'm line-editing, I **test every sentence against the question "What purpose does this serve?"** (You can do this too, as TRUCK #8.) If it's not necessary — if it's something we already know, or something extraneous to the story or the point, or if it's not showing us more about the world or the character that is important for the story or point — I will often suggest cutting it.

If it *is* necessary, I want to be sure it's phrased in the very best way possible to communicate the meaning to readers. Here's an example that's not from *Emily*, but from the first draft of a translation I edited:

> Choosing this tiny, two-story Victorian with its dingy blue columns and faded shutters, wedged between two even more run-down houses, was especially odd since every business worthy of the name had long ago deserted the street.

The point of this sentence, the key information it was meant to convey, was simply that the Victorian house was an odd choice for the buyer to make. But that's being obscured by the long description of the house between the "choosing" and "odd," and the many other tidbits of information that distract the reader.

The easiest way to emphasize something in a sentence or a paragraph is to say it in a standalone declarative clause at either the beginning or end. Remember when you did topic sentences in school? How the first sentence in a paragraph establishes your thesis, and the rest of the paragraph supports that? Or how you were supposed to write a concluding sentence to sum up your argument in a particular paragraph, and then go on to the rest of your argument? The same structure can be applied to fiction. The first or last sentence in a paragraph — or even the first or last phrase in a sentence — should give a sense of what you're talking about and the circumstances in which the action is taking place. So the translator and I put the "odd choice" together and upfront to get:

> It was an odd choice of location for a bookstore — a tiny, two-story Victorian house with dingy blue columns and faded shutters — especially since every other business worthy of the name had long ago deserted the street.

And I hope you'll agree that that is an improvement, as it now states that key information in a manner that's easy for the reader to comprehend. This is where the detective's work and the editor's are most alike: They're all about paying attention to details. To quote Holmes one more time: "It is, of course, a trifle, but there is nothing so important as trifles."

If you'll look at Figure B now, we'll go over some edits Arthur and I made to the first scene of *So Totally Emily Ebers*.

This is from the first draft, and you'll see that compared to the other drafts, there aren't a lot of line-edit notes here. That's because, as a rule, we don't do a lot of line-edits on first draft — too much can change with

FIGURE B

Emily Ebers Explains Everything
By Lisa Yee

⑧ First draft
January 2006

Page 2 of 245
1/6/06

June 7

Dear Dad,

Today was the last day of school, and the second saddest day of my entire life. AJ
and Nicole were crying and crying, and I was crying, and then Mrs. Spence
started crying. This freaked everyone out because teachers aren't supposed to cry.
The only other time a teacher at Wilcox Academy has cried was when Mr.
Kinnoin from grade three won the lottery. Trembling, he stood on his desk and
shouted, "Okay, you little weenies, you're never going to see me in a classroom
again!" Then he burst into tears.

My whole class had made me a humongous card, and everyone wrote nice
things, even Seth. When I finished reading it, I began bawling so hard that a long
string of boogers flew out and dangled from my nose. As it swung back and forth,
Nicole started wheezing so badly that Mrs. Spence was convinced she was having
another asthma attack. AJ and I offered to take Nicole to the nurse.

"Girls, go directly there," Mrs. Spence instructed. "And hurry!"

As soon as we got outside, we began laughing hysterically -- and that's when
it happened. I lost it. Yes. I peed in my pants. Again. AJ gave me her jacket to tie
around my waist, and Nicole reminded me that she peed in her pants during that
flesh-eating movie, where Rex Rock fights off the zombies with a pair of
tweezers. I suppose, if you must pee in your pants in public, it's better to do it in
front of your best friends than worst enemies.

AJ Schifman, Nicole Kwan and I have been together since kindergarten. That

[handwritten margin note:] maybe this is a girl thing, but Jim put off by this. It's not that funny to me & it makes EE unappealing. We're not her best friends yet.

[handwritten note at bottom:] Something Dad ought to know? Maybe phrase as reminder, or question "Can you believe...?"

FIGURE B continued

makes seven years of best friendness. It is beyond ultimate sadness that we are being ripped apart. I think I have set a new world record for crying. Tonight as I squeezed out what little tears I had left, I stared at myself in the bathroom mirror for so long my face looked like it was morphing into monsters. It was bizarre and interesting and depressing at the same time.

Well, it's after midnight. The house is empty. The movers came today. Mom trailed them around saying, "That's fragile!" and "Do you have any idea what it would cost to replace that?" She's conked out in a sleeping bag next to the fireplace. Guess I'd better get to bed, too. Tomorrow's going to be rough.

Goodnight, Dad.

Love,

Emily

the story and point still, so it's not worth messing with specific language. (I'd also like to note that the vast majority of *So Totally Emily Ebers* didn't require as much editing as you'll see here. . . . This was the first chapter, so it was absolutely essential that we get it right, and we spent a lot of time on it.)

Arthur commented on the "pee your pants" paragraph. That's because peeing your pants is intrinsically a little gross, right? And on the very first page of the book, we readers don't know Emily well enough to go there with her, so it put Arthur off (me too, I admit).

I commented on the fact that Dad ought to know who Emily's best friends are, so if Emily has to *tell* Dad her best friends' names, that makes me not believe in Emily's closeness to her dad. But the point of this whole book, as we said earlier, is Emily recognizing that her closeness with her dad wasn't all that real from the beginning. That means the reader needs to believe it at the beginning, just as Emily does, and so I asked Lisa to change this. On the other hand, we needed to establish the girls' friendship upfront for the reader, since friendship is also an important theme of the book. . . . Watch for this sentence in future drafts.

Figure C shows the line-edit of that same first page in second draft. First, note the changes Lisa made here. She cut the "pee your pants" paragraph; added the line "I know you can never remember my friends," then described them; and added the paragraph about the Elmo tape recorder on p. 2. That was a direct result of a discussion in the editorial letter about Emily's relationship with her dad — the Elmo recorder establishes their closeness. On the other hand, the "never remember my friends" line undercuts that closeness, so I asked Lisa to consider dropping it.

Running down through the other edits on that page:

- "The only other time a teacher . . .": Remember what I was saying about topic sentences above? The first scene in a book serves as sort of the topic sentence of that book, as it establishes the narrator, the setting, and the main idea quickly for the reader. Therefore you really want to stay focused in that first scene, especially early on. Here the anecdote about a teacher we don't know and who will have nothing to do with the action of the book interrupts the establishing process, so I asked Lisa to cut it.

- "I began bawling so hard . . .": Basically the same problem as "pee your pants" above; I don't know and love Emily so much at this point in the book that my fondness for her overcomes my disgust at her telling me about her boogers! Better to cut.

- "Girls, go directly there!": This was a case of misplaced dramatization, as the point of this scene is showing the reader how close A.J. and Nicole and Emily are, and therefore how sad Emily will be to leave them. Given that, Mrs. Spence is

FIGURE C

Emily Ebers Explains Everything
By Lisa Yee

Page 2 of 283
3/1/06

⑨ Second draft
March 2006

June 7

Dear Dad,

Today was the last day of school, and the second saddest day of my entire life. AJ

and Nicole were crying and crying, and I was crying, and then Mrs. Spence

started crying. This freaked everyone out because teachers aren't supposed to cry.

> The only other time a teacher at Wilcox Academy has cried was when Mr.
> Kinnoin from grade three won the lottery. Trembling, he stood on his desk and
> shouted, "Okay, you little weenies, you're never going to see me in a classroom
> again!" Then he burst into tears.

I love this incident, but the first paragraph of the book seems a bit early for a digression!

My whole class had made me a humongous card, and everyone wrote nice

things, even Seth. When ~~I finished~~ reading it, I began bawling ~~so hard that a long~~ *and*

~~string of boogers flew out and dangled from my nose. As it swung back and forth,~~

Nicole started wheezing so badly that Mrs. Spence was convinced she was having

another asthma attack. AJ and I offered to take Nicole to the nurse.

EWW — not sure about having something this gross this early?

~~"Girls, go directly there," Mrs. Spence instructed. "And hurry!" As we left~~

~~the room, she started saying, "Your summer assignment . . ."~~ We waited until we

were halfway down the hallway ~~and then~~ burst out laughing hysterically.

AJ Schiffman, Nicole Kwan and I have been together since kindergarten.

> That makes seven years of best friendness. I know you can never remember my
> friends, even though they are so totally different. So I'll tell you again, for old
> time's sake. AJ has shoulder-length light brown hair and blue eyes, and is always
> singing. Nicole is half Chinese and half French, has green eyes and wavy dark

Instead of focusing on the girls' looks (and Dad's disappointing EE already by never remembering their names), perhaps you could have EE reminisce a little

about activities they've done together, so readers know why the relationship has meaning for EE? Or better still, continue the scene after they burst out laughing hysterically? How do best friends act when they're about to be

FIGURE C continued

~~black hair, and is allergic to everything.~~

It is beyond ultimate sadness that we are being ripped apart. I think I have set

a new world record for crying. Tonight as I squeezed out what little tears I had

left, I stared at myself in the bathroom mirror for so long my face looked like it

was morphing into monsters. It was bizarre and interesting and depressing at the

same time.

Again, a bit too early for anecdotes not driving action. Also see p. 6 — introduce LJ idea here?

Well it's after midnight. The house is empty. The movers came today. Mom

trailed them around shouting, "That's fragile!" and "Do you have any idea what it

would cost to replace that??!!!" She's conked out in a sleeping bag next to the

fireplace. I guess yelling at moving men is exhausting.

When I got home from school,

To set up EE's movement through the day

I'd better get to bed, too. Tomorrow's going to be rough. I wish you were

here to sing me to sleep like you used to do when I was little. In a box labeled

"Emily's Most Important Things," I packed my Elmo tape recorder. It has the

cassette of you singing *The Emily Song* in it. That's the first thing I'm going to

unpack when we get to ~~Rancho Rosetta~~ California.

Goodnight, Daddy.

B/c their overall geographic destination is more important than town name right now, OK?

Love,

Emily

important only because she sends the girls out of the room — we don't need to hear her words directly.

- "That makes seven years of best friendness": To the explanation on the page, I'll add that as a paragraph of solid description, this stopped the action dead — not something that should happen in the first scene! So I asked Lisa to establish the girls' characters through their dialogue rather than their appearances, as the dialogue reinforced the girls' friendship, thus serving the point of the scene.
- "When I got home from school": This created a transition from the school day to evening at home.
- "I packed my Elmo tape recorder": Again, just moving the important information to the front of the sentence.

Figure D shows the third draft line-edits, and again, note the changes Lisa made from the previous draft: Besides the little corrections, she replaced the physical description of the girls with emotional dialogue binding them together (using the Mr. Kinnoin anecdote that had been in that first paragraph), and added the line about the hamster, which flows nicely into their all crying again and "beyond ultimate sadness." At this point, we've gotten the content in such strong shape that my edits here are really coming down to individual words and little tiny emotional reactions, as you can see.

- I suggest running the first two paragraphs together because (1) You don't want to give readers a place to stop until they're thoroughly hooked in the book; and (2) ending the paragraph with "teachers aren't supposed to cry" makes that thought sound really important and pithy, and while it *is* funny, the emphasis here should not be on the teacher or thoughts about teachers, but on Emily's sadness at leaving her friends. Putting those two paragraphs together changed the focus of the paragraph to just that.
- Here I suggested adding "After we stopped laughing" for the same reasons we added "When I got home from school" above:

FIGURE D

⑩ THIRD DRAFT MANUSCRIPT WITH CHERYL'S EDITS

June 7

Dear Dad,

Today was the last day of school, and the second saddest day of my entire life. AJ
and Nicole were crying and crying, and I was crying, and then Mrs. Buono started
crying. This freaked everyone out because teachers aren't supposed to cry. My whole
class had made me a humongous card, and everyone wrote nice things, even Evan.
When I finished reading it, I began bawling and Nicole started wheezing so badly
that Mrs. Buono was convinced she was having another asthma attack. AJ and I
offered to take Nicole to the nurse.

> **Deleted:** [cherykle 6/26/06 4:09 PM]

We managed to wait until we were halfway down the hall to begin laughing
hysterically. [Suggest adding "managed" (or something like that) to more
directly suggest the conspiracy among the three girls, and therefore their
friendship, which is reinforced by moving up the next sentence:]

> **Deleted:** ed [cherykle 6/26/06 4:10 PM]

  A.J. Schiffman, Nicole Quan and I have been best friends forever. After we
stopped laughing, A.J. brought up the time we were in first grade and Mr. Kinnoin
won the lottery. [This "trembling" is a great showing detail, but sounds more
like a novelist speaking than like Emily?] He stood on his desk and shouted,
"Okay, you little weenies, you're never going to see me in a classroom again!" Then
he then burst into tears and ran out of the room.

> **Deleted:** Then [cherykle 6/26/06 4:13 PM]
>
> **Deleted:** Trembling, he [cherykle 6/26/06 4:13 PM]
>
> **Deleted:** He [cherykle 6/26/06 4:14 PM]

  Nicole reminded us how in second grade we dressed as the three little pigs for
Halloween, and whenever anyone asked us anything, we'd just make piggy noises.

> **Deleted:** made us laugh when she [cherykle 6/26/06 4:14 PM]
>
> **Deleted:** embered [cherykle 6/26/06 4:16 PM]

FIGURE D continued

Then I remembered [AL recommended changing this word as "recalled" didn't

sound like Emily's diction, so I suggest changing "remembered" to

"reminded us" above, and this to "remember" instead—OK?] when A.J.'s

hamster died and we had a funeral for her, and then we all started crying all over

again.

[Don't need to state this so baldly, I don't think . . .]

Now it's after midnight. The house is empty. The movers came today. When I

got home from school Mom was trailing them around shouting, "That's fragile!" and

"Do you have any idea what it would cost to replace that??!!!" She's conked out in a

sleeping bag next to the fireplace still clutching her clipboard. I guess yelling at

moving men is exhausting.

I'd better get to bed too. Tomorrow's going to be rough. I wish you were here

to sing me to sleep like you used to do when I was little. I packed my Elmo tape

recorder in a box labeled "Emily's Most Important Things." It has the cassette of

you singing *The Emily Song* in it. That's the first thing I'm going to unpack when we

get to California.

Goodnight, Daddy.

Love,

Emily

---

cherykle 6/26/06 4:14 PM
Deleted: recalled

cherykle 6/26/06 4:15 PM
Deleted: It is beyond ultimate sadness that we are being ripped apart. AJ Schiffman, Nicole Quan and I have been best friends forever. I think I have set a new world record for crying.

cherykle 6/26/06 4:17 PM
Deleted: It's

It created a transition from one setting (or in this case, emotion) to the next.

* Both "Trembling" and "recalled" sounded out-of-tune with Emily's slightly dizzy voice, so we cut them both, which with "recalled" necessitated some word juggling to avoid repetition.
* The "It is beyond ultimate sadness" paragraph: This was something that the reader could understand by this point without Lisa having to state Emily's feelings outright, so we didn't need these three lines.
* And the last two paragraphs are again just perfect.

Figure E reveals the text more or less the way it appears in the final book.

For the record, all of those edits are the result of at least two and usually three reads of the manuscript. Ideally, I read a draft once to form my reactions to it; once more to write preliminary line-edits; once more to put in final line-edits, and oftentimes a fourth time to be sure all of my notes are in tune with each other and with the accompanying letter. So if you ever wonder why an editor takes so long to respond to your submission — it's because we're putting in so much time on the books we already have!

After I finish my line-edits, I write a cover letter that reviews the big things we need to concentrate on in this draft, and I ship the package off to the author. And we repeat this process until we get the book where it needs to be and I turn it in to the copyediting department.

Now, not everybody likes revising. In fact, some people hate it. If you are one of those people, I'd like to offer some ways to think about your edits, whether they're ones you initiate yourself or ones recommended by your writing group or your editor.

1. Everyone gets edited. Katherine Paterson? Edited. J. K. Rowling? Edited. Your editor? Edited. It happens to everyone worth reading. (Anne Rice, in her later novels? Not edited. Tells you something, doesn't it?)

FIGURE E

JUNE 7

Dear Dad,

Today was the last day of school and the second saddest day of my entire life. A.J. and Nicole were crying and crying, and I was crying, and then Mrs. Buono started crying. This freaked everyone out because teachers aren't supposed to cry. My whole class had made me a humongous card, and everyone wrote nice things, even Evan. When I finished reading it, I began bawling and Nicole started wheezing so badly that Mrs. Buono was convinced she was having another asthma attack. A.J. and I offered to take Nicole to the nurse.

We managed to wait until we were halfway down the hall to begin laughing hysterically.

When we could breathe again, A.J. brought up the time we were in first grade and Mr. Kinnoin won the lottery. He climbed up on his desk and shouted, "Okay, you little weenies, you're never going to see me in a classroom again!" Then he burst into tears and ran out of the room.

1

FIGURE E continued

Nicole reminded us how in second grade we dressed as the three little pigs for Halloween, and whenever anyone asked us anything, we'd just make piggy noises. Then I remembered when A.J.'s hamster died and we had a funeral for her, and then we all started crying all over again.

It's after midnight now. The house is empty. The movers came today. When I got home from school, Mom was trailing them around shouting, "That's fragile!" and "Do you have any idea what it would cost to replace that?!?!" She's conked out in a sleeping bag next to the fireplace, still clutching her clipboard. I guess yelling at moving men is exhausting.

I'd better get to bed too. Tomorrow's going to be rough. I wish you were here to sing me to sleep like you used to do when I was little. I packed my Elmo tape recorder in a box labeled "Emily's Most Important Things." It has the cassette of you singing "The Emily Song" in it. That's the first thing I'm going to unpack when we get to California.

Good night, Daddy.

Love,

Emily

2

2. The edits are not a personal judgment on you or your authorial worth. In case it bears saying: Your editor does not hate you. Your editor does not think you're stupid because your work needs revision. Your editor does not care if you make copyediting mistakes, and you do not need to apologize for them. Editors are here to help make your book *work*. That's the only thing we care about.

If I identify a problem in a manuscript, the writer does not have to take my specific revision suggestion on how to solve the problem. I am fine with my suggestion being ignored. BUT he does have to either fix the problem another way, or convince me it's not a problem at all. An editor's greatest joy is a writer who can recognize his own weaknesses and respond with an intelligent revision.

3. It is perfectly okay to be upset about cutting things, as long as you ultimately do what's best for the story. If you receive a suggestion to, say, cut Mr. Fluffy, and you think "No! Never! Mr. Fluffy *has* to stay!", sit down and think why you feel this way. Is it because Mr. Fluffy is truly essential to the story? Or is it because you spent five hours writing that scene with him?

If it's important to you for a writing reason, look at why your editor wants to cut him. Suppose she points out that he doesn't seem to be doing much within the text. In that case, is there a way to solve his character so he serves a function in the book? If there is, then it might be worth keeping him. But if having Mr. Fluffy in there is important to you only for personal reasons, because of the time you've invested in him or your relationship with him personally — then you have to sigh and be a grown-up about it, in the name of good art and a good book. (Editorial Anonymous has an excellent blog post on this at <u>http://editorialanony-mous.blogspot.com/2008/10/just-saying-no-to-your-editor.html</u>.)

Don't waste too much energy on negative emotions. The most important thing for an author (and editor) should be making the book work for its readers. And really, if you hate cutting that one line or plot development because it's so perfect and you spent so much time on it:

4. **Remember: It's just disappearing from this work. It's not disappearing from the world.** You can use it again somewhere else. And this
leads me to:

TRUCK #9: Keep a copy of everything.
This is probably obvious, but: Save every draft in a new file, or transfer
anything significant that you cut to an OUTTAKES section at the
bottom of your document. You never know when you might need the
backup, or if you may want to add it again in revision, or when that one
line will provide the title or the idea for your next book.

Finally, whether you're writing a first draft, editing an old draft, or
about to send off a brand-spanking-new draft, try:

TRUCK #10: Give it time.
Time to absorb the suggested changes, so they grow in the bones of
the revision; time to experiment with trying new things or directions;
time to make your work the best it can be. Editors get suspicious when
authors return revisions too quickly, because it usually indicates they're
only surface changes — the author hasn't really thought the changes
through.

If you print out a fresh draft of your manuscript and want to send it
to me, please: Stick it in a drawer for a week and reread it then. If there
are things that still need to be fixed, they'll be more apparent when you
approach them with a fresh eye than immediately after you've finished
the corrections; and if it's ready to go — it will still be ready to go in a
week. (Or twenty-four hours, if you can't stand to wait seven days.)

And if I go to the trouble of asking for a revision of your manuscript, I'm not going to lose interest in it because you get it to me in four
months instead of two. I'd rather have an author who took the time to
write a good revision in four months, than one who rushes it right back
to me without thinking it all through.

So that brings us to the end of our parade of TRUCKs. I hope you
have found things in it that will be helpful to you. I said at the beginning
that the editor's work and the detective's aren't very much alike. But we

are both searching for that elusive truth, in life or in fiction. Or the best of all, fiction that readers love as much as life, for all the truth it contains.

As Holmes says, "What one man can invent, another can discover." And "My life is spent in one long effort to escape from the commonplace of existence." I live for the great stories that lift us out of the commonplace of existence; and if yours do that, I look forward to discovering your inventions.

FOUR TECHNIQUES TO GET AT THE EMOTIONAL HEART OF YOUR STORY

July 5, 2009

I am in various composition stages on one-two-*three* different editorial letters right now . . . so of course I'm going to procrastinate and write a blog post. But these are some of the models I'm using to figure out the hearts of these manuscripts — the core character change (aka Emotional Plot) that needs to occur — and then to think through the Action Plot that overlies them to see where we may need to add events or motivation or subtract unnecessary story elements.

1. Conflict, Mystery, Lack. I go on about this at length in various talks elsewhere, so I won't spend much time on it here, but simply: Which model is your central plot and each of your subplots? Are all the narrative requirements of those plots set up at the beginning (e.g. a clear antagonist, a defined mystery, a hole of some kind in the protagonist's life), developed through the middle (escalating antagonism, clues, the filling of the hole), and satisfactory at the end (a clear victory for one side and/or reconciliation, an answer to the mystery, emotional wholeness at last)?

2. What Does the Character Want? (I admit I sometimes append "Dammit" to this.) Not all plots have or should have a character with a big goal, taking action to get it. . . . The best novels are like life, and often we don't know what we want in life and have to figure it out, and the dramatization of that figuring-it-out can be fun and fascinating if the people are real enough in it. (Case in point: *The Treasure Map of Boys* by E. Lockhart, which I read in one long, enjoyable trip around New York yesterday.) But if your plot *does* allow your character to want a specific thing from the beginning, and readers know what that thing is, *boy*, that makes the dynamics of the action so much easier and the character instantly attractive to readers, and gives you a strong narrative spine on which to hang all sorts of other subplots.

3. Compulsion vs. Obstacles. A formula I first heard from Laurie Halse Anderson:

+ What action or emotional pattern is the character compelled to repeat over and over?
+ What obstacles will keep him/her from doing it this time, and/or will force him/her to change this pattern? That is your frontstory.
+ What personality or life circumstances have formed him/her that way? That is your backstory.

4. Problem, Process, Solution. I talk about this as a picture-book-story technique in "Words, Wisdom, Art, and Heart," but it's proving enormously useful for novels as well — basically "Compulsion vs. Obstacles" once the ending has been defined, which helps to identify the steps that actually make a difference in getting to the Solution. Those steps are the Process, and there ought to be at least one of those steps, in some form, in every chapter.

And three rules of thumb: **A novel ought to be at least 75 percent Process.** Once the Problem is defined, it's time to start solving it. Don't spend valuable narrative time rehashing it, or too much time celebrating or talking about the Solution once it's been reached. (I love *Emma*, but the scene where Mr. Knightley reads Frank Churchill's letter and apostrophizes upon his faults drives me crazy — a rare authorial slip in an otherwise perfect book. I can only imagine that Jane Austen, too, adored Mr. Knightley so much that she indulged him in this fit of moralizing for the pleasure of spending more time with him.)

The main character ought to drive at least half of that Process. Either through mistakes or conscious action, and whether he or she knows it or not.

Every scene has to have a point, which is often an emotional point.

This is the moment where someone finally says the thing they've been meaning to say, or misses the moment where they ought to say it, or does something else that makes a difference in the action or the characters' relationships. Often writers will either cut scenes off before this point is reached or just let scenes lollygag on and on without getting to this point . . . at which point the scenes are ripe for the "Justify Your Existence" test, and in danger of getting cut or combined with another scene if they flunk.

Back to my mss.; good luck with yours.

WORDS, WISDOM, ART & HEART:
Making A Picture-Book Cookie

I gave this talk at the Los Angeles SCBWI Speakers' Day in April 2007. My thanks to James Monohan, the below-mentioned Kathryne (Katy) Beebe, Joshua Hatton, and Ted Salk for their help and support, and Thuy Nguyen, whose website hosted the Flash player for the pictures in the online version of this talk.

This talk is called *Words, Wisdom, Art & Heart: Making a Picture-Book Cookie*. Now, making a story is never as straightforward as a recipe — put in these ingredients and out it pops. Each story depends upon the personality of the cook, the quality of his or her materials, and the unique way the cook chooses to combine them. But like recipes, all stories have common ingredients — characters you care about, doing things that make a difference in their lives; an order to follow, from beginning to end; and basic rules of procedure — techniques you can learn through apprenticeship, study, or stealing, which help you along the way to the desired result. And that result is something that satisfies not just the palate — the taste buds seeking sweet or savory, the mind seeking adventure — but the soul, in the emotional effect that arises from the experience.

I want to draw your attention to that distinction, between the surface experience of a work of art and the larger emotional effect. You may know I talk a lot about the two different kinds of plot — the Action Plot and the Emotional Plot. The Action Plot is what happens in the story: A little boy in a wolf suit sails to the land of the Wild Things, where he is king and there is a wild rumpus, until he decides to come home. The Emotional Plot is what the story means, how it makes you feel: A little boy who has been sent to his room, made to feel his own lack of power, travels to a place where he has nothing but power — and discovers that power isn't the greatest good, that he wants to be where someone loves him "best of all."

All good stories — and this isn't just picture books, but novels too — have both an Action Plot and an Emotional Plot. And they are most satisfying when they work together, playing off each other, to create a story you can't put down, a story that fills you up . . . exactly like a good dinner or a great dessert.

So I thought the best way to discuss picture book making would be to start with an actual picture book manuscript. Suppose I'm a writer, and I've decided I want to write a picture book about me and my best friend Katy. And I'm just going to tell the story of something we do together — a shopping trip, say. So I write a story called *Two Friends Together*.

TWO FRIENDS TOGETHER
(a.k.a. Bad Picture Book Draft #1)

Cheryl and Katy were best friends.

One day they were sitting around their glamorous apartments trying to decide what to do.

"I know!" Katy said. "Let's go have salads!"

So they went to the local diner.

Katy had a Caesar salad.

Cheryl had spinach with pears and goat cheese.

"That was fun," said Cheryl. "What should we do next?"

"I know!" Katy said.

"Let's go get facials!"

So they went to the spa.

Katy had a deep pore purifying facial.

Cheryl had a restorative facial peel.

"Mmmm, a clean, soft face," said Cheryl. "What should we do next?"

"I know!" Katy said. "Let's go shopping!"

So they went to Bloomingdale's jeans department.

Cheryl tried on a pair of Juicy Couture.

Katy tried on a pair of True Religion.

Cheryl tried on a pair of Diesel.

Katy tried on a pair of Morphine Generation.

Cheryl tried on a pair of Susana Monaco.

Katy tried on a pair of Primp Clothing.

Cheryl tried on a pair of Foley Corinna.

Katy tried on a pair of Nadia & Nadya.

Cheryl tried on a pair of Little Giraffe.

Katy tried on a pair of Blue Cult.

Finally Cheryl decided to buy a pair of Seven for All Mankind.

And Katy chose a pair of Citizens of Humanity.

They toasted their new purchases with martinis —

Clink! —

And talked about their stupid ex-boyfriends.

It was a wonderful day!

So, problems with this story? None, right? It's totally perfect and publishable?

Good heavens no! There are many, many problems with this story. I'm going to break them down into six categories, which we'll talk about one by one, and we'll look at a couple different versions of this manuscript as we try to fix those problems. And hopefully by the end of this analysis, you'll have a better sense of how picture books (and indeed all stories) are structured, what a perfect picture book can and should do, and how you can improve your own work to bring it up to those standards.

So, I was just talking about Action Plots versus Emotional Plots. What's the Action Plot of this story? Two friends eat salads, get facials, buy jeans, and drink martinis. And the Emotional Plot? They have a nice day together. And this is all very well and good for these two twentysomethings, but for a picture book, there's a huge issue here:

Problem #1: No Child Interest / Appeal.

The picture book is an amazing art form, and it doesn't *have* to be for children; many adult artists work in the book form. But as a financially viable, commercially publishable form, almost all picture books *are* for children. And this means it has to speak to a child, give delight or meaning to a child, to be fully artistically successful. It should do this in both its Action Plot and its Emotional Plot.

In terms of its Action Plot, it's good to have a child or child stand-in as the protagonist. And the action could deal with experiences kids have — friends, school, pets, brothers and sisters, going to sleep. (Though you do need to be careful with stories about pets, bullies, and monsters under the bed, as those topics have been so well covered they're almost clichés.)

In terms of Emotional Plot, think about the emotional dimensions of those common childhood experiences. For instance, at its heart, a pet book — a story about a goldfish, say — might actually be about dealing with death once the goldfish passes away. A book about monsters under the bed could be about fear: how the child protagonist learns to deal with things outside of his or her control. A book about bullies might really be about power: the lack of it that might cause one child to feel frightened, or the rush of how good it feels to bend another's will to your own. Indeed, a lot of children's stories are actually about power, because it's the number-one thing kids don't have. *Where the Wild Things Are*, *Harry Potter*, all those other fantasies about evil overlords and orphaned children chosen for great destinies . . . Those kinds of books provide a safe, imaginative space for the child to identify with the protagonist, act out his desire for power or frustration at its lack, overcome difficulties, and finally learn more about the wise use of power, whether he has it back in the real world or not.

So how can a writer create a story with child interest? Study child psychology. I am not kidding about this. Kids go through certain stages in life where they respond to certain phenomena in terms of Action Plot — that's why there are so many books for three-year-olds about fire trucks; or where they need certain forms of reassurance, or they can handle certain levels of fear or challenge, in the Emotional Plot. A good child psychology book can cue you into which ages are ready for what types of stories.

But that speaks to the general, the mass of kids. Once you have those principles, you, as a writer, have to ground them in the specific — a real character or conflict. And often that starts with what *you* know of the world and what *you* remember of your childhood. Reach back into yourself — beyond the easy memories and clichés — and think about:

- What is your first memory? Your favorite memory?
- What was your favorite thing to do by yourself, or place to be?
- Who were your friends? What did you do together?
- What scared you most?
- What made you happiest?
- What were your dreams or fantasies? What did you want to be when you grew up?

And build a story around those emotions or events. I'm not saying that you should solely write what you know, but that your truest story begins with your own experience —"a writer's way of being in the world," as Zadie Smith says — transposed into an imaginary context and characters.

Now, obviously, I have not chosen an imaginary context and characters for *Two Friends Together*. But there is one thing that is true and meaningful about the story that kids might connect with: the characters' friendship. When I was a child, I was passionately devoted to my friends. I can still name most of my best friends throughout elementary school; I shared best-friend necklaces; I wrote stories about adventures we had together; and the years I was unhappiest were the years when I was without a best friend. And this dedication to my friends continues today: Katy has been my best friend for eleven years now, since we were suitemates our freshman year of college.

So the fact that the story is about best friends is a plus. But what are the friends doing? They're eating adult foods, getting adult spa services, buying adult clothes. This has nothing to do with children's lives or psychology, so these activities will seem entirely foreign to the child readership, if not boring or even repugnant. I'd like to write a story about friendship, but I need to find some plot for it that has child appeal.

Is there something else Katy and I could do together? Well, as you might tell from our very first activity in the story — we like to eat. So I decided I was going to revise this story so she and I are still the main characters, but instead of being about salads and shopping, it's about making cookies. (Note: I would LIKE to revise this so it has child main characters, but I'm going to show some illustrations for it at the end, and for that I needed to use us as grown-ups. But you can imagine it with children if you like.)

CHERYL AND KATY AND COOKIES
(a.k.a. Bad Picture Book Draft #2)

Cheryl and Katy were best friends.

One day, they decided to make cookies at Cheryl's house. And not just any cookies, but their favorite banana oatmeal chocolate-chip cookies.

Katy brought the bananas, the sugar, the nutmeg, the cinnamon, and the egg.

Cheryl supplied the flour, the baking soda, the salt, butter, oatmeal, and chocolate chips.

Katy measured

And Cheryl sifted.

Cheryl mashed
And Katy poured.
Katy accidentally broke the egg
And Cheryl cleaned it up.
"It's okay," she said, going to her refrigerator,
"I have another egg in here."
She took the egg out and broke it into the bowl.
They took turns beating the mixture until their arms were tired
And then finally Katy poured in the chocolate chips
And Cheryl folded them into the batter.
They each spooned great lumps onto cookie sheets,
Stuck the sheets in the hot oven,
And washed all the dishes.
Fifteen minutes later,
They pulled the cookie sheets out,
Poured themselves tall glasses of milk,
And scooped up the hot cookies.
Yum!

So, as a piece of writing for children, is this better or worse? I would judge it marginally better, because it does at least deal with things children are interested in, like cookies and baking. But we still have numerous problems going on . . . the number one being — there's not much going on! It is what editors often identify as a "slice of life" story: It neatly captures the activities of these two friends, but *nothing happens.* Either action-wise: They make cookies. Big deal. Or emotionally: They're friends. Big deal. So the two issues we're looking at right now with *Cheryl and Katy and Cookies:*

Problems 2. & 3.: No emotional journey, and no narrative shape

Actually, I need to pause here for a moment and talk about the two different types of picture books, because many picture books do not have plots at all. A plot, in the classical sense, is defined by a *change*: Things are different at the end of the story than they were at the beginning. This might be a change in the protagonist's circumstances; it might be a change in the protagonist himself. Often it's a change in both, as the character has learned something, or gained something, or gone somewhere new. And this change — in a picture book — is always for the better: The character is better equipped to live his or her life happily because of the experience we've seen.

There are many lovely picture books that may have narrative development, but they do not demonstrate any sort of a meaningful change in the main character's circumstances, if they even have a main character at all. These books fall in a category I call "Now" books, meaning that all of their story action takes place in the present moment, and they're often designed to do something besides give pleasure through storytelling. For instance, they will celebrate or describe something, like the wonderful *Everywhere Babies* by Susan Meyer and Marla Frazee, or *Charlie Parker Played Be-Bop* by Chris Raschka, or Richard Scarry's Look books; or they will teach something, as concept books and many nonfiction books do.

The other kind of picture book is a story book, which is what we're discussing here. Any book that focuses on a character we follow and are interested in, and then shows the solution to his or her problem or captures his or her experience, is a story book. Some of my favorites in this category are *Owl Moon* by Jane Yolen, illustrated by John Schoenherr; *The Gardener* by Sarah Stewart, illustrated by David Small; and *Julius, the Baby of the World* and *Kitten's First Full Moon*, both by Kevin Henkes.

So going back to the problem I identified with *Cheryl and Katy and Cookies*, I said that it had no emotional journey, and no narrative shape. In a picture book, these two things are identical.

All stories, whether in picture books or novels, need to have a beginning, middle, and end. Or as I prefer to think of it when it comes to story books: **"Problem, Process, Solution."** The story starts by presenting its protagonist with a problem that must be solved. Then it shows the process by which that problem is worked out; then it arrives at a solution and its consequences.

A perfect example of a book like this is *Don't Let the Pigeon Drive the Bus* by Mo Willems. On the front endpapers and the title page, the bus driver charges us readers to keep the pigeon from driving the bus; that means that what the pigeon wants is to drive the bus, and that's the problem that must be solved for him by the end of the book. Then we have thirteen spreads of process, where the pigeon asks again and again to drive the bus, getting madder and madder and madder, and we readers have the great pleasure of saying no, and no, and no. The process section climaxes when the bus driver comes back and drives away; the pigeon didn't get what he wanted, which means his problem is unresolved. But then he changes the problem: What he really wants is to drive a RIG! And that offers a solution, because it keeps the hope and the dream alive.

Note that picture books should have just ONE problem; there is not really room for subplots in the text. Subplots might happen in the art, as in Peggy Rathmann's hilarious *Good Night, Gorilla,* where a mouse trails along after the gorilla and security guard, enacting a sweet little story of his own. But such subplots are mostly for the artist to determine, not the writer. And, to repeat myself: A change should happen in all plots, in the character or his circumstances, as the problem gets resolved.

Coming back to *Cheryl and Katy and Cookies*: Hrmm. We seem to be missing a story here — a problem to solve — and any sort of change. So we have to invent a problem. It could be something simple, like Katy forgot to bring the egg and has to go back out and buy one. But that would be sort of boring, and add length to the story without involving any sort of change. The most interesting problems for stories are not external or physical conflicts, like the lack of an egg, but internal or interpersonal situations to be explored. Often such stories might be *prompted* by external or physical conflicts: For instance, if Katy forgot the egg, and Cheryl got annoyed and snapped at her about it, then we'd have an interpersonal situation to explore. But the more easily your story can be solved, the less interesting it is.

Many plots fall into one of three categories: a Conflict, where, say, Cheryl and Katy might fight; a Mystery, where, perhaps, one doesn't know where the other is; or a Lack, like one misses the other. From those premises, the story could go in multiple directions. For instance, suppose my plot problem in this book was a Lack: Katy misses Cheryl. Then the action of the book — the process — would be about the two of us reconnecting in some way. And the solution would be our satisfaction once that happened.

If my plot problem were a Mystery, that, say, Cheryl doesn't know where Katy is, then the process would be the search for Katy, and Cheryl could walk around the neighborhood yelling "Katy! Katy! Hot cookies here!" And the solution would be us sharing cookies together. (The real Katy read an early draft of this talk, and she said that if this Mystery actually involved me yelling "Katy! Katy! Hot cookies here!", it would be a very short book, because she would come running for the cookies and we'd have our solution.)

But just for the heck of it, I'm going to go with the problem of Conflict: Cheryl and Katy fight. Process: They figure out a way to apologize and make up. And solution: They're friends again, better than ever, because they've both learned something about themselves and the nature of friendship.

Why would Katy and I fight? Again, there are many possible directions here. But Conflict plots always come down to one thing: what one character wants vs. what another character wants. And this problem of our fight, the reason behind it, is going to be the emotional problem of the story — the real, deeper conflict that needs to be resolved as we're tussling over cookies or whatever.

So I could say that she borrowed something from me and never returned it and I want it back and she doesn't want to give it to me. But that is an external conflict like forgetting the egg; she returns the item and the story is over. Or we could fight over a man — but that would not be appropriate really for a children's book, being a grown-up conflict rather than a childhood one.

We could each want to take charge of the baking — which happens a lot when Katy and I work on things together. Or after we're done baking, we could each want the last cookie — which also happens a lot when Katy and I eat dessert together. And both of those last two things are interesting, kid-friendly problems, actually, that could have equally interesting processes and solutions.

But here I was working under the limitation that I wanted to write a story involving Katy and cookies, and she was in England, and hence not available to pose for illustrations with me. So I made up a conflict where one of us is in a bad mood — namely me — and I am mean to Katy. I admit this isn't as interesting as, for instance, us both trying to take charge of the baking, but:

- It is one singular problem, as a picture book needs;
- It can be resolved by the process of cookie-making, as I wanted;
- It has a change, as I go from bad mood to good.
- And I'm the main character, as was necessary for my illustrations here.

Whether you write picture books or novels, an editor might sometimes ask you: "Whose story is this?" And the answer is: "Whichever character experiences the emotional change." So if you write a novel where a girl is struggling with her alcoholic father, and the father enters rehab, recovers, and apologizes to his daughter for hurting her, but the girl doesn't forgive him and stays angry: It is the father's story, not the daughter's, that's interesting there, because the father is making a major change and the girl isn't. And if you want this to be a book where the girl is the protagonist, you'd need to revise the novel to address that.

Anyway, our problem now is, I am in a bad mood, and this makes me mean to Katy. So let's look at draft number three.

WHEN CHERYL MAKES COOKIES
(a.k.a. Bad Picture Book Draft #3)

Katy and Cheryl were best friends. Cheryl wore glasses and had blonde hair. Katy had a wide smile and dark hair. And though Cheryl lived in New York and Katy lived in Oxford, England, they talked on the phone every Sunday — Cheryl on her shiny red cordless phone, and Katy on her little black cell phone.

One Sunday, when Cheryl dialed Katy's number, she was in a very bad mood. She had been to the grocery store after church, and they were out of her favorite soft drink, Fresca, and her favorite cookies, McVitie's Plain Chocolate Digestive Biscuits; but she still bought orange juice and chocolate and bread and bananas. She had to carry the heavy bags back to her apartment all by herself, and her arms were tired — so tired she found it hard to hold up the phone.

Katy said, "Hello?"

"I thought you'd never answer!" said Cheryl.

"I've had a very tough week," said Katy. "I've been teaching these silly undergraduates who don't know the difference between a friar and a chicken. I even told them my frequent-friar-miles joke and they didn't laugh!"

"That's a stupid joke anyway," Cheryl said.

"My husband Josh has a cold — "

"He should take some cold medicine!"

"And it's been raining all week."

Cheryl rolled her eyes. "That's why they call it Old Blighty."

"And then the other day, when I was walking down Catte Street, one of the silly undergrads threw a bright yellow banana peel over his shoulder, and I slipped and fell and landed on my knee, and it hurt!"

Cheryl laughed and said, "Hee hee hee! I bet you looked like an ox."

Katy said, "Well! If you're going to be rude to me, I'll just hang up." And she did.

"Well!" Cheryl said. "I didn't really want to talk to her anyway! I hope Josh sneezes and wheezes all over her." But she was still in a very bad mood. She stomped across the apartment and kicked her toe on the table.

"OWWWWW!" Cheryl yelled. "I WANT COOKIES!"

But the grocery store hadn't had the right cookies, so she decided to make some — her special banana oatmeal chocolate-chip cookies. She got out the bananas, the oatmeal, the sugar, the flour, the cinnamon, the baking soda, and of course, the chocolate chips.

And she lingered for a long time over her music collection, choosing just what album she should listen to while she worked: *A Little Night Music? The College Dropout?* Or perhaps *Bruce Springsteen's Greatest Hits?*

After selecting the Boss, putting the CD in the CD player, and turning the music on, Cheryl began making the cookies.

First she set the oven to three hundred fifty degrees.

Then she measured out all the dry ingredients except the oatmeal, one by one, and stirred them together. She added the egg, beating it thoroughly into the dry ingredients, with the oatmeal after that.

As she was mashing the banana, she remembered Katy's fall and how she had laughed at it. *That wasn't very nice of me,* Cheryl thought, and she felt the tiniest twinge of shame.

She mixed and mixed and mixed some more, then folded the chocolate chips into the batter. Once everything was blended, she took two teaspoons and spooned the batter onto the cookie sheet, though she ate a little of the dough herself (using a clean teaspoon, of course). Then she put the cookies in the oven and set the timer for fifteen minutes.

Cheryl picked up her photo album and looked at all the pictures of things she and Katy had done together through the years. There was Katy in her wedding dress in Oxford, and Katy barefoot on the beach in Coney Island; Katy looking out at the water by the Brooklyn Bridge, and Katy and Cheryl on a mountain in the Peak District of England.

Cheryl remembered that Katy was the best friend she'd ever had. She felt very sorry she'd been so rude, and she knew she needed to make it up to Katy.

The timer beeped. Cheryl took the cookies out of the oven and ate one, just to see if it was done. It was delicious, and the taste put her right out of her bad mood.

"Boy, Katy would really like these!" Cheryl said.

She decided she would send Katy a box of the cookies to say she was sorry. She got a box and packing tape and wrapping paper and a Sharpie, and once the cookies were all finished and cooled, Cheryl put them into the box one by one, with waxed paper to fill up the gaps between them and foil to keep them fresh.

Then she labeled the box "Katy Beebe, Oxford, England," and took it to the post office. She knew Katy would be happy with the cookies . . .

. . . and indeed, Katy was.

When they talked the next week, Cheryl apologized, and they were friends again.

So this is our story in terms of Action Plot:
- Problem: Cheryl fights with Katy.
- Process: Cheryl makes cookies.
- Solution: Cheryl sends Katy cookies; they are friends again.

And in terms of Emotional Plot:

- Problem: Cheryl is in a bad mood, and hurts Katy's feelings.
- Process: Cheryl is distracted from bad mood by pleasure of making cookies and by remembering her good times with Katy, and she comes to feel sorry for what she did.
- Solution: Cheryl sends Katy cookies; they are friends again.

And we see that all happen here. If you know the book *When Sophie Gets Angry — Really, Really Angry*, you can think of this as *When Cheryl Makes Cookies — Many, Many Cookies*.

So now I'm feeling pretty good about my story structure, since everything's in place. But, you probably noticed, I introduced a number of other issues into this draft, all of which reflect issues I see a lot in picture book manuscripts.

The first one is still related to story structure: **The ending goes on too long.** Where does the action problem end? When Cheryl and Katy make up. Where does the emotional problem end? When Cheryl's bad mood is gone. Are these the exact same point in the story? No. But as a rule of thumb, **a story is over once the emotional problem is resolved.**

This has been Cheryl's story, not Katy's; Cheryl's bad mood, not her best friend's. We don't actually need to see the two of them reconnect to feel the satisfaction of the change happening and the story being complete. So the story more or less ends with "Cheryl decided she would send Katy a box of the cookies to say she was sorry." And if I were the editor on this book, I would just cut all the following lines.

The second new issue in this draft: **unnecessary dramatization.** In novels, I love to see emotionally significant conversations and actions played out in full. Novelists must construct a whole imaginative world in the reader's mind, and they have as much space as they need to do so. It's the same for short stories: You have time and space to offer explanations, flashbacks and flash-forwards, insights into a character's brain, full descriptions of dress and action.

But picture books are different. They're only thirty-two to forty-eight pages altogether, in which most of the page will and should be taken up by the illustration. There must be something to illustrate, which means there has to be more outward action than inner action — it's boring to see pictures of someone thinking or making a decision. And that action must always drive FORWARD: The reader reads the book in one direction only, and the action must always move in one direction as well. That generally means no flashbacks or flashforwards to things in the past or future; you can show only present action. All of the visual information and description will be shown in the illustration, so there shouldn't be a lot of description. And in general, you want to have as tight and short a text as possible. Writers never like this, but it's true when it comes to picture books: The shorter, the better. It's not a trend, it's a fact.

So, *When Cheryl Makes Cookies* as it stands at present is more like a short story. I describe what Cheryl and Katy look like, and even what phones they use. I have a flashback to the grocery store, explaining why Cheryl was in a bad mood. I offer lots of irrelevant detail, like what Cheryl's favorite cookie and soft drink are, and what CDs Cheryl is choosing among for her baking music. I spell out every single action, like setting the temperature on the oven and putting the CD in the CD player.

I also do something that would be equally awful if I *were* writing a novel or short story: I say, "Cheryl was still very angry," and "Cheryl felt very sorry she'd been so rude." That is, I *tell*, as opposed to *show*. Right after the line, "Cheryl was still very angry," she stomps across the apartment — that's showing. And then I mail a box of cookies to Katy — that's showing. So those lines describing my emotional state are redundant with those actions, and I could cut them.

Spelling out every single action and feeling here also creates another problem: **The pictures will be redundant with the text.** This is one of the most difficult parts of picture-book-making, and what makes the picture-book form so unique: The factual and emotional information in the book does not come solely from the words. So all we writers, illustrators, and editors of picture books are on a quest we cannot accomplish alone: to marry the words and pictures perfectly, inextricably, so nothing is redundant or wasted. The emotional experience grows out of both parts equally, and the whole is indeed greater than the sum of its parts.

If I say in my text "Cheryl smiled," and I show this:

That's a boring illustration, because it's telling us something we already know from the text. Or it's boring text, because it's telling us something we already know from the illustration. Whereas if I say, "Cheryl had an evil plan," and I show the exact same picture, the text is telling us what's going on plotwise, but the illustration is showing how I feel about it. It would also show you something about my character — that I *like* being evil, that I take pleasure in it. And it would provide the humor of the unexpected.

In his marvelous book *Writing with Pictures*, Uri Shulevitz says, "A picture book says in words only what pictures cannot show. In a picture book, the pictures extend, clarify, complement, or take the place of words." The way this breaks down is that pictures should provide:

- **Visual characterization:** What the characters look like, what their expressions are.

- **Visual detail:** I don't need to say in my text that Cheryl had a shiny red cordless phone while Katy had a black cell phone, because the illustrations will show that.

  o There is a long debate about whether authors can include visual notes — things the illustrations should include that do not belong in the text. Editors dislike such notes because, I must tell you, it often feels like if you give an author a visual inch, he will take a mile. He will describe shot angles. He will write character descriptions. And obviously the only thing keeping him from illustrating this book is the fact that he can't draw. So if you can avoid having visual notes, do. But if you can't, and if the visual action is essential to the story, describe that action in your cover letter or in brackets at the appropriate point in the story, *briefly*. Then let the rest of the manuscript stand on its own.

- **The key moments of the action:** A good illustration shows the highest point of emotional interest and active tension in a scene. Suppose a text reads, "Cheryl ran through the park, leaped across the ravine, somersaulted through the daffodils, stood up, and started running again. But the bear was still behind her." In a graphic novel, the illustrator might use several frames to show all five of Cheryl's actions on a single spread. But in a picture book, the illustrator has to choose just one of them — and so she'd probably go with the point where Cheryl was leaping across the ravine, because that's the moment with the most tension and excitement. She would also need to add the bear chasing Cheryl in clear focus, as that's the source of all this suspense and action.

- **Visual perspective:** the distance, the angle, the size of the action we are seeing on the page. A spot has different meaning than a full-page single illustration, which has different meaning than a spread, because they each give a different emphasis to the action shown.

+ And what this all adds up to is the **visual atmosphere** of the book: whether it looks sunny, bleak, detailed, vague, scary, joyous.

Meanwhile, the text provides:

+ **Story and structure:** We've already gone over this.

+ **Verbal and behavioral characterization:** who a character is, as seen in her words and actions.

+ **Sound and dialogue:** what sounds the main character can hear; what two characters are saying to each other.

+ **Plot focus:** What overall action is happening on each spread, as the moment is frozen in time by the illustration; what matters in an illustration action-wise. Suppose we go back to that line I cited above: "Cheryl ran through the park, leaped across the ravine, somersaulted through the daffodils, stood up, and started running again. But the bear was still behind her." The placement of the line about the bear at the end of that paragraph (and probably the last line on the page) indicate that it's important; readers should remember the animal and focus on it, even if it's not the biggest image in the illustration.

+ **Emotional focus:** What matters in an illustration emotionally. That line "The bear was still behind her" indicates that the predominant emotion here is still suspense: Will Cheryl be able to escape the bear?

+ Most importantly, they provide **language with a certain sound, rhythm, and pleasure to it.**

A good picture book text does not simply report the action in a flat tone: "Katy had a deep pore purifying facial. Cheryl had a restorative facial peel." And in fact, that was failing #6 of that text: **Extremely boring language.**

Good picture book texts demonstrate a strength of personality equal to that of the illustrations. They have lyricism, rhythm, humor, attitude, a special form — something to make the language as interesting as the stories they tell. The rhythm of a text is especially important; the prose should be easy and pleasing to read, not unnatural or forced; and the story itself should have a rhythm in the places where repeating elements in the text appear. (This will be illustrated shortly.)

Many picture book texts are written in rhyme, and often at writers' conferences or on Internet bulletin boards, you will hear people say "Editors hate rhyme." This is not true. A more accurate description would be that we are *extremely suspicious* of rhyme. This suspicion grew out of the fact that so many people (and baby boomers especially) grew up on Dr. Seuss, that their definition of "picture book text" equals "written in rhyme." And this means many first-time writers think, if they just write in rhyme, their book is a picture book.

The suspicion also comes from the fact that most rhyme is not very good. In fact, it is frequently awful. It will be out of meter, forced, awkward; it often muddies up the action through the writer's having to manipulate his language to rhyme one line with the next, or it imposes a jaunty tone inappropriate to the events it describes:

> So then, you see, my dear old Pops,
> He closed his eyes and died.
> I felt his crumpled hand grow cold
> And I cried and cried and cried.

And altogether, rhyme often ends up detracting from the story rather than enhancing it. So the rule is, you are not allowed to write rhyme unless:

1. You're very, very good at it, and you have verification of that from someone who knows something about poetry and would not lie to you.

2. It's right for the story you're telling, and not imposing the wrong emotional tone a lá the Pops verse above.

3. And it adds something to the story you're telling — you're not doing it just because you like writing in rhyme.

If those three qualities don't apply to your project, stay far away from it.

So what are we going to do, then, with *When Cheryl Makes Cookies?* We are going to cut the heck out of it. Here's my final draft:

THE BAD MOOD BANANA COOKIES
[a.k.a. Bad Picture Book Draft #4 (final working draft)]

Katy and Cheryl were best friends, even though they lived thousands of miles apart.

One day Cheryl was in a bad mood.

When Katy said, "Hello?" Cheryl said, "I thought you'd never answer!"

While Katy talked about her week, Cheryl sighed loudly and said, "Yeah, yeah, yeah, get on with it!"

And when Katy said that she had slipped and fallen on a banana peel, Cheryl said "Hee hee hee! I bet you looked like an ox."

"Well!" Katy said. "If you're going to be rude to me, I'll just hang up."

And she did.

"Well!" Cheryl said.

She stomped around her apartment.

She kicked her toe on the table.

"OWWW!" Cheryl yelled. "I WANT A COOKIE!"

So she decided to make some.

She got out the flour, sugar, salt, baking soda, cinnamon, and nutmeg; the butter, egg, bananas, oatmeal, and of course, the chocolate chips.

She measured, poured, stirred, and measured a little more.

As she was mashing the banana, she remembered Katy's fall.

It wasn't very nice of me to laugh, Cheryl thought.

She spooned the batter out — not all of it onto the pan — set the timer, and put the cookies in the oven.

Cheryl picked up her photo album. There was Katy by the Brooklyn Bridge, and Katy by the beach, Katy in her wedding dress, and Katy and Cheryl on top of a mountain.

The timer beeped. The cookies tasted like banana and chocolate and love.

And Cheryl knew the best way to say sorry.

I'm now going to run through a quick comparison of this draft to the text of *When Cheryl Makes Cookies* and identify and explain some of the changes I made. In the first paragraph: Everything's gone except a very basic explanation of who these characters are and why they call each other rather than getting together. The second: Again, everything's gone except the emotional information: Cheryl was in a very bad mood. It doesn't matter who called who, and the reason why Cheryl is in a bad mood only matters if the story will address that directly. This story doesn't deal with the causes of her bad mood — she doesn't get McVitie's and Fresca in the course of the book — and therefore we don't need it. The conversation between the two characters has been cut to a nubbin. The fact that Katy has a husband and teaches undergraduates would cause a child reader to identify less with her, and indeed most of what she's saying is only important because Cheryl reacts to it rudely — showing the effect of her bad mood.

The decision to make cookies: I got rid of "She was still very angry," to let the action show that, and thinned the rest down a bit. We know Cheryl is feeling nasty — we don't need to show it again through the wish about Josh. The cookie-making: I'm not describing every single step here, and I'm trying to give some rhythm and interest to what IS still there. This will become important when we look at the illustrations in a moment. Remember that line, too, "not all of it into the pan."

Looking at the album: Besides cutting out all the description of Cheryl's feelings, you see I rearranged the order of Katy's pictures from one draft to another, putting the wedding dress next to last. That way the pictures build in emotional significance, from the beach to the bridge to the wedding dress, and then to Cheryl and Katy together, which implicitly reminds Cheryl of all the good times they've had. And finally, in the conclusion, rather than just saying "It was delicious," I tried to describe a little of the emotion attached to the cookies — rather bluntly, I admit. I cut those last seven lines about packing up the cookies off the end. And this last line, "the best way to say sorry" — remember that too. A great picture book will have a great last line, so the reader closes the book with an "Ah!" of satisfaction. This line is just OK, but it'll do.

So now that I have a text I can work with, I need to paginate the manuscript. All picture books must be a multiple of eight pages to work in the standard bookbinding process. The most common page count, and the one you should start working in or from, is thirty-two pages. It's extremely rare to see a hardcover American picture book shorter than that; and the book's subject or story will need to justify its length if it goes beyond forty pages. (Many nonfiction picture books are forty-eight pages.) When I'm considering a picture-book manuscript editorially, I always divide the text up over thirty-two pages to see if there's enough story to fill out all thirty-two pages, where the main action of the story lies, what moments would need more visual time or page space (and might therefore even need more text), etc.

There are three ways to paginate a text. The easiest is just to insert page numbers in the text where you think the page turns should be. Remember you need to leave at least one page (usually the single page at the very front) for a title page, and at least one page for the copyright information and dedication; that even-numbered pages are left-hand pages, and odd-numbered pages are right-hand pages; and that picture books are viewed in spreads rather than individual pages. Thus you don't necessarily want to have text on every single page, as you'll likely want a nice mix of spots for small moments, single pages for larger incidents, and spreads to illustrate grand vistas or turning points. To this end, it's good to divide the text up into spreads rather than single pages. For *The Bad Mood Banana Cookies*, my paginated text would look in part like this:

p. 1 < title page >

2 < copyright page >

3 <dedication >

4-5 Katy and Cheryl were best friends, even though they lived thousands of miles apart.

6-7 One day Cheryl was in a bad mood. When Katy said, "Hello?" Cheryl said, "I thought you'd never answer!"

8-9 While Katy talked about her week, Cheryl sighed loudly and said, "Yeah, yeah, yeah, get on with it!"

10-11 And when Katy said how she had slipped and fallen on a banana peel, Cheryl said "Hee hee hee! I bet you looked like an ox."

12-13 "Well!" Katy said. "If you're going to be rude to me, I'll just hang up."

And she did.

Etc. The excellent picture-book writer Anastasia Suen actually teaches her students to write their picture book texts this way, in a thirty-two-page framework, so they're thinking about page turns and story balance from the very beginning. You might find that structure useful for future projects too.

Once you have a paginated text, it's often useful to picture-book writers to take the next visual step and create thumbnails or a dummy. Thumbnails are like an animator's storyboards — many small, quick sketches that show the visual development of the book over the allotted number of pages. Once an illustrator has worked up some satisfactory thumbnails, he or she will expand them into sketches, and then into a dummy — full-sized, detailed sketches of every piece of art in the book. Some illustrators go ahead and bind the dummy up so that s/he and the editor can experience the page turns and be sure the book will have the right visual effect.

To make thumbnails for a thirty-two-page picture book, draw fifteen double-size rectangles on a page, with one half-size rectangle at the beginning and the end, like this:

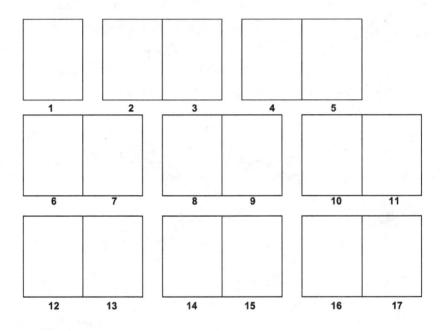

(You can download this thumbnails template as a Microsoft Word doc at http://www.cherylklein.com/thumbnails.html.)

To make a dummy, stack sixteen pieces of paper together, fold the stack in half, then attach the pages together on the fold in some way. (I've used staples, tape, and needle and thread at various times.) Number all the pages in either the thumbnails or dummy.

Then distribute the text (including the title page, copyright, and dedication, remember) over the space of all thirty-two pages. If you're doing thumbnails, write the text in the boxes as appropriate. When I make text dummies for the projects I work on, I usually print out the text, then cut up the individual lines or text blocks and tape them to the pages as I go. Once you've arranged the text so it feels right — which may take some time or involve some rejiggering — you might even sketch in stick figures so you have visual images of a sort to accompany your words. Then take a hard look at the proto-book that results, and ask yourself:

- Do you have enough story to spread out over thirty-two pages? Too much? (You *can* add pages at this stage, going up to forty or forty-eight; but you should be sure that the narrative is more or less perfect just as it is, per all the other questions below, and thus those pages are absolutely necessary for the right rhythm of the book.)
- Does the action develop smoothly over the full course of the book? Or does it all clump up in the beginning or end?
- Picture the illustration that would have to go with each spread: who or what would be pictured on it, what the characters would be doing. If they stay in one place for a long time or repeat the same action over and over again, do the illustrations get repetitive? (This is something to watch for with conversation, especially — you don't want five consecutive spreads of people sitting and talking, because that's rather visually boring.)
- Are there moments that deserve more emphasis textually than you're giving them? Or moments that need less text, because the illustration can carry the emotion or description? Where are the turning points?
- Where should the page turns be? Can you rewrite the text to use those turns more effectively?
- Have another smart reader read the book. What's their sense of how the story moves?

Then make any revisions that seem necessary, and start the dummy process over again. You should still be prepared for an editor to ask to change your text, or for an illustrator's pagination to be different from your own, as they'll have a distance from the project that you won't have. But you will have done the best you can to make the book visually effective, and to identify and correct any weaknesses of your text.

I not only paginated the manuscript for *The Bad Mood Banana Cookies*, I "illustrated" it as well, with the help of my boyfriend and my digital camera, and Katy, her husband, and *her* digital camera. You can see the results in the pages that follow. I will say right off: I make no claims to this being a good picture book. I'm an editor, not a creative writer, so the text is still pretty flat; and it contains some of the worst pictures of me ever committed to pixel. Some of that is the fault of the manuscript, as you'll see, and some of it is the fault of the pictures. But it does do some things right, so I hope you find it useful and interesting to think about, at the very least.

1

The Bad-Mood Banana Cookies

by Cheryl Klein
Pictures by James Monohan,
Joshua Hatton, Cheryl Klein,
and the Internet

CBK Books
Brooklyn, New York

Page 1. Title page. Not much to say about it.

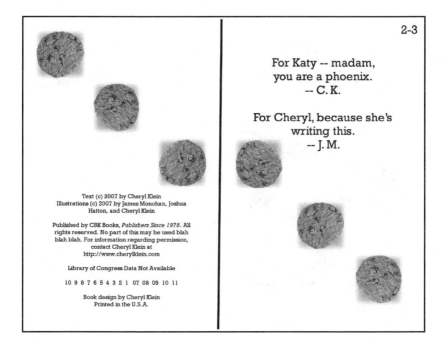

Text (c) 2007 by Cheryl Klein
Illustrations (c) 2007 by James Monohan, Joshua
Hatton, and Cheryl Klein

Published by CBK Books, *Publishers Since 1978*. All
rights reserved. No part of this may be used blah
blah blah. For information regarding permission,
contact Cheryl Klein at
http://www.cherylklein.com

Library of Congress Data Not Available

10 9 8 7 6 5 4 3 2 1 07 08 09 10 11

Book design by Cheryl Klein
Printed in the U.S.A.

2-3

For Katy -- madam,
you are a phoenix.
-- C. K.

For Cheryl, because she's
writing this.
-- J. M.

Pages 2-3. Copyright and dedication. A perfect picture book starts developing the story from page 1 — or even from the endpapers, if the book has printed ends. Even though the action hasn't started yet, the title page, copyright, and dedication are the illustrator's opportunity to set the stage, introduce visual motifs, and start drawing readers into the world of the book. Here, you see, I'm doing that with dancing cookies.

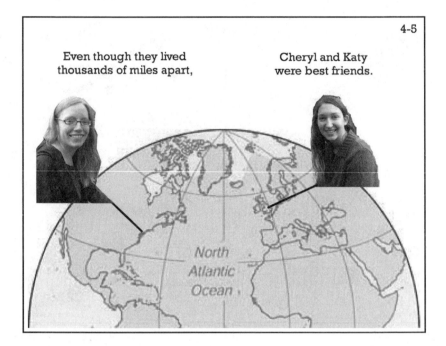

Pages 4-5. These illustrations, you can see, are so lame they're rather funny, but this communicates the idea visually that the text explains verbally.

Note that I reversed the phrasing of this first line from the manuscript so that the last phrase on the page — the idea the reader takes into the next spread — is not their distance, but their friendship; and I reversed the order of "Katy and Cheryl" so that the text matches the visual read from left to right.

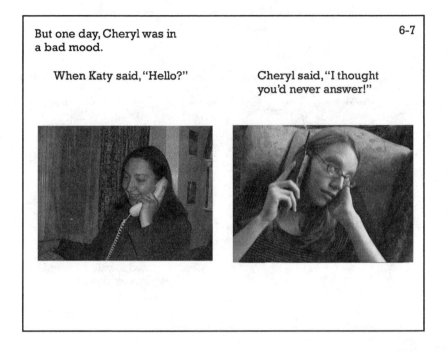

Pages 6-7. The conversation starts . . .

Pages 8-9. And continues . . .

Pages 10-11. And continues . . .

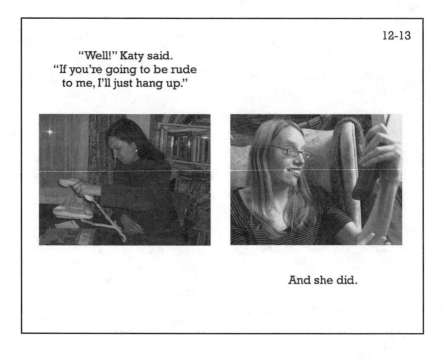

12-13

"Well!" Katy said.
"If you're going to be rude
to me, I'll just hang up."

And she did.

Pages 12-13. And ends. You remember how I said earlier that conversations in picture books can be very boring? You have just witnessed why! Repetitions like this can work if something significant is changing each time — e.g., if Cheryl is getting madder and madder and madder, and Katy is getting sadder and sadder and sadder, and everything else is staying the same. That's what I was going for here. But even so, four spreads is a long time, picture-book-wise, to show the same images and layout.

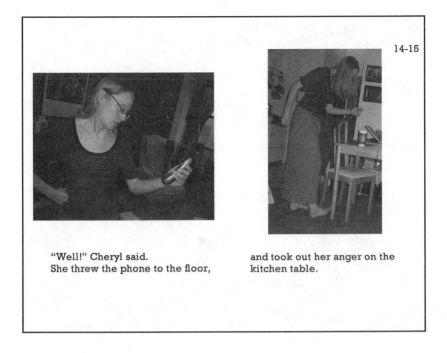

14-15

"Well!" Cheryl said.
She threw the phone to the floor,

and took out her anger on the
kitchen table.

Pages 14-15. Cheryl stomps around and kicks the table. Nice to vary the action a bit, isn't it? Here's an alternate design for that same page:

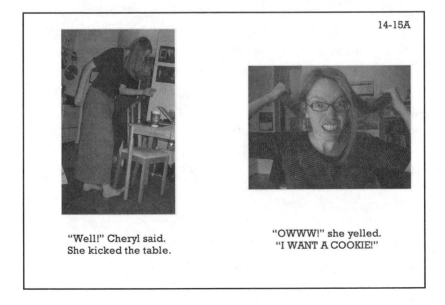

14-15A

"Well!" Cheryl said.
She kicked the table.

"OWWW!" she yelled.
"I WANT A COOKIE!"

Pages 16-17. Cheryl's point of highest emotional distress. I had originally intended to have this text on the previous spread, after the kicking the table, and you can see this original layout on the previous page at bottom. But when I was assembling my pages here, I realized I hadn't actually created a spread for 16-17, so my book was going to be a spread short.

So instead of getting a single-page picture of Cheryl screaming, we have a full spread of Cheryl screaming. And this actually worked out well, as ugly as this picture is, because this is really the first turning point of the book, the end of Act I: We've reached the end of the Problem (Cheryl's in a bad mood) and are about to go into the Process of getting her out of it (making cookies). Thus we mark the end of Act I with the first spread we've had since p. 4-5, so you can feel the intensity here, through the full-bleed illustration, the extreme closeup, and the bright type. It's much more effective at showing Cheryl's distress than **Pages 14-15A**, isn't it?

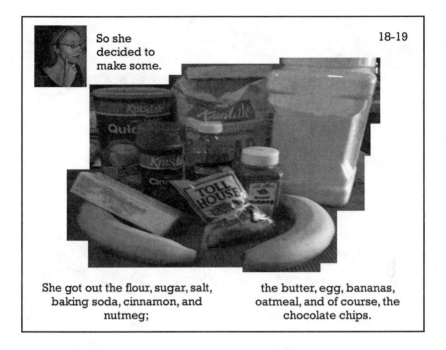

So she decided to make some.

18-19

She got out the flour, sugar, salt, baking soda, cinnamon, and nutmeg;

the butter, egg, bananas, oatmeal, and of course, the chocolate chips.

Pages 18-19. The assembly of the ingredients. The illustration in the top left corner — someone thinking. Boring! This is why picture-book texts need to focus on external action. This text, and this illustration, could be cut with very little loss — certainly no emotional loss, since there's nothing emotional (or even interesting) about this picture.

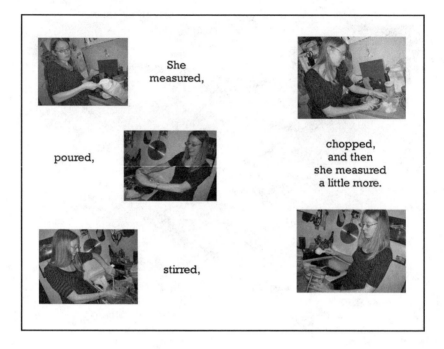

She
measured,

poured,

chopped,
and then
she measured
a little more.

stirred,

Pages 20-21. Here's a pretty good example of using spots to make a boring text more interesting. The eye bounces around the page, as does Cheryl's position. If I had planned this out properly, you could see my facial expressions get less and less angry as I get deeper and deeper into the baking. Alas, I did not plan this properly — but so it goes.

I have a lot of lists in this manuscript: the list of what Katy and I were saying to each other, that rhythmic bouncing back and forth; the list of ingredients; the list of actions here; the list of pictures of Katy later. That's about three too many. Lists work best when you can use them to establish a rhythm, as in the conversation with Katy earlier, or when they can be used in action, as here.

And in all cases, they must advance the plot. This list serves the Action Plot, I suppose, as you do see me making cookies; but as with the list of ingredients, there's nothing emotional about it, and it could probably go.

It wasn't very nice of me to laugh, Cheryl thought.

As she was mashing the banana, she remembered Katy's fall.

22-23

Pages 22-23. And here you see me mashing the banana. Again, it's a full-page spread. I chose this deliberately because this is the turning point for Cheryl's attitude towards Katy; it's the first time she thinks, *Oh, I made a mistake,* and I wanted to emphasize the importance of that moment for readers. (Though it's undercut here by the fact I'm smiling, I admit. That was supposed to be smiling at the pleasure of mashing.)

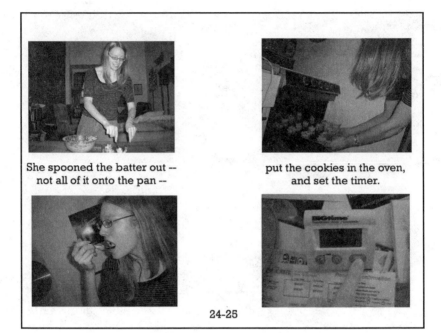

She spooned the batter out --
not all of it onto the pan --

put the cookies in the oven,
and set the timer.

24-25

Pages 24-25. Spooning out the batter —"not all of it into the pan." The bottom left picture is one of the few good things in this book — a place where the illustrations and text work together just as they should, and you need both to understand perfectly what's happening. I like that. A real illustrator would always show the character's face, of course, and not have her looking like Cousin It in that top right picture. And the bottom right is a little boring.

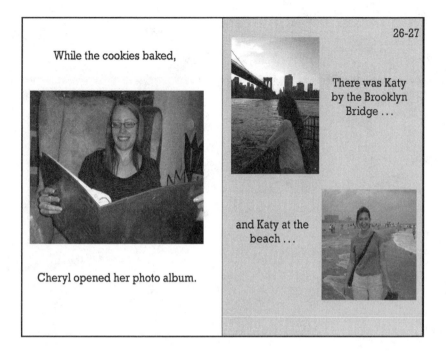

Pages 26-27. The page on the right is supposed to have a pink background as a visual signal that we've shifted out of the regular world of the picture book, the world we've been in thus far, into the visual world of the album, which is also pink on the outside.

Again, it's a little too early for me to be smiling so hugely here.

28-29

Katy in her wedding dress,

and Katy and Cheryl
on a mountain.

Pages 28-29. The climax of the book emotionally: seeing Katy and Cheryl together. This is the kind of unity in friendship they're supposed to have, and it calls Cheryl back to her purpose on the next page:

30-31

The timer beeped.

The cookies tasted like bananas and chocolate and love.

Pages 30-31. We're back in the real world (no pink) and we're using an almost-full-spread here, because I wanted to give the text and illustrations close to equal weight. If the illustration just showed Cheryl smiling at the cookie, on a full spread, then we would know she was happy with the cookie, but the fact that her happiness was tied to her thinking about Katy might have gotten lost. But if the text gets equal space with the illustration, then we know that the text is just as important here — and that the friendship and love are what's making her happy as well.

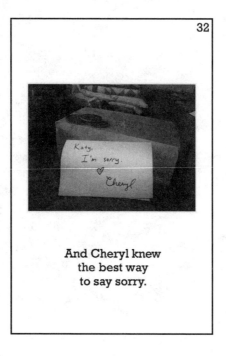

**And Cheryl knew
the best way
to say sorry.**

Page 32. And again, a good combination of text and art, where the page wouldn't make sense without the two working together. The text saying I'm sorry with the picture saying "I'm sorry" is a little bit redundant — the note should perhaps say, "Friends?" or something like that instead. And the cookies in the top left are McVitie's rather than the actual cookies, because I, um, ate all the real cookies before I took this picture.

The 2008 Caldecott winner it isn't — but I hope it's served its purpose here.

So, to tie things up: A perfect picture book:

- Will speak to a child's external and emotional concerns.
- Has a clear narrative through-line,
    - o Whether Problem-Process-Solution if it's a Story book
    - o Or another form of organization if it's a Now book.

- Is tightly written, with no unnecessary dramatization or redundancies with the illustration.
- Has illustrations that vary in perspective, layout, size, position on the page, etc., as appropriate for the story.
- Allows you to follow the action simply by looking at the pictures — you don't need to see the words.
- But also has words that add another level of depth and interest to the pictures,
    o And the two of them work in harmony to create an emotional experience as well as an artistic one.

A picture-book manuscript is an incredibly challenging form — perhaps the very hardest form of writing out there, because it requires so much tautness of text, such imagination on the writer's part to give up his words in favor of the pictures, and then the humility and willingness to do so.

But when it works, through the writer's words, and the illustrator's art, both their intelligence and wisdom, and all the love in their hearts, you create books that live in children's hearts forever — cherished, pored over, passed down through the generations, like a beloved family cookie recipe. Those are the kind of picture books I want to make, and I hope I have the chance to do that with some of you.

Thank you.

A FEW THINGS WRITERS
CAN LEARN FROM
HARRY POTTER

———❖———

I wrote this talk as a keynote speech for the Terminus Harry Potter fan conven-
tion in August 2008. It draws on ideas from a child_lit and blog post entitled
"Seven Reasons People Love Harry Potter," which you can read online at http://
chavelaque.blogspot.com/2007/08/seven-reasons-why-people-love-harry.html,
as well as material from "The Rules of Engagement" and "Finding a Publisher
and Falling in Love" earlier in this volume. If you have not read the books, note
that there are spoilers for the series in this talk. And all these ideas are solely my
own and do not represent the intentions, opinions, or interpretations of J. K.
Rowling or her publishers.

My name is Cheryl Klein, and I'm a senior editor at Arthur A. Levine
Books, an imprint of Scholastic Inc., and the continuity editor for the
U.S. editions of the Harry Potter books.

And it is a great pleasure to be with you here today, because before
I was any of that — before I started as Arthur's editorial assistant, or
moved to New York City, or even thought about being in children's
publishing — I was a Harry Potter fangirl.

I discovered the series nine years ago this month, in August of 1999,
in a white Dodge Dynasty, as I drove from Missouri to Minnesota with
my best friend for our senior year of college. She was driving, and I was
sitting in the back. So I picked up this book she'd been raving about,
Harry Potter and the Prisoner of Azkaban, just to see why it was such a
big deal. And when I read "Harry Potter was a highly unusual boy in
many ways," followed by the detailing of all the ways he was so very, very
strange, it didn't take long: I was hooked.

My friend noticed I was awfully quiet all of a sudden, and she said, "Are you reading my book?"

"No," I said.

"You are! You are! That's mine!"

And it got to the point where neither one of us wanted to drive because we both wanted to read.

When we finally reached school, I bought *Sorcerer's Stone* along with my fall course textbooks. I read *Chamber of Secrets* over winter break. I haunted the Unofficial Harry Potter Fan Club for news about Book Four — do any of you remember that website? Run by Jenna? It was the Leaky Cauldron/Mugglenet of its day. And I waited in line at midnight for *Goblet of Fire*.

When I was hired at the end of the summer of 2000 as Arthur Levine's editorial assistant, I literally jumped up and down, knowing I might get to work on Harry Potter. And doing so has been the biggest honor and excitement of my editorial life. And the greatest pleasure, too — the pure reading pleasure that all of us have shared, as we followed this series over the years of its unfolding.

There have been lots of wonderful talks here at Terminus exploring the characters, world, and philosophy of J. K. Rowling's books and the fandom they've spawned. In this talk, I'd like to go back to the books themselves to explore how that pleasure was created — the narrative techniques that make these books mean so much to us all, focusing on the big four elements of fiction: Character, Voice, Theme, and Plot. And, for you fiction writers out there, I hope to offer some practical suggestions on how you can develop these elements in your own writing.

I am so very honored to be here. I want to say thank you to Amy and the Terminus staff for inviting me, and thank *you* very much for your kind attendance and attention; I'll try to make it worth your while.

So I'm going to start with Character. The first thing that J. K. Rowling does well at the beginning of *Harry Potter and the Sorcerer's Stone* is so basic and so invisible that it's very easy for us readers to take it for granted. But it's absolutely essential to everything that follows, and masterfully done here.

And that is that she gets us readers to identify with her hero. Because Harry is real and interesting to us, we care about him; because we care about him, we want to know how his story will come out; and we want to know that so much, we eventually line up at bookstores at midnight wearing funny hats.

So how does she make us care about Harry? First, she gets us to sympathize with him by making him live with the horrible Dursleys. It's easy to forget sometimes, looking back over the whole series, that the first book doesn't begin with Harry or magic at all. It begins in our Muggle world, with Muggles who think they are perfectly normal, thank you very much. But who instead are perfectly awful: gossiping, greedy, disapproving, cheating, and unloving to their orphaned nephew/cousin. What happens here is basic literary math: We readers dislike the Dursleys, and the Dursleys dislike Harry, so we automatically like Harry.

The second step in getting us interested in Harry: Ms. Rowling gives him an intriguing backstory and destiny. The first non-Dursley people we meet in the book are Professor McGonagall, Professor Dumbledore, and Hagrid: people who can transform into cats, put out streetlamps with the flick of a lighter, and ride motorcycles through the sky. *Much* cooler and more interesting than the Dursleys! And they dislike the Dursleys too, you'll note. So we readers now have someone to identify with — the magical people.

These magical people talk about Harry as a child with a great mystery behind him: "How in the name of heaven did Harry survive?" Professor McGonagall asks. And a great future ahead of him: "I wouldn't be surprised if today was known as Harry Potter day in the future!" she says later. This past and future together sets up the plot that will drive all seven books and further increases our interest in Harry: What's the solution to this mystery? And what will happen to this heroic child next? *I want to know.*

And finally—the third technique J. K. Rowling uses in getting us to identify with Harry — she makes him a good person. For me this is exemplified by the Brazilian snake scene in Chapter Two. You all know how this goes: Dudley whines, orders, and moans at his father to get the snake to move, but nothing happens. Then: "Harry moved in front of the tank and looked intently at the snake. He wouldn't have been surprised if it had died of boredom itself — no company except stupid people drumming their fingers on the glass trying to disturb it all day long." Harry goes on to have a conversation with the snake, where he empathizes further with it and finally sets it free.

We've seen a lot of reverse characterization of Harry in the book up to this point — we like him because we dislike the Dursleys, who treat him terribly. But this is simple positive characterization: He sympathizes with the snake, of all creatures, and puts himself inside its head rather than being self-centered like Dudley and demanding things of it. And then he lets it go, showing his kind heart. And of course, he can talk to snakes, period! *Tres* cool.

These three things — sympathy, mystery, likeability — make his story nearly irresistible to follow, and are three tools for you writers to remember in establishing your own protagonists and plots.

Many writers have used these techniques before and since, of course — *especially* since, to the extent that when I read a fantasy manuscript now, I have to say, I often roll my eyes at the moment when someone prophesies a great destiny for our put-upon boy hero. This is a moment that happens in about seventy-five percent of fantasy manuscripts, if not more.

What makes the HP books different is the unpretentious honesty that accompanies the prophecy. Note that Dumbledore says the fame that leads to "Harry Potter day" would be *awful* for Harry — it would "turn his head" and it's better if he grows up away from it. That's hardly the expected start to a heroic narrative!

And there are wonderful side details that anchor all of these characters, even the Dursleys, in reality. Mr. Dursley strokes his mustache when he thinks. Dumbledore likes lemon drops. Harry gets excited about a treat like the zoo. These are people whom we readers recognize because they share the habits or tastes or emotions that we nonfictional people have ourselves, or know to be within the bounds of reality.

Once we're interested in Harry, and he's established as fictionally real, J. K. Rowling uses these techniques — unpretentious honesty and an eye for the well-observed detail — to develop him and his friends and relations through all seven books. Even as the magical world becomes ever wider, she keeps deepening the psychological reality of her characters by showing how their innate qualities — their personalities and their histories — drive the action, and by letting them make mistakes.

In terms of personality, in the first couple books, Harry is sort of the Barack Obama of children's literature (Barack Obama in 2007, I should say). He's a nice guy who everyone likes, a hero for his interesting biography and good looks, but a little bit of a blank slate beyond that essential goodness — someone on whom people project what they want to see.

But he acquires real personality and depths — or rather, we come to see the personality and depth that was always there — as the series progresses and he is tested: not always making the right choices, but learning from all of his choices on the way. We discover his virtues, like his bravery in going after the Sorcerer's Stone in Book One, his kindness to Dobby in Book Two, his sense of justice when he won't kill Sirius in Book Three, his loyalty to his friends throughout. And we find out his flaws, which are often the flip side of those same virtues.

One of my favorite moments in Book Five is when Hermione says to Harry, "Don't you think you've got a bit of a — a — *saving-people thing?*" right before they take off for the Ministry. It's the author's explicit acknowledgement of the double-edged sword in her hero's personality, that he loves his friends and proto-family so much, having been without friends or family for so long, that he has a tendency to plunge in without getting all the information or thinking his decisions through. This sort of acknowledgement is an incredibly brave thing for a writer to do, because it invites the reader to step away from Harry's point of view and examine his choices — to stop identifying with him if we think he's making a mistake. And of course he *is* making a mistake here — one that leads indirectly to Sirius's death.

In Book Seven, the same test happens again, when the Deathly Hallows are revealed to Harry. He can indulge his impulse to act — to seize the Elder Wand and defeat Voldemort, becoming the Master of Death and saving all his friends. And the Harry of Book Five would do that very thing. But in Book Seven, tempered by the deaths of Dobby and Wormtail (and, I daresay, that experience in Book Five), he chooses *not* to act — to continue instead on the course he was set: trusting Dumbledore, even without all the information at his disposal. That moment is the surest sign that Harry has grown up, and one that leads directly to his ultimate defeat of Voldemort.

I've often heard adult readers get indignant about the fact that the HP series is classified as children's or young adult literature, arguing that they're adult books in the complexity of their plots and themes. I have to say that this is not an argument I have much sympathy with. First of all, it assumes that children's or YA books can't have complex plots and themes — that those qualities belong solely to adult literature, which is condescending and wrong. But more importantly, what makes a book adult vs. children's vs. YA is the psychological age of the protagonist and of the emotional journey he undertakes — how it forces him to change and grow, and what he changes and grows into.

And the seven books of the Harry Potter series are a classic young-adult emotional journey, from the simple "Yay School!" atmosphere of Book One, to the emphasis upon choices in Book Two, to the revelations of family history in Book Three, to dealing with death in Book Four, to Harry's discovery of seemingly every single adult's feet of clay in Book Five (not to mention the irrational anger and hilariously bad first romance there), to his losing the most important grown-up in his life and facing his mission in Book Six, and finally his taking control of his destiny and becoming a grown-up himself in Book Seven.

It's a growth process I think all of us can see in our own lives, even though the details are different for us Muggle non-orphans. And the Harry Potter series wouldn't have experienced even a quarter as much success as it did if J. K. Rowling weren't able to make us care about Harry and his friends at the beginning, and to keep them real and their lives recognizable over the course of their growing up. To restate something I said at the beginning: The plot may have kept us turning the pages, but our knowledge of and love for the characters is what makes that plot matter.

So if you're a writer, and you've got an awesome idea for a plot, by all means develop that. But I urge you to spend at least an equal amount of time thinking about character. What sort of character will grow the most within the sort of plot you've created? What are her virtues? Her flaws? How will those qualities drive her actions, and therefore that plot journey? What are the telling details that will make her real? And then give her the freedom to be who she is, without you the author getting in the way: overexplaining who she is or why she's doing something, or worse, protecting the character from the consequences of her actions because you love her so much.

And this leads me to the way in which the story is told — the narrative Voice. We editors and writing teachers toss one particular adage out over and over again: *Show, not tell.* Telling is the writer's informing the reader of a particular quality or circumstance, and showing is the writer's dramatizing this idea for the reader.

For instance, if Ms. Rowling had written, "Draco Malfoy was an extremely spoiled and unpleasant boy," that would be Telling. But instead, within thirty seconds of meeting Harry, Draco says "I don't see why first-years can't have their own racing brooms. I think I'll bully Father into getting me one and I'll smuggle it in somehow." That's Showing. And — what a jerk!

As that example demonstrates, Showing is much more powerful than Telling because it allows the reader to react to the action based on first-hand experience, rather than having to take the author's word for it. And the Harry Potter books are almost entirely Show. We readers are there with Harry every step of the way, seeing what he sees, experiencing the class, the Quidditch game, the kiss, the battle right alongside him, and therefore feeling the joy or terror he feels, without Ms. Rowling having to say "Harry felt terrified."

When I'm reading manuscript submissions, I'm always alert to the use of the word "felt," especially in the first ten pages, because if you-the-writer are having to tell me how your character feels, then that probably means you haven't succeeded in getting me in the character's head. That means I'm not feeling those emotions alongside the character; and I read books precisely to get out of my own head and emotions into the experiences and feelings of these imaginary people.

The lesson for writers, I would *like* to say, is "Do not use the word 'felt,'" but rather show me how the character came to feel however he or she feels. Let me get to know him, and put me in the action with him, so when he sees the girl of his dreams pashing another guy, I feel the kick in the gut the same way he does.

Now, Ms. Rowling does use "felt" fairly often, as I'm sure you know. But if you look closely at when that happens, the Telling there usually serves as a confirmation of emotion for the reader, directing the emotional takeaway from whatever just happened — a emotion we were likely feeling already. The truth is, both Showing and Telling have their place in fiction, because sometimes readers need the plain straightforward direction of Telling to elucidate the point of all that Showing.

How many of you learned about topic sentences in school? A topic sentence is the first sentence of a paragraph, which sets forth its main idea or hypothesis. It's mostly used in nonfiction or expositional writing, but it's a wonderful structure for description or narration as well, because it makes each paragraph function almost like an argument. You set forth your premise, which is often Telling: for instance, "The dungeon was, most unusually, already full of vapors and odd smells." Then you back it up with evidence that supports the point you're making — the Showing.

> Harry, Ron, and Hermione sniffed interestedly as they passed large, bubbling cauldrons. . . . They chose the [table] nearest a gold-colored cauldron that was emitting one of the most seductive scents Harry had ever inhaled: Somehow it reminded him simultaneously of treacle tart, the woody smell of a broomstick handle, and something flowery he thought he might have smelled at the Burrow.

Then you conclude the paragraph and move the story forward: "A great contentment stole over him; he grinned across at Ron, who grinned back lazily." That structure recurs over and over again throughout the books. Indeed, I think it's Ms. Rowling's natural narrative voice.

And I'd argue that one of the main reasons HP has been such an unprecedented worldwide phenomenon is precisely this abundance of Showing. Ms. Rowling describes things so thoroughly, and we're in Harry's head and in the action so completely, that my experience reading, say, *Goblet of Fire* was very similar to those of readers in England and Germany, Japan and Australia, because we were all seeing the same things and caught up in the emotions of the story the same way.

And this leads me to the third element of fiction I'd like to discuss — Theme. Or, the Big Ideas. How many of you read the epigraphs to *Deathly Hallows* before diving in to the text? How many of you just started with Chapter 1? Well, if you read them, you saw this quote from William Penn:

Death is but crossing the world, as friends do the seas; they live in one another still. For they must needs be present, that love and live in that which is omnipresent. . . . This is the comfort of friends, that though they may be said to die, yet their friendship and society are, in the best sense, ever present, because immortal.

Those of you who read the epigraphs — how many of you saw that and thought, "OK, that's it, Harry's gonna bite it?" I know I did, the first time I read the manuscript. And then I got teary-eyed over that page more than once after reading the book, because the ideas of death and love are central to the series — even more central than power, I would say. The whole story happens because Voldemort does not want to die — as simple as that. He tries to kill Harry because Harry is supposed to kill him. But Harry is protected by his mother's blood — the physical manifestation of her love.

On Harry and the reader's end, each one of the books introduces, in a fashion appropriate to their age and understanding, a way of thinking about or dealing with death. From the first three, when he's seeing the images of his parents and the past everywhere around him — literally, in the mirror of Erised, the diary, and the Marauders; to *Goblet of Fire*, where Harry witnesses death in person; to *Order*, which brings the deaths closer, and introduces him to the idea of his own in the prophecy ("Neither shall live while the other survives"); and finally *Half-Blood Prince* and *Deathly Hallows*, which introduce the Horcruxes — Voldemort's instruments of avoiding death — and the Hallows — the objects the Peverells literally take from Death.

And with Book Seven, we saw that Ms. Rowling's slow approach to the subject, the slow accretion of character and backstory, was all preparing Harry for his own death on behalf of the people he loves — teaching him that, as Dumbledore says in Book Five, "There are things much worse than death" . . . like the *loss* of people we love. And, at the very beginning of the whole story, back in Book One: "To the well-organized mind, death is but the next great adventure."

This sort of thematic richness in a writer's work grows out of serious engagement with the questions that are important to that writer and to us all, about what matters in life, what's the right way to live, how we should treat each other, what we live for. And if you are a writer, then you can do worse than starting from these questions, constructing a story to explore the options or illustrate your answers. Or, if you have a solid draft of a story in hand, asking yourself, "What do I want to say here? What point do I want to make? Is my plot at present accomplishing that?"

Novels are really philosophy books in narrative disguise. And — presuming greatly here — I think Ms. Rowling's philosophy might ultimately be expressed in something else Dumbledore says: "Do not pity the dead, Harry. Pity the living, and above all, those who live without love." Not looking back at the past, at the dead, but looking forward, to the life we all share, and the good we can do each other within that.

And the idea of looking forward brings me, finally, to Plot. Truly I could have started with plot, and made this entire talk about the plot of the Harry Potter books, because I don't think anyone since Dickens has plotted like J. K. Rowling, and even Dickens spun his story across only one book, not seven. To toss out some literary theory here, I believe there are basically three kinds of plots:

- A Conflict: Two people or forces in opposition to each other. This can be an internal conflict and/or an external conflict.
- A Mystery: Where some piece of information needs to be found out — the name of the murderer, the location of an object on a quest.
- And a Lack: Where something is missing from the protagonist's life at the beginning, and it is earned or fulfilled by the end.

One of the reasons the series as a whole works so brilliantly is because it offers readers all three types of plot across all seven books:

+ The Conflict: Harry vs. Voldemort
+ The Mystery: Why Voldemort couldn't kill baby Harry, and how the grown-up Harry can eventually defeat him
+ And the Lack: Harry going from not having friends or family to being surrounded by them at the end of Book Seven

And then each individual book has at least one internal Mystery or Conflict, like the identity of the Heir of Slytherin, or the Triwizard Tournament, or the search for the Horcruxes, that provides propulsion and story for that book even as it contributes to the overall course of the action.

Now, if you are a writer trying to plot out your work, and looking to the HP books as a model, you might very easily just throw up your hands and quit. Because how do you compete with that? (It's worth remembering J. K. Rowling spent seven years working on the first book and the series as a whole before any of it was published.) Still, I think there are two useful lessons you might take away here — one theoretical, one practical.

First, the theory. (I really love narrative theory, in case you can't tell, so I hope I'm not boring you with this.) In *The Poetics* by Aristotle, the first major work of literary criticism in Western civilization, Aristotle defined dramatic action as "the change from good fortune to bad, or bad fortune to good." The key word here is *change*. That means your protagonist's circumstances are different at the end then they are at the beginning — for better or for worse. Otherwise, you will have made a reader plow through two hundred pages to discover nothing is different. And that would be infuriating. But more than that, your *character* must change as a result of his experiences, growing in some way — kinder or more bitter or wiser or more insulated.

When I read the manuscript of Book Seven for the first time, I cried as I have never cried at a book before in the chapter "The Forest Again," when Harry goes to meet Voldemort with his parents, Sirius, and Lupin. Correction: I didn't cry. I wept. I bawled. I sobbed. I almost couldn't see the pages through my tears, though of course, I also couldn't stop reading. And I realized later that this was because I identified with Harry so thoroughly (Character) and I was so completely in his point of view (Voice), that it was like I was going to my death as well. And it was horrible but necessary to save everyone else Harry loved. And that, of course, is Ms. Rowling's theme — that as scary as death is to us, love is stronger and more important.

My point here is, Ms. Rowling constructed a plot in which her hero would, in the whole course of the seven-book action — thanks to the loss of his parents and Sirius and Dumbledore, the search for the Horcruxes and the conquering of his desire for the Deathly Hallows — come to discover her theme. And this is what good plots do: They provide a structure and events through which your protagonist has painful experiences, learns from them, grows, and triumphs in a way that conveys the Big Idea the author has in mind.

Since we readers identify with the main character, we are making those mistakes along with him. And then we learn the same emotional lesson that he learns from the experience, and we come away changed as well. The theme is ultimately the Big Idea the character, and the reader, takes away from the plot.

So, if you're a writer, ask yourself: "How do my character's circumstances change? And how does the character himself or herself change? What do the events of my plot teach my character? Is he discovering my theme or point for himself, as a result of what he learns through the action? Or are the events just one darn thing after another?" And if the latter, you may need to tweak your plot or your theme to fix that.

The second thing — the practical thing — I think writers can take away from J. K. Rowling's plotting is the value of planning and outlining. Now, I do not mean to say that you have to think out every step of your book from the beginning. There are some writers who do that, in sort of the classical music model — very structured and controlled. And there are others who literally make everything up as they go along, in the jazz model — improvising, freewheeling. Most writers, I think, fall somewhere in between, what I guess we'd call the "American Idol" model: They have a sense of the overall tune, but what makes it interesting is the variations on the way. And all of these writing models are totally fine: What's important is finding the one that works for you.

J. K. Rowling, clearly, is a classical musician on the order of Mozart or Bach in the way she planned and ordered all the plots in the series. She outlined all the books from the beginning, which allowed her to weave a plot of this complexity. But if you aren't a plotter of this type — you're more of a jazz musician or Adam Lambert — or if you do outline everything, but then find yourself deviating from that as you write, then I suggest that, *after* you finish your first draft, you go back and outline the entire book, chapter by chapter. Describe the key action and plot or character-development points of each chapter and write down key thoughts or lines. This is commonly known as a book map.

I do this with each and every novel I edit, because it allows me to see how the conflict develops, where the clues to any mysteries are being laid, how the protagonist is getting what he needs. And more important, it lets me see how the book *isn't* working: where the author is going for long periods without introducing any new developments or information, where characters are behaving inconsistently, where there's a dialogue scene that's fun but sort of pointless, or where two scenes in a row establish the exact same plot points, so one isn't necessary.

Thanks to the book map, I don't get caught up in the language of the book, so I can get a more global view of the kind of plot the author is developing — a Conflict, Mystery, or Lack — and all the little subplots within them. And then I can also keep track of whether they've fulfilled the essential requirements of that plot: Has the heroine overcome the enemy — or vice versa — in a Conflict plot? What is the answer to the

Mystery? Has the hero gotten what he needed in a Lack plot? I can also look at the themes the author is developing and look for points where those ideas might be underlined or strengthened.

I'm going to wind up here with two last things that writers can learn from the Harry Potter series. The first is, take your time. I wrote the author biographies that appeared in the back of the American editions of the last three books — my immense contribution to Potter lore — and with *Deathly Hallows* I made an especial point of including the following sentence: "J. K. Rowling has been working on the Harry Potter series since 1990." That was *seventeen years* from the initial idea till the publication of Book Seven. It was five years between the idea and the completion of *Sorcerer's Stone*. And in all that time, Ms. Rowling was working out her plots, deepening her characters and themes, writing and rewriting . . . eager to be published, no doubt, but also giving herself time to get it right, as she ultimately did.

And that brings me to my final point: Have fun, and write what you love. When J. K. Rowling wrote the first Harry Potter book, and my boss, Arthur A. Levine, bought the American rights, fantasy wasn't "hot." Children's books weren't "hot." British books weren't "hot." And publishing people sort of thought Arthur was nuts. But he just knew he loved this book, that it was one of the most fresh and wonderful things he'd ever read.

And that magic happened because Ms. Rowling wasn't writing to please the market. She was writing to please herself. And she did that across all seven books, in spite of the pressures of fans and reporters and the Internet and critics, keeping true to her vision every step of the way.

So don't write what you think is going to sell, what you think the market wants — because that's going to change by the time you publish anyway. But rather write the story you've always wanted to hear, the one you've never read anywhere else, the one that scares you with the pleasure of writing it. It will happen in a world that you alone can create — maybe a fantasy world, maybe the town next door — and with people that you alone can fill it with: characters you come to know and love through their experiences and the way they grow and change. And of all that grows out of *your* unique experiences, the way *you've* grown and come to see the world, a perspective unlike anyone else's on earth.

You have to take joy in the work of writing, for it is hard work, but when you can find that just-right word, that perfect plot twist — there are very few greater pleasures.

And then, even if your book is never published — or if it is published, but never quite achieves four hundred million copies in print — you will still have the story you always wanted, a little bit of yourself forever in the world. Because a book is kind of like a good Horcrux, if we can imagine that — a piece of the writer's soul, preserved in a physical object for all time, and changing the lives of all those who come in contact with it.

I know that nine years ago, in a white Dodge Dynasty somewhere in the wilds of Iowa, my life was changed forever, thanks to Harry Potter and J. K. Rowling. And I know that many of you can say the same. If you are writers, I wish you all the best with your own Horcri.* For all of you, I thank you for your kind attention. And I hope that all of us can say, in the end, "All was well."

*A Harry Potter fan community in-joke inspired by my friend John Noe, who insisted the plural of "Horcrux" should be "Horcri."

QUARTET:
Four Elements of Fiction

I wrote these next four talks over a period of two years, and revised them into a whole for the Missouri SCBWI and Western Washington SCBWI retreats in 2009. It was a pleasure to have the chance to think and speak about all four of these important elements of fiction, and then to put them together and think about how they play together in books (mostly novels). All of them have been revised extensively for this book.

The talks draw heavily on examples from four novels, two of which I edited and all four of which I greatly admire: *Bobby vs. Girls (Accidentally)*, a funny third-person realistic contemporary chapter book by Lisa Yee (co-edited with Arthur Levine, 2009); *Marcelo in the Real World*, by Francisco X. Stork, a first-person realistic contemporary YA novel (2009); *Graceling* by Kristin Cashore, a third-person YA fantasy set in an imaginary world (Harcourt, 2008); and *The Hunger Games* by Suzanne Collins, a first-person dystopic YA science-fiction novel set in the hopefully far future (Scholastic Press, 2008).

QUARTET:
Point

—————— ·◆◆◆· ——————

We're going to get started with a writing exercise very first thing. Please take three to five minutes to write a brief scene incorporating the following five elements:

A girl   A ball   A boy   A tree   A cat

You can name them, age them, set them anywhere or in any time you like. This can be the beginning of a story, the middle or the end. Don't try to polish it or make it pretty. Just write more or less the first thing that comes into your head. We're going to call the story and characters that result here the "Basic Book," and we'll refer back to it occasionally throughout the talks that follow.

At the end of the three-to-five minutes, look at the scene you wrote. Can you restate it in one line as follows? (Feel free to adapt the structure as necessary.)

___[Character]___ ___[Action Verb]___, as ___[Another Character]___ ___[Another Action Verb]___, which the reader sees from the perspective of ___[Point of View]___.

For instance, "Jenny climbed the tree to rescue her brother Joseph, as Snookums snickered from behind the bushes, which the reader sees from the perspective of an omniscient observer." Or "The tree tried to bend away from Jenny, Joseph, and Snookums as they attacked it with knives and claws, which the reader sees from the tree's perspective."

I'm asking you to restate the story in this way because that highlights the three most important elements of fiction: the Voice, the Characters, and the Action, also known as the plot. All of these things come together in a novel to convey what I call its *Point*. The point of the novel is not its theme — though it can be. And it's not its moral — though it can be that too, if the point of your novel is impart an idea about how to live in the world.

What I call the point is the idea or experience that the novel is built to convey. It might be to scare the bejeezus out of your reader. It might be to make them roll on the floor laughing or crying. It might be to teach a lesson, like, say, attacking trees with knives and claws is bad. Or it might be to explore an idea: why people have to suffer, what happens after we die, whether the joy caused by love is worth its pain. And it might be — indeed, probably ought to be — more than one of these.

Every decision that you make as an author should ultimately be in the service of the novel's point, going toward the end you want to achieve for yourself and for the reader. These decisions get made in the three main areas we've already identified:

- The plot — the structure of the book's story
- The characters — the people who bring the story to life, and who must come to life themselves
- The voice — the consciousness and rhythm of the story's telling. David Mamet said, "All art is where you put the camera," and we're going to explore that idea in detail later.

A lot of these decisions are made unconsciously: You hear a voice in your head, and that becomes the voice of your main character. Or you're writing a magnetic older man, and you automatically make him look like your incredibly charismatic father. Here we're going to investigate how these aspects of fiction work, so you can make these decisions more consciously and choose the right ones to illuminate your point, or revise the ones you have to illumine it better.

Now I want to be clear about two things related to point:

1. For many writers, the point of their book, what they most want it to achieve, is to be published. Which makes perfect sense — you've put in all this labor, you want it to be seen and read and to make money. But we're going to set that aside in these talks and just think about the book as a work of art here that a reader will experience, not as an object for sale to that same reader.

2. The point of your book does not have to be the points most often found in beautiful hardcover literary fiction. That is, an emotional journey in which — to offer the most clichéd example of a Newbery winner — a Southern girl comes to terms with a relative's death or her own mortality. You may realize, in writing, that what you like writing most is not necessarily going to win the Newbery. That's fine! You just need to know what you *do* want your work to accomplish, and then make that the very best book that it can be. Whether a book is *Captain Underpants* or *Because of Winn-Dixie*, a book ultimately just has to meet one standard of quality: to fulfill the reader's expectations for it.

All that said, the thing I edit most and think about most is children's and YA literary fiction, so those are the expectations and standards I'm going to talk about most here. These are books in which:

- The action of the plot is driven primarily by the characters.
- The characters themselves are complex and interesting.
- The voice and prosody are distinctive — the thoughts and the rhythms of the thought could belong to only one writer or character.

Besides pleasure, what I'm looking for most in the fiction I read is reality about life — the truth as polished by art. Even in a fantasy or science-fiction novel, I'm looking for that reality. I want to be sucked into this imaginary world and believe these people are real and their actions are real. And I want the flow of the language around me to be like water to a fish — transparent, so I see right through it to the truth of the action, and so immersive that I take it for granted.

When I edit a novel, nearly everything I do is for more truth or more transparency. So these talks will try to lay out the principles that guide my editing for those ends, so much as I can articulate them, and how you can apply those same principles to your book.

Now, to return to my earlier points about point. I think there are actually two kinds of points in fiction. The first is what I'll call the **emotional point:** what you want your reader to feel as a result of the book, what kind of emotional experience you want him to have. Terrified? Exhausted? Exhilarated? Do you want them to have learned something? Thought about something? Or just to have had a good time? Clearly each individual scene of your novel will be driven by its own emotional point. But when you think about the overall project, what is the one specific adjective or couple of adjectives — besides "brilliant" or "beautiful" or another generically good term — that you want a reader to use after they finish your novel? Romantic? Spine-tingling? Quirky? Inspiring? That is your novel's emotional point.

The second kind of point is what I call the **thematic point:** what you want your reader to think about as a result of the book, what subject is at the heart of your work, what kind of questions you want to inspire or answer. The writer David Lodge said, "A novel is a long answer to the question, 'What is it about?'" — so, what is yours about? In the classical model of plotting, the events of the story come together in a way that makes the reader, or the character, or both, recognize a truth they hadn't previously understood, and often, this truth forces your character to change themselves or their life in one particular direction. In modernist fiction, with its more fragmented view of human life and consciousness, stories are often less about the development of character and the wholeness of the truth revealed than the evocation of a particular experience for a reader, which may just raise more questions to be asked. Either way, there is likely something larger here that you wanted the events of your book to come together to show.

So I'm guessing that all of you have a completed draft of a book somewhere. To that end, please take a few minutes and complete these two sentences:

My Emotional Point is:

My Thematic Point is:

These are things that might very well evolve as you think about your book from different angles. But we're putting them out there as starter statements, starter ideas, getting whatever intentions you have for this book into words.

I put such emphasis on figuring out the point of your novel because, in revision, it is a yardstick by which you can measure everything else in the book. (And I would emphasize "in revision" there because I think most writers discover the point as they write the first draft, which is as it should be.) Once you know the point, you can isolate the individual parts of the book and see how each of them is contributing or not contributing to that point. Or, of course, you can see what IS working and adapt your point to fit. If your point is to write a rip-roaring action adventure, but your main character is a wet noodle (literally or metaphorically) — that's not going to work out. Or suppose you want to write a deeply sad novel about a girl who's dying of leukemia, but you can't help cracking potty jokes every four lines; again, you're going to have to adjust either your point or your voice to tell a wholly emotionally successful story, in one direction or another.

This is always more or less the very first thing I try to identify with my authors: what exactly they want to do in their books. And then I can figure out how to help them do it. And now that you all have your tentative points written out, hopefully, we can figure that out for you too.

QUARTET:
Character

Before we get started here: I hope you saved the exercise you did during the Point section, with the girl, the boy, the ball, the cat, and the tree, because we're going to refer back to that in more writing exercises. You should also keep one of your works-in-progress in mind — ideally a completed draft of a novel. When writing exercises appear in the text, you can either expand on the material of the boy-girl-etc. exercise, or you can use it to go deeper into your own work-in-progress, whichever you prefer.

So, as you know, my name is Cheryl Klein, and I'm the senior editor at Arthur A. Levine Books, an imprint of Scholastic Inc. I am also the daughter of Alan and Rebecca Klein; the older sister of Melissa Jackson; the girlfriend of James Monohan; and the best friend of Kathryne Beebe. I was born September 22, 1978. I graduated from Raymore-Peculiar High School and Carleton College in 1996 and 2000, respectively. I'm a Virgo, a Horse, a runner, a writer, a Methodist, a Brooklynite, a Democrat, and a blonde (chemically enhanced).

Every day I put on a silver watch and a ring that says "In my beginning is my end." I love reading more than any other activity on earth. I get really, really anxious when I'm running late. I am easily distracted, insanely detail-oriented, and something of a workaholic. I want to own an apartment in Brooklyn, visit India, and edit a Newbery Medal winner. I attend church, even though I struggle with my faith. I take care of my friends. I get somewhat annoyed at people who repeat themselves. And I have secrets I'm not telling.

And I have just listed these things in such detail because this is my character: who I am, as best I can define it in words. I could go on for much longer, of course, listing all the books I've read, the experiences

I've had, all the people I've been in love with and why, and how each of those things has changed me over time, and affected the way I will act in the future . . . and sure, I'm tempted to do just that. But as interesting as such a monologue would be for *me*, it wouldn't be relevant to the story we all find ourselves in now: the story of this talk, which should be all about your fictional characters and not my real one!

And when you're writing fiction, you have to make the same decision that I just did. You have a character who is bursting with life, with possibilities and contradictions, and you either have to follow the whims of that character and see where she takes you, which may be nowhere you ever intended; or you find a way to make those whims work within the story you want to tell. So we're going to discuss how to create rich, round characters that connect with a reader, and how to make those characters function within a story, to result in the kind of fiction we all want to read, with characters we love, having experiences that make us laugh, cry, and in the end, cheer.

What is a character? It is a human being who inhabits a story. And that is how you should try to think of them: human beings just like you, every one of them as complex and emotional and real as you; and it is your job as their creator to bring out all of those complexities and emotions within the boundaries of the plot.

And what makes a good character? I'm going to begin with theory here and go on to practice. A character can be defined the same way as a spoon can: by what he is (essence) and by what he does (action). A spoon is, according to Webster's, "an eating or cooking implement consisting of a small shallow bowl with a relatively long handle." But it is just a small, shallow bowl with a handle until it is *used*. The thing that makes it more than a small shallow bowl with a handle — its very spoonness — consists of its utility in stirring, measuring, and eating.

It's the same way with a character in fiction. She can have all these charming quirks, all the personality and kindness in the world—a truly wonderful essence — but they don't matter until she begins to do something within the novel — her actions. Yet at the same time, if she didn't have that personality, there would be nothing to distinguish her from a robot or an animal, or any other creature capable of carrying out the function she serves in the story. What makes a character come alive on the page is the unity of essence and action.

So let's look at these two things together. First, Essence — who the character is. I think there are five factors to keep in mind here. (This is an aspect of *my* character: I'm very into lists.)

1. Facts: The basic situation of the character. Is your character a boy or girl? How old is he/she at the time of your book? What is his/her ethnic background? Sexuality? Who is in his/her immediate family, and what is their socioeconomic status? Where do they live?

2. Identities: The roles the character plays in his/her life. This is an concept I learned from Kathi Appelt, author of *The Underneath* and *Keeper*, at the Vermont College of Fine Arts retreat in 2008, and I've found it extraordinarily useful in my thinking about character ever since: How would your protagonist define his or her primary identity in life? It will likely be different in different circumstances, of course, but you should be able to pick out one key role that reflects the primary action or relationships your character pursues in the book. I said at the beginning that I'm a senior editor at Arthur A. Levine Books, a daughter, a sister, a girlfriend, a best friend, a Democrat, a runner, and a Methodist, and I can be all of those things in the course of a week. But for the purposes of this talk, the identity that matters most is that I'm a writer, because that defines what I'm trying to do right now — write words are true — and the rest of those identities are irrelevant in this circumstance.

Once a character's primary identity is established in their own mind, that identity can become a wonderful driver of plot conflict, if another character or the society at large disagrees with the protagonist's defini-tion; if the protagonist is forced to prioritize one identity over another, to the latter's detriment; or if the protagonist's identity is threatened or changes according to outside factors. Looking at our example books, we can see that in *Bobby vs. Girls (Accidentally)*, Bobby has always defined himself partly as "Holly Harper's best friend"—in secret, of course, because boys and girls can't be best friends in public. But as they head into fourth grade, the gender roles are getting more calcified and contentious, so Bobby and Holly are each coming to define themselves more as "boy" and "girl" than "best friends," and suffering from the resulting loss of their friendship and connection. In *Graceling*, Katsa has always defined herself as a fighter, even a killer, foremost; and when she falls in love, and learns the young man loves her back, she's forced to consider an identity as a lover instead—even possibly a wife and mother, which causes her considerable distress. In both these novels, a change in identity drives the conflicts in a way that feels very true because it's so integral to the characters.

Exercise: List all of the identities of the protagonist of your WIP at the beginning of the book, then rank them by their importance to him/her at that point. How are those priorities reflected in the plot? Will they change by the end of the book?

3. Internal Qualities: The internal factors that shape how the character acts and reacts. Internal Qualities are any kind of behavior determinant that comes from within your character. Such a determinant might be in his DNA, or it might have been learned through or created by external forces, or the causes might, of course, overlap.

Qualities can be broken down into five loose categories, which might also overlap with each other, as each reflects a facet of the same essential whole. The first is basic **personality drivers:** the combination of deep-seated desires, needs, and fears that drive an individual's approach to the world and show themselves in smaller personality behaviors. (The second category *is* those smaller **personality behaviors.**) I said of myself earlier, I'm easily distracted, insanely detail-oriented, and something of a workaholic. These behaviors are all manifestations of two of my personality drivers, that "God is in the details" and "It's vitally important to get as much right as possible"—indeed, that it might be dangerous if I *don't* get something right, that if I make a mistake, everything could fall apart. Thus I have to pay attention to everything and work all the time. In our example book *Marcelo in the Real World*, Arturo Sandoval is a highly successful lawyer — the partner in his own law firm — who attended Harvard Law and made his name and fortune representing small Mexican companies in patent cases. We could surmise from this that his personality drivers involve a lifelong quest for ambition, achievement, and worldly money and power; and indeed those qualities reveal themselves in every aspect of his behavior, most especially his occasional discomfort with his son Marcelo (a deeply spiritual young man with something like Asperger's syndrome), and his desire for Marcelo to integrate into "the real world," which precipitates the plot of the book.

Both personality drivers and the behaviors that result from them could be described as weaknesses or flaws, but the reality is, as with most human characteristics, they can also be our strengths. Being easily distracted means I multitask well; insane detail orientation means I usually catch typographical errors; working all the time means I get a heck of a lot done. But: It might take me longer to finish things because I'm trying to do so many things at once; I can obsess over details and miss the larger picture; and I can get downright grouchy when I feel stressed. Thanks to his ambition and desire for achievement, Arturo is not even close to being as morally good a person as Marcelo is, but one of the surprises of the novel is that he's nonetheless right about his son's need to join the real world. As you create your protagonist's personality drivers and resultant personality behaviors, be sure to think about both the positive *and* negative ways they can play out in his/her life and story.

The third category of Internal Qualities: the character's **ethics/ morals/values**. That is, what they will and won't do for whatever it is they want. Will they steal, lie, cheat, kill? Where are their boundaries? What will push them to those boundaries? Editor Molly O'Neill posed an interesting question on her blog once: What is the thing your character knows absolutely to be true? What happens if that turns out to be false? Maybe at the beginning of the book, the character is willing to steal to get money for his grandma's AIDS treatment — but by the end he's found someone he *can't* steal from. Or maybe he's not willing to steal at the beginning but it seems perfectly justifiable to him by the end. Choosing between two values like this (love of grandma vs. wrongness of theft) creates a plot concept called "moral dilemma," which I love madly and will discuss at more length in the plot section later.

A fourth category of Internal Qualities is **the character's degree of self-awareness**. Suppose your main character is a thief, as we were just discussing. Is he aware that's bad and he gets a charge off it? Aware it's bad, but he's able to rationalize it out? Or does he just not think about it? That can really affect how a reader reacts to your character's behavior — the degree to which the reader subscribes to the rationalization. In both *The Hunger Games* and *Graceling*, the heroines have to kill to survive, and they spend a lot of time thinking about (agonizing over, even) the fact that they're taking others' lives. Which is how we non-killers can accept it as well: We know they aren't monsters, because this behavior is considered and painful for them.

The last category of Internal Quality I'll mention here, and by far the least important one, is **Tastes**: the character's favorite food, color, video game, sport, movie star, kind of shoe, vacation spot, breed of chicken, you name it. Tastes provide useful details to know for small touches of character throughout your book — that he wears red on days when he needs luck, or that she loves ginger ale but hates Fresca — but unless the choices the character makes in relation to these tastes are impacting your plot in some way, you probably don't need to spend a great deal of time developing these.

Don't be afraid to have two qualities that are COMPLETELY CONTRADICTORY. The most interesting characters usually are. They might publicly define their identities as vegetarian Buddhists, but then sneak a cheeseburger; be jerks at home, but sweet-talkers at school; shy with people, but at ease with animals. One of my favorite quotations regarding character comes from Samuel Johnson: "Inconsistencies cannot both be right; but imputed to man, they may both be true."

4. External Qualities: Those aspects of the character that can be seen from the outside. There are two subcategories here. The first is **appearance.** We base our first impressions of people off what we see and what they say — so your descriptions of your character's appearance *can* be important to establishing him in the reader's mind. I say "can" because too much emphasis on appearance can cut both ways. There's a terrible cliché in fiction where the main character will stop and look in a mirror and catalogue his or her features somewhere in the first chapter in order to establish the person visually in the reader's mind. But that never really works for me — partly because it's such a cliché that it annoys me and marks the writer as less interesting than s/he could be, and partly because that description defines the character in the reader's mind as someone who likely looks different than the reader, which perhaps weakens the reader's identification with the character. (None of Sarah Dessen's book covers feature the faces of her protagonists, at her request, because she wants readers to be able to imagine themselves into the lives of her characters.)

On the other hand, there are certain types of novels — fantasy especially — where you really want to have the characters described so the reader can visualize them, because the point of the book is that the reader falls into this world and experiences it fully. Or, if your novel is written in first person, we want to see what that main character sees when she looks at other people, which will help characterize those other people for us (and characterize your main character by showing us what she notices about others). So it depends on the point you're going for whether you'll want to spend time on appearances.

The second subcategory here is **manners of speaking/patterns of behavior.** These are often manifestations of the smaller personality behaviors we discussed above. Because I'm easily distracted, I often stop myself in the middle of saying something to correct a previous

thought or chase down another thought. Like the dog in the film *Up* —
SQUIRREL! They can also just be small distinctive gestures: Marcelo in
Marcelo in the Real World opens and closes his hands when he's stressed
to help him physically release tension. Note that this isn't the *content*
of what the character says or does — only the pattern, the overt things
readers would see from the outside. I actually think this category is
much more important than the character's physical appearance, because
these patterns often provide the little details that, in their humanity and
recognizability, make a character real.

5. **History — also known as backstory.** Where was your character
born? What was his first grade teacher like? When is his birthday?
Where did his mother grow up? All of these questions might reasonably
be classified as backstory, as each of them could have some effect on his
character or behavior if one of the answers changed who he was. And in
general it is good for you the author to know as much as you can here,
because it helps the character come to life in your mind.

However, the only history your *readers* need to know is either what's
relevant to your plot or what's relevant to how your character will act
in that plot. If you were writing a middle-grade novel about a softball
star and her quest for the championship, for instance, it's important
to include an account of the team's performance the previous season,
because that will influence the character's drive now. But you don't
necessarily need to include her spotty GPA the year before — unless
that's something that will keep her off the team this year or it's causing
tension with her academically overachieving family.

Plotwise, backstory is commonly used as mystery, where you can
tantalize the reader by referring to some fact the characters know but
the reader must discover, or keep that part of the story hidden for the
character to work out the mystery himself. Indeed, a great part of the
brilliance of the Harry Potter series is that every book works in two
opposite directions: Harry investigates a mystery that involves some
backstory about either his parents or Lord Voldemort, which in turn

contributes to his frontstory as he moves forward through the school year. Or consider the first two lines of *Graceling*: "In these dungeons the darkness was complete, but Katsa had a map in her mind. One that had so far proven correct, as Oll's maps tended to do." From just these lines, we can deduce a great deal of Katsa and Oll's backstory: One is the Woman of Action, the other the planner and highly competent; they've done this before, which means there's a history and expertise here, and expertise is a very attractive quality; and Katsa is in some dungeons, a place of great danger, which promises a great story . . . so already *I'm* interested in what they'll do next.

Finally, backstory can also be used — and SHOULD also be used — as emotional context. There's a great example of this early in *The Hunger Games*, where the heroine Katniss is reflecting on what she knows about a young man named Peeta, a baker's son, who will be her fellow representative of District 12 in the Games. She remembers a time when she and her family were starving and she came to the bakery to beg bread. His mother turned her down, but shortly thereafter, Katniss heard a shrieking inside the bakery, and Peeta brought out two partially-burned loaves of bread . . . which he apparently burned deliberately, suffering a beating in consequence, in order to be able to give it to her. That sort of backstory inclines us readers to like Peeta very much, however much Katniss may profess to be neutral about him.

Too much backstory can easily swamp a frontstory — your main plot. Concentrate on getting the frontstory out to the reader, then use the backstory to show the reader how the character became who she is, what his or her relationships with other people are like, and why the frontstory matters to her.

An important note about all three of these latter things — Internal Qualities, External Qualities, and history. When editors say they want you to show, not tell, in relation to a character, we usually mean we want the character's Internal Qualities to be demonstrated through their

External Qualities and action rather than through blunt statement of fact. For instance, rather than saying "John hated to deal with anything related to his father's death," we want you to dramatize a scene where John's mom or best friend tries to approach the topic, and we see John pull away or change the subject.

You CAN get away with telling if you have showing to back it up. For instance, if you spent a paragraph talking about how John couldn't think about the accident his father was in, couldn't even name the place or the month or the color of the car in his head — you would have earned the right to say at the end, "John hated to deal with anything related to his father's death," and the sentence would serve as the conclusion to your argument. (Or you could put it at the beginning of the paragraph, and it would serve as a thesis statement that you then supported with evidence.) But you would need to be careful then that that sentence wasn't redundant with what the reader already knew.

Two of my very favorite writers start their books by telling about the characters: Jane Austen with Emma and J. K. Rowling with the Dursleys. But they quickly follow it up with action demonstrating the qualities they just told the reader about. And what matters, and what the reader remembers, is not the telling but the showing. The rule of thumb here is: Let your characters' words and actions speak for themselves.

And that leads us nicely out of the Essence qualities — what a character *is* — and into the Action qualities — what the character *does*. The essayist Michel de Montaigne said "Anything we do reveals us," and these three qualities all reveal the essence of a character through the action he takes.

1. Desire: What the character wants. To find the bad guy, to get the girl, to be the smartest person in the room, to make a ton of money, to find their father, to live a normal life. . . . The possibilities are as wide as human experience. I sometimes think of this as the "primary value" (and it will likely align in some way with the primary identity from earlier):

If you knocked this person out, when they woke up, after their basic needs were met and they knew everyone else was okay — what would be the first thing they thought of?

What the character wants reveals quite a bit about them — their philosophy of life, the scope of their imagination, where they are in their lives. For instance, a kid who wants a dog is at a different point in his experience than a kid who wants to feed starving children in Africa, and both of them differ further from the kid who wants to do both and can't decide.

Many (maybe all) interesting characters want more than one thing. Marcelo wants to go to his special school, Paterson, but he also wants to keep a good relationship with his father, who'd like him to attend a regular school. Katniss wants to survive the Hunger Games, but she also wants to rebel against the Capitol. This double desire is a tremendously effective device not only because it's realistic — don't we *all* want more than one thing? — but because it instantly creates internal conflict when the character has to choose to pursue one desire above the other, or choose between two competing values, or choose among the people who represent those values and desires to him. Of course, desire quite often creates external conflict as well, when one character's desires clash with another character's — like Marcelo's and his father's differing ideas about the right school for him. Either way, your reader will expect to see those conflicts worked out in some manner in the course of the book. If that *doesn't* happen — if the character's desires are neither fulfilled nor frustrated nor changed in the course of the book — you'll need to have a good reason for that, or else you'll have a dissatisfied reader on your hands.

Question: What is the key desire of the main character in your novel at the beginning? What is his/her primary value?

2. Attitude/Energy: The attitude a character brings to a situation. This is deeply tied to the internal and external qualities we discussed in

Essence. But this is the *content* of what the character will say, as well as the way they say it, so much as those two can be separated.

Suppose your character is the new kid in school and he's heading into the lunchroom. His interior monologue could be: *Oh gosh, will anyone ask me to eat with them?* Or *Which of these losers has earned the right to my presence at their table?* Or *I have to find that cute Jamie — I'd love to eat with him.* And all three of those things reveal his character through his attitude: his approach towards new situations and other people, and his approach toward life in general.

At the beginning of a novel, I think it's really important that your main character show either positive energy (meaning they approach life optimistically) or interesting negative energy (that is, they approach life pessimistically, but they're interesting or funny about it). Because generally, if the reader wouldn't want to hang around with a character in person, the reader also won't want to hang around with them in a novel. Katniss in *The Hunger Games* is extremely pessimistic at first about her chances of survival, which equals negative energy. But she also has great *fight* and motivation, and we readers can see that she has more skills than she knows, and that (along with all the other great things about the book) keeps us going.

Question: How would you characterize the overall attitude or energy of your protagonist at the beginning of your book?

Exercise: To figure out a character's attitude and energy, try journaling a regular week in the life of that character. What would they write about? Not write about? What would they say that no one else would say? Do they have any characteristic phrases? This is an especially good exercise for supporting characters, because it can be very easy to just think about your protagonist and forget that the people around him or her need to be just as real.

3. Action: What the character does to get what they want. Action is the result of Desire plus Attitude. If your character wants a dog, but has a negative attitude, he probably won't figure out a way to get it or believe that he can. But if the character wants a dog, and has a can-do attitude, she'll keep going after it until it happens.

It says a lot about a character if she talks about something all throughout the book and never goes after it; your readers will sense that, and it eventually grows into a sense of contempt for the character, I think, the same way it's easy to lose respect for any big dreamer with no action. So if your character has a defined desire, she also needs to have some follow-through.

Question: What are three concrete actions that your protagonist takes in service of getting his/her desire?

If you struggled with answering that at all . . . Lack of action on the protagonist's part may not be the number-one problem I see in novels, but it's definitely in the top ten. Usually this is because the character is mostly observing his world, particularly either a backstory mystery (why his mom won't talk to his grandma, say) or a present-day situation involving someone else (his parents are getting a divorce). Or his desire is impossible for him to accomplish — for instance, his desire is for his parents NOT to get a divorce, which is a situation no action of his might help. If this is a problem in your own work, then I have two suggestions:

1. Show the character acting out against the situation. This is what happens in *So Totally Emily Ebers* by Lisa Yee. Emily wants her parents to get back together, or, at the very least, for her dad to give her a call. But she can't control either of those factors, so in her depression, she starts shopping with the credit card her dad gave her. And shopping. And shopping. And shopping. This eventually causes TWO crises that unite the main threads of the book: friendship, when Emily's new "friends" expect her to buy them something really expensive; and family, as her dad finally calls her to complain about the credit card bill.

2. Give the character another desire where she CAN take action. In other words, add a subplot where she is the prime mover . . . and strongly consider making it your primary plot, and turning whatever situation involves these other people into a subplot. For instance, suppose your main character's brother has run away, and they're waiting around for him to come back. The novel could easily devolve into her observations of everyone's behavior in this situation — which might be interesting and beautiful, but isn't necessarily action-filled. So if you're going for action-filled, add a subplot where she wants to get to know the cute new boy in school. Or she wants to try out for the lead in the class play. Or she wants to run away herself and starts planning that. All those things would give you some action in your book that the main character can effect while she waits for the larger emotional situation to be fulfilled. Kate DiCamillo's lovely *Because of Winn-Dixie* follows this model.

One of my favorite exercises for writers is to have them write the flap copy for their own books, because whenever you have to write flaps, like I do, it becomes really obvious *really quickly* if the main character doesn't have a desire or never does anything — there is no action to write about. So, **Exercise:** Try writing the flap copy for your book — a 250-word summary with a strong emphasis on the situation at the beginning, the reasons that situation will change, and the action your protagonist will take in response.

That is all the theory of how to create a character, and we can put it into practice by simply coming up with one answer for each category. In fact, you're going to make up a character right now. Grab a piece of paper and a pencil, and without thinking about it very much (that is: write down more or less the first thing that comes into your head), answer these questions:

FACTS
+ Is your character a boy or girl?
+ How old is s/he?
+ Ethnic/racial background?
+ Family situation?

+ Where does s/he live?

IDENTITY

+ List five roles s/he fills, in descending order of priority for the character.

INTERNAL QUALITIES

+ Name one driver of his/her personality.
+ Name one resultant behavior from that.
+ Identify one of his/her ethics/morals/values.
+ On a scale of 1-10, with 1 being a Neanderthal and 10 Woody Allen, what's his/her degree of self-awareness?
+ Identify one of his/her tastes.

EXTERNAL QUALITIES?

+ What does s/he look like?
+ Describe a distinctive pattern of speech or behavior.

HISTORY

+ Come up with an emotionally interesting item from his/her history.

ACTION

+ What does s/he want? (What is his/her primary value?)
+ What is his/her attitude?
+ What action will s/he take to get what s/he wants?

The more you add under each category, the more well-rounded and interesting your character will be. Another easy way to add depth is to ask the question "Why?" You said under what s/he wants: _____. Now write out *why* s/he wants that. What experiences gave her the attitude you identified above? What are his parents like, that he has the ethical rule you named here?

Here are three more questions I love in exploring character:

+ What keeps him/her alive? (What's the character's joy?)
+ What's his/her pain?

♦ What's his/her name? Why?

I adore the name question in particular because a name says so much about a character's parents (that they would choose that name), family (that this name reflects a particular history and culture), and history (especially if the character has a nickname or chose a name for him/herself).

And in the end, what we have here is, in the very loosest form, the plot of a novel:

♦ How s/he overcomes the pain — the _____
♦ And gets the want — the _____
♦ By means of the thing that keeps her alive — the _____

So you've probably created someone who's pretty interesting, right? We could go through and run this chart for each of the characters in your novel — the parents, the siblings, the friends and teachers — and we'd have a complex web of conflicting desires and actions — which, again, adds up to a novel. This is actually really important to remember: Everyone is the hero of his own story. To the minor characters in your book, the hero of your book isn't your main character — it's *them*. This even applies to your villain: No one is the bad guy in their own story. Everyone has reasons for doing the things they do, and you need to know those reasons.

And you can create dynamic minor characters simply by giving each one a desire and a distinctive external quality or two (as presumably we see these minor characters mostly from the outside). So every time one particular character shows up, the reader thinks, "Oh yes! This is the kid who wants to win the soccer championship and has pink hair." You don't want to overplay those qualities — that becomes repetitive and annoying. And everything should definitely remain relevant to your plot. But if you need to characterize someone fast, those are useful tools.

Time for another, more extensive writing **Exercise.** Think about either the Basic Book exercise we did earlier — the boy/girl/cat/ball/tree scene — or the most recent scene you wrote in your own WIP. Take one of the characters and fill out that character chart we just used according to the standards set in your scene. For instance, if you wrote a Basic Book scene where the boy got angry at the girl and threw the ball at her cat in the tree, that might mean the boy is naturally mean. Such people exist in the world. But it might also mean that his father is dying of cancer and he's really frustrated and scared by the whole experience, and this is his way of acting out at something that he *can* have power over — the cat — since he *can't* have power over death and cancer. So his greatest desire, under the Action category on the chart, is for his father to survive.

Take three or four minutes, use the chart as a starting point, and freewrite everything associated with this character that you can. Then do it again for one of the other characters in your book or in this scene. Then you will have these two characters, and know what they want and what they'd do to get it. Hold those thoughts — we're going to use them in a later talk.

So I was rattling on about thematic points and emotional points earlier, and you might be wondering "Well, Cheryl, what does that have to do with character?" First of all, to achieve an emotional point, you have to construct a character readers want to follow. Because if they're not interested enough in that character, they're not going to read your story, and then they're never going to reach the emotional point you had in mind.

How do you get a reader to be interested in your main character? (Credit where it is due: Many of the following ideas were drawn from Orson Scott Card's excellent *Characters and Viewpoint*.)

1. Make the character new. I read a lot of manuscripts, as do all of my editorial colleagues, and I have to say, oftentimes the desire, the voice, the Internal Qualities, the entire character just feels so familiar and been-there-done-that, even from Chapter 1, that I quickly lose interest. This is particularly a problem in fantasy, where we see so, so many underappreciated kids missing one or more parents and fated for a great destiny.

One easy way to make interesting, new characters is to change one of the Action qualities above to something you wouldn't expect in a novel of its kind. For instance, instead of a boy who wants a dog, change his Desire so he wants a cat instead — or a kangaroo, or an ostrich. Instead of a girl who hates moving because she's leaving all her friends behind, change her Attitude so that she's really, really excited to get out of town. Instead of a boy who wants to keep a dog as a pet, perhaps he kills the dog (changing the Action itself). All of these things would make me read on with interest, because they're intriguing variations on these standard plots, and thus they promise interesting action and psychology as I discover why the character wants, feels, or does such a thing. In Francisco X. Stork's *The Last Summer of the Death Warriors*, you learn in more or less the first ten pages that the main character, Pancho, is planning to kill someone. And that made me sit up and take notice, because I don't see a lot of wannabe murderers as sympathetic protagonists in YA fiction, and yet I *totally* sympathized with this guy from the very beginning.

2. Make your main character the viewpoint character. Of course, part of the reason I empathized with Pancho was because he was the lens through which I saw the action. When your main character is our primary point of view, either in first person or a limited third-person, we readers have to depend on that character in order to see and experience your fictional world. This has its own dangers in first person, which we will discuss more when we get to Voice. But it's definitely a way to draw readers into your protagonist's world.

2a. If the book is in first person, give the character a distinctive voice, or in limited third, the habit of noticing or thinking interesting things. Marcelo's voice at the beginning of his book is clipped, stiff, sometimes repetitive — a little "off," altogether. I wanted to know why his voice sounded like that, so I read on. In the first paragraph of *Death Warriors*, Pancho is surprised by how long it takes to get where he's going, but "Maybe it was a short drive that seemed long because Mrs. Olivares would not stop talking. Mostly she told him how lucky he was to be going to St. Anthony's rather than a juvenile detention center." There's a prickly, realistic energy to the line about Mrs. Olivares, and if he was supposed to be in a detention center, clearly this is a guy who makes trouble — worth finding out about.

3. Give the character a cause that readers can root for. That is, give the character a Desire that creates readerly interest or sympathy in the character, because that Desire is so interesting (wanting a kangaroo as a pet) or ethically right (standing up to the mean girls, working for a homeless shelter), or it has such high stakes. In both *The Hunger Games* and *Graceling*, the main character is fighting for her survival, and the survival of the man she reluctantly comes to love. And because I like both those characters so much, those are causes I can get behind.

4. Have the character take action and show energy. Action is inherently attractive because it makes things happen in the book, and readers read to see things happen. (They can watch paint dry in real life.) Bad guys are often sexier than good guys because they *do things*, they cause trouble, in going after what they want. Flip that around and have your good guy do something in going after what he wants.

5. Put them in pain or jeopardy (anticipated pain). At the end of the first chapter of *The Hunger Games*, Katniss volunteers for a competition only one contestant will survive. That jeopardy makes her instantly sympathetic, even as the terms of her volunteering also fulfill qualities #1-4 above: She's a hunter (not the most common female YA protagonist — #1), who narrates the story in a first-person voice full of sharp observations (#2 and 2a), and volunteers for the Games (#4) in order to save her sister's life (#3). As a result, the reader is deeply attached to Katniss, and that's part of what drives readers so swiftly through the book.

But this "jeopardy" technique can be applied to novels with less action-oriented stakes as well. In *Millicent Min, Girl Genius*, by Lisa Yee, Millicent is a child prodigy who can't admit how much she wants a friend. In a flashback early in the novel, she's in the lunchroom at her elementary school, and other kids begin to throw food at her, particularly tater tots. Up until that point, Millicent as a narrator and character has been funny, but sort of a pill; she's so well armored behind her intelligence that it's hard for the reader to get close to her. Seeing her get hit with tater tots shows us her loneliness and vulnerability — her pain — and makes us sympathize with her emotionally, even as we still recognize the mistakes she's making socially. It's such an iconic moment for us at Arthur A. Levine Books that we refer to the point at which a character experiences pain and becomes real and human as a "tater tot moment."

With that said, it is usually not good to actually start a novel with pain, to have the first line of Chapter 1 be something like, "'Ow!' I cried as Mama's belt rained down upon me." I mean, I am wincing already, but I don't really know the character enough to thoroughly identify and sympathize with them, and I'm as likely to be turned off by the in-your-faceness of the violence at that point as I am to want to keep reading.

A substrategy here: Surround your good guy with unlikeable characters (that is, people who cause him pain). It's easy to forget that *Harry Potter and the Sorcerer's Stone* (and thus the saga as a whole) doesn't open with Harry. It actually opens with the Dursleys, who are shown to be small-minded, snotty human beings — characters the reader can enjoy feeling superior to. Then when we meet Dumbledore, we automatically like him, because he is obviously much wiser and kinder than the Dursleys; and when we meet Harry, we like him even more, because the Dursleys *don't* like him, and therefore he must be good.

Another word about pain: To be a writer, you need to be able to both feel with and kill your characters at any moment. I mean this absolutely. You have to give them free rein to run around and be stupid, to have awful things happen to them, to have them make awful things happen to others. You are not your characters' mother. You have to have a heart of stone.

But you also have to show how they feel when awful things happen to them, or when the effects of their actions rebound upon them, or when they make dumb decisions. Don't protect them from those effects, because nobody in real life would protect them from those effects; and that is the way they will learn and grow.

I *love* suffering in a novel. I am a total pain junkie for bad things happening to good characters. It is, in fact, the way some writers plot a novel: Come up with a character, think of the worst thing that could possibly happen to him, and then do it. Molly O'Neill's suggestion above about identifying the thing your character knows absolutely to be true, and then turning around and making that false — that's one of the worst things you can possibly do to a character. And *really interesting.*

And what do thematic points have to do with character? In many situations, you're constructing a character *who does not know the thematic point yet* and learns it in the course of the action.

There is a lot of forgetting that goes into being an author. You have to balance knowing what the whole book is about — the point and plot — and yet not-knowing when you're writing from the point of view of that character. And in particular, you must not-know what the thematic point is. Instead, you have to illuminate what the character is like and his or her life is like at the beginning, and then you have to construct the sequence of events that would cause that person to learn the point — that "sequence of events" also known as the plot.

In *Marcelo in the Real World*, Marcelo listens all the time to his Internal Music, or IM, which is like a radio station straight from God . . . not that it tells him what to do, but it's just beautiful and peaceful and pure. He is protected from the real world by not just his autism, but by his family's wealth and his ability to attend a special school where his differences are indulged.

But then his father decides that he wants Marcelo to work in the mail room of his law firm for the summer, and Marcelo comes in contact for the first time with real suffering. Or, for the first time, it matters to him. Later he articulates specifically the question that is the theme of the book: "How is it possible to live with all of the suffering in the world?" There the thematic point comes together: That to be a good citizen of the real world, one must work to alleviate that suffering. Marcelo must participate in the real world, not just observe it from his protected place. And by the end of the novel, he has figured out how.

So how do these points get conveyed to the reader? Again: Pain. Growth through suffering is a terrible cliché, but it's also a true one. As John Keats says, "Do you not see how necessary a world of pains and troubles is to school an intelligence and make it a soul?"

Katniss watches her friends die and herself kills several people in the course of the Hunger Games. Marcelo experiences great mental and spiritual anguish in the course of coming down from his tower. Katsa nearly loses her lover; Bobby *does* lose a character who becomes his confidante after Holly Harper's defection. And it's because we care so much about these characters that the thematic points of their stories come through to us. We are right there in their heads, having these experiences with them, sharing their pain; and as a result we share their growth as well.

I've been speaking here as if your novel will always start with a character for whom you will then discover a point. But of course, sometimes your stories don't start with a character — they start with a situation. A boy serves as a soldier in George Washington's army. A girl attends a unicorn-training academy. A girl's mother is dying of ovarian cancer. A boy wants to become a powerful chef. When you have a compelling situation like this, you need to create a character who will be equally compelling in that situation — who will turn up the volume, as it were, on an already interesting plot.

Before you do that, though, it's good to work through your situation to make it as interesting, compelling, and original as possible. Let's say you want to tell a story about a boy who's been kidnapped by pirates. You might ask yourself:

Has this situation been done before? Yes.

What would the reader expect from the situation? Boy to bond with the pirates; boy to defeat the pirates; boy to escape from the pirates. (In a boy vs. pirates Conflict plot, which is what you're setting out here, those are pretty much the three options: join 'em, beat 'em, run away.)

So: How can you mess with those expectations and still be dramatically interesting? This is especially important since we said "Yes" to the first question about whether this has been done before; and unless you're deliberately setting out to rework or evoke *Treasure Island*, say, I doubt you want to follow in other writers' footsteps. So maybe it's a girl who gets kidnapped by pirates. Maybe the boy kidnaps the pirates, not the other way around. Maybe the boy reforms the pirates. Maybe the boy isn't kidnapped but deliberately sets out to find the pirates. Work through all the possibilities in order to find something that excites you and will excite the reader with its fresh take on an old story.

Not every writer will want to do this, but: You might also consider if there are any thematic ideas here you want to explore. For instance, a book about a boy who runs away to join the pirates is probably going to deal with ideas about family — whether he belongs with his family, or whether he can create a new family with the pirates, or whether he needs a family at all. Or it might be about freedom, and where people truly find their freedom: in civil society, or outside it, as pirates are. The point is, if you're interested in and excited by those big moral and psychological questions, how might you construct this premise to explore those?

Once you feel comfortable with your premise, work up a one- or two-line summary of the story arc and maybe some themes you'll want to touch on. I would strongly advise you NOT to plot out the entire premise here, because then you will be creating actions for your characters to perform before you have the characters to do the actions. Then you must turn to creating those characters, and the two questions to ask here are:

1. Why? That is, how did this premise come about? Why would the pirates want to kidnap this child? It might be for revenge against his parents (or maybe his nanny, a former pirate herself, if you wanted to shake things up). It might be for ransom against his rich parents (or maybe the country, if he were a prince of the realm). Perhaps he has a treasure map tattooed on his back (and how would this have come about?). Perhaps they need a housekeeper and they saw this urchin sweeping the walk in front of a store for bread (so how was he orphaned, and why didn't the child just steal the bread? Who or what in his past gave him the moral character to want to work for it instead?). Each answer will open up more questions that reveal more about the character and circumstances of your protagonist, and more possibilities for his story to follow.

2. Who would suffer most from this situation? (We're coming back to the idea of pain here, and the need for a heart of stone.) This question doesn't refer to physical suffering, because everyone goes through physical suffering, and it isn't very interesting — *nobody* likes swabbing the deck. I mean emotional, mental, or moral suffering, the kind of experience that forces a character toward growth and change. That sort of suffering lifts your premise from a story, which is a sequence of events, to a plot, which imbues those events with meaning. (We'll explore these ideas more in the next section.)

So — what kind of boy would suffer from being kidnapped by pirates? Enough that he grows in an interesting way?

+ A spoiled brat made to swab the deck would suffer because his ideas of his own importance would be challenged.
+ A son of a Royal Navy captain who grew up on his father's ship

would suffer because he might hate the pirates' disorder; he'd have to work through the competing value systems of what he was taught then and how he has to live now.

+ A kid who grew up believing his father was a pirate hero, but it turns out his father is actually the terrible scallywag Brownbeard, whom his pirate cohorts marooned on an island ten years ago, would suffer from the loss of that illusion, and the pain of having to rebuild his vision of who his father was, and who he is in turn.

And each of those suggests further refinements on the situation or places it could go. Truly, there is no shame in jerry-rigging a character to serve a situation or plot. There is only shame in not doing it well.

I've heard writers say that they have a great premise, they'll be writing away — and suddenly the characters will take on independent life and want to go haring off after something besides what the plot requires. Should they follow the character, or stick with their planned plot?

There is no one-size-fits-all final answer here. It depends on what you're more excited about — the character or the situation. But even if you're more interested in the situation, I suggest giving the character their head for five pages or so just to see what it might turn up. This whim might end up connecting back to your situation in a new, interesting way. Or it might turn out to be more interesting than the situation you originally conceived — and because it is character-driven, it will be deeper and more emotionally powerful too.

The difference between starting with premise and starting with character is usually that in a premise plot, the character has something done to him or her from the outside; and in a character plot, the character is the one who causes the action, thanks to the Desire. While books on writing (including this one) tend to praise the latter over the former, readers themselves don't much care so long as they get a good story — and premise-driven plots are excellent at delivering story. In our example books here, *The Hunger Games, Bobby vs. Girls,* and *Marcelo* are all done-to-him plots, where another character involves our hero in action he wasn't seeking and doesn't particularly want. You can get away with having mostly "done to him" and the character not instigating the action so long as the action "done to him" is really, really cool; the "him" is relatively likeable and definitely real; and when he *is* called upon to take action, he steps up to the plate and does what's necessary with skill and class. And all of those things are true of our example books.

And whether you are writing a story that starts with character or a story that starts with a premise, there's one more thing you must keep in mind: the character's development. That is, how he or she changes emotionally or morally over the course of the novel, through what happens to him, or what she causes to happen, and the events that result, all of which should get the character, or reader, to your emotional and thematic points of the book. I especially encourage you to pay attention to the character's flaws here, the Internal Qualities that might result in bad decisions and terrible mistakes, because what do those cause? SUFFERING! And suffering causes change, and moral growth.

In *Marcelo in the Real World*, one of Marcelo's Internal Qualities is detachment — mostly the result of his Asperger's-like syndrome, certainly, but it's reinforced by his tastes, his habits, his family's socio-economic status, the way his whole life has been constructed. Then at his father's the law firm, he comes in contact with real suffering — a girl whose face has been ripped apart by a windshield, whose manufacturer the law firm represents. He connects with her, his detachment is broken at last, and he must make some tough decisions about responding to this girl's need vs. his father's profits, staying in his place of safety or pushing beyond.

The book has a happy ending not because his new situation is unequivocally good; some things are in disarray, outside that place of safety. But Marcelo has been tested by the real world, and he's found connections in it, outside of his detachment; and with those, we know he can handle whatever challenges might come next. It's as Richard Peck says: "A good YA novel ends not with happily ever after, but at a new beginning, with the sense of a lot of life yet to be lived."

The most important things involved in creating a character are truthfulness and time. Be realistic, and be truthful about what you've observed of the world. Readers respond to characters and feelings they recognize. That doesn't mean that the characters have to be people they've met or things they've experienced themselves, but things that ring emotionally true, that fall within the realm of human possibility. Everything I've said here about internal and external qualities, identity, history, desire and so forth goes toward that goal of making that person seem real. The best way of making your characters real is to base them on your observations of real life, your knowledge of yourself and of other people, how we all change and grow, combined with your own marvelous imagination and view of the world.

And all these things take time. You COULD start a novel with a checklist like the one above: My character is named Abby, she's twelve, her identity is a big sister, her internal quality is impatience, her external quality is tapping her finger on her lips when she thinks, her pain is her parents are divorced, and so forth. But it's far more likely you'll find out all those things as you write her — especially as you see her take action and react to other people. Because really, it doesn't matter whether you can create the character in a checklist if you can't bring her to life on the page. And you need to give that time. It's the same way you get to know a good friend: multiple experiences together, multiple conversations — multiple drafts, frankly.

Honestly, unless you're really starving for ideas, I think the time this checklist of character qualities may be most useful is after you finish your first draft. Then you can come back and look at this and ask yourself:

+ Does the character have internal qualities that influence her behavior?

+ What is this character's identity? How does she define herself, versus how other people define her?
+ Does she have a distinct way of acting or speaking, different from everyone else? If a reader looks at a line of her dialogue — could only she have said it?
+ Can you offer a brief history of her life?
+ What does she want?
+ What is her attitude?
+ What action does she take in the novel?

Such questions might help you cross-check her roundedness, her character, against what is already on the page. And if you can't come up with answers for the last three, then you might need to take a serious look at the manuscript and think about who she is and what's driving your plot.

Saul Bellow said, "The main reason for rewriting is not to achieve a smooth surface, but to discover the inner truth of your characters." And you keep digging down until that inner truth is revealed.

QUARTET:
Plot

A quick outline of where we're headed here: I'm going to go over some large principles of plot and then present two different ways to approach the subject, one character-based, one structural. Different methods speak to different writers, so I hope you'll find that one or the other is effective in helping you think about your own work. I'll refer occasionally to examples from the plot of *Harry Potter and the Sorcerer's Stone*, because it's familiar to most modern readers and writers, and we will also return to both the Basic Book boy/ball/girl/cat/tree examples and the books mentioned earlier. And I'll be asking questions that you can use in thinking about your own plot problems, so you should keep pen and paper out, and your work in progress in mind. Finally, while this was written with novels in mind, I think much of it can apply to story-driven picture books too, in terms of overall changes and deep emotional structure.

First, a highly theoretical definition of plot. If you were an English major, you might have studied some of this in college, so if you know all of it already, thank you for being patient.

T. S. Eliot, one of my very favorite poets, was also a literary critic. He wrote a famous essay called "Hamlet and His Problems" in which he asserted that "Hamlet" was an artistic failure. (If only we could all fail so well, right?) Why did he judge it a failure? Because Shakespeare failed to get us into Hamlet's mindset and have us participate in his emotions. Eliot writes: "Hamlet (the man) is dominated by an emotion which is inexpressible, because it is in *excess* of the facts as they appear." In other words, before the ghost appears, Hamlet is more upset than he ought to be given the facts that the reader or playgoer can see — that his dad is dead and his mother married his uncle. Eliot continues:

> The intense feeling, ecstatic or terrible, without an object
> or exceeding its object, is something which every person of
> sensibility has known; it is doubtless a study to pathologists.
> It often occurs in adolescence; the ordinary person puts those
> feelings to sleep, or trims down his feeling to fit the business
> world; the artist keeps it alive by his ability to intensify the
> world to his emotions.

(All you YA novelists should love the fact that he cites adolescence as a time of intense feeling, "ecstatic or terrible.") So how does the artist "intensify the world to his emotions"? Mr. Eliot:

> The only way of expressing emotion in the form of art
> is by finding an "objective correlative"; in other words, a
> set of objects, a situation, a chain of events which shall be
> the formula of that particular emotion; such that when the
> external facts, which must terminate in sensory experience,
> are given, the emotion is immediately evoked.

Or put more simply: To express emotion in art, you must find the right imaginary objects and events for your purpose and make them real and meaningful enough that they evoke the feeling you want to create in the reader. Characters, moving through a setting, are the imaginary objects that we're playing with here. A plot provides the imaginary events. And we want to be sure you choose the *right* imaginary events for your purpose — the ones that will pull forth the right reactions from the reader, based upon the reader's relationship to your characters and their experiences. The "right reactions" are the reactions we identified as your emotional point. And that's what we're going to keep working towards, discussing those right events here.

Now, some basic principles about plotting, with questions to be applied to your work.

1. The story of the book is what happens in that book — the basic events. The plot of the book is the deep structure of those events, which give the action shape and meaning. In *Harry Potter*, the story is about an orphaned boy, who is an outcast even in his own family, being chosen to go to a magical school, where he makes friends, takes classes in magic, learns to play Quidditch, discovers that an evil overlord wants to kill him, and has that first encounter with the overlord. The plot is about a boy who is unloved and abused, basically, finding a place where he can be respected and have emotional support, and discovering a larger challenge that threatens this new place of stability.

Put yet another way, the story is a sequence of events; the plot is the larger change that happens through those events. Which leads to:

2. We can identify a plot by a change: Your protagonist's circumstances change over the course of the novel, and so does he. If you don't have a change, you don't really have a plot. You might have a story, and the story, indeed, can be fabulous all on its own; but if it ends with the characters coming home the same as they were before, it's not reaching the depths it could achieve.

The surest way to damn a book at Arthur A. Levine Books is to compare it to *Alice in Wonderland*, because neither Arthur nor I like stories where a lot of random stuff happens and nothing really changes. Those stories might have nice little emotional points: Some readers love the experiences of meeting the Mad Hatter, watching the caterpillar smoke his hookah, the craziness of the Red Queen, and that's enough for them. But it does not have a thematic point. Alice goes back to the real world, and she takes up her regular life with her sister, and that's it — she hasn't changed in any way. And I think that leaves the reader unchanged as well, other than entertained; there's nothing larger to take away. (If you have ever had a manuscript rejected for being a "slice-of-life" story, what that means is that there was no larger change.)

Question #1: Does a change of some kind happen in the course of your book?

3. **The protagonist of the book is the person to whom the change happens and in whom the change occurs.** Suppose you have a story about a twelve-year-old girl and her alcoholic father. The father goes to rehab and comes out a changed man, but the daughter refuses to forgive him. It doesn't matter if you write that whole novel from the girl's point of view — unless she forgives him, or their relationship changes in some other way, the dad is the protagonist of that plot.

Question #2: Who changes in your WIP?

4. **The two dimensions of the plot are the Action Plot and the Emotional Plot.** The **Action Plot** is the change in the character's circumstances. For instance, Harry Potter is plucked from obscurity and hardship, told he has a great history and destiny, and sent off to wizard school, where he becomes a hero. The **Emotional Plot** is the change within your protagonist himself. For instance, once Harry is there, he makes friends and finds new courage within himself.

Another way of thinking about this: You can regard the Action Plot as challenges that are imposed upon your protagonist from the outside by his circumstances; the Emotional Plot is the challenges that come from the inside, who he is. Or simplifying it even further, the Action Plot is the story, in the boy-goes-to-wizard-school sense; the Emotional Plot is character.

So, **Questions #3 and #4**, which may not be so easy to answer immediately: What is your protagonist's change in circumstances from the beginning to the end of the novel? And how does he himself change?

5. **Your plot will begin when one of these changes does.** When the character moves to a new town and makes a new friend. When the character decides to set out at last on that journey to find his father. When the character discovers that his mother isn't actually his mother but an alien cyborg. (He doesn't have to do anything about that knowledge, but the knowledge alone would change him, and that's the start of the Emotional Plot.)

Novels often have a scene set before the change starts to establish the circumstances at the outset, the better to show how things are different by the end. This is tricky but OK. The first scene of *Marcelo in the Real World* is set in a doctor's office, where Marcelo's brain is scanned and he slips into his "internal music." That music will be greatly disturbed by the end of the book, by everything he sees at the law firm. So that scene sets the emotional stakes for the book, because it shows what Marcelo will lose. And when we were talking about character-hooking-in strategies in the previous essay — Marcelo is so compelling as a character, with such a distinctive voice, that you can get away with not having a lot of action there, I think.

Likewise, *The Hunger Games* starts with Katniss hunting with her friend Gale on the morning of the reaping. From a character perspective, she's showing us her strength, resourcefulness, and hunting ability. From a plot perspective, we're seeing what she stands to lose: a life where she is the provider for her family. Suzanne Collins further plants the seeds of the change by having Katniss and Gale talk about the selection that day, and slipping in the rules of the competition.

Alternatively, you can start with an action scene showing the beginning of the change, then set up the backstory in Chapter 2. This is what happens in *Graceling*, where the heroine Katsa meets her match, another Graceling, in the midst of breaking into a king's dungeons. The change might even have already begun when the book does: In *Bobby vs. Girls (Accidentally)*, Holly Harper has already become more of a (gasp!) *girl*, with straight hair and shopping trips, when Bobby runs into her in Chapter 1, so that opening scene establishes both the depth of their friendship and the new tensions between them.

Question #5: Where do the changes for your protagonist begin? How close to the beginning can you set those events? (The answer is probably closer than you think.)

6. And while the entertainment of a book may come from its Action Plot—the chance for the reader to go to wizard school with Harry, to

ride broomsticks and raise dragons and face down an evil overlord — **the deeper emotional effect and meaning of the book comes from its Emotional Plot** — how much you the reader care about this character, and the chance to see him change and grow.

Not all books have both kinds of plots, or balance both kinds of plots equally — and that's fine. If you're writing a rip-roaring fantasy adventure novel, you will want more Action Plot than Emotional Plot. If you're writing a novel about a boy dealing with his grandfather's death, that's going to be heavier on Emotional Plot than Action. The important thing is to try to have enough of each to keep the story moving forward, and yet developing the reader's connection to the character and consequent response to what happens to him.

Now that we have those principles out of the way, I am going to present the character-based view of plot, in which a good book develops its story in five simple steps:

1. The book establishes a character — someone with:
   - a flaw of which he or she may not be aware (some possibly destructive Internal Quality)
   - Or something to gain or lose (a Desire, often)
   - Or both
2. The story presents that character with a situation
   - that will evoke the flaw — again, possibly unbeknownst to the character
   - Or in which the thing that can be gained or lost, *will* be gained or lost
   - Or both
3. And then it forces that character to make a choice or take some sort of action.
   - John Gardner: "Real suspense comes with moral dilemma and

the courage to make and act upon choices. False suspense comes from the accidental and meaningless occurrence of one damned thing after another."

+ Remember when I was talking earlier about *Alice in Wonderland*? *Alice* is "the accidental and meaningless occurrence of one damn thing after another."

+ Moral dilemma is when you have two equally good or equally bad choices and you have to pick one. *Hard* choices.

     o In *Marcelo*, Marcelo eventually has to choose between doing a good thing for someone for whom he cares deeply, and hurting his father's law firm. In the *Hunger Games*, the choices are survival and death. And both of these books are compelling because the choices are so important, painful, and real.

4. In the new situation engendered by the results of #3, the plot repeats steps 2 and 3, until

5. The flaw in the character is faced and dealt with or

+ the thing to be lost or won is lost or won

+ or both.

"Dealt with" does not necessarily mean "corrected" — the character can and probably will make mistakes involving that flaw again, after the book ends. But it does mean, I think, "recognized and acknowledged," so that the flaw no longer wreaks its havoc unconsciously; there has been some form of growth.

This view of plot is based upon one outlined by Laurie Halse Anderson in a 2008 talk for writers. She said there that "Plotting is compulsion vs. obstacles": what your character, by his very nature, is compelled to do, versus the thing that is keeping him from doing it.

So, **Question #6**: What is your character's flaw that keeps getting him into trouble in the plot? What is your character's compulsion? And **Question #7**: What is your character's thing to be gained or lost? (This could be the same thing as the Desire we identified in the character talk: What does your character want?)

You don't have to have both. Harry Potter in Book One is actually a pretty much perfect boy. He has a penchant for mischievousness and getting in trouble, certainly, but he doesn't really show any deeper flaws at this point. But still, he does want something, and he does have something he could gain or lose: emotional support, a family. And while in Book One, he just makes friends, the project of the whole seven-book series is to supply him with exactly that. Moreover, by Book Five, we know him well enough and he has suffered enough that we do see the outlines of a compulsion: what Hermione calls his "saving-people-thing," which wreaks damage by the end of that book, and then changes his behavior significantly in Books Six and Seven.

The thing that can be gained or lost in the course of the action is the **stakes.** And there should be stakes for both your Action and Emotional Plots. The four books we have here demonstrate how wide-ranging stakes can be, depending upon the author's interests and the story s/he wants to tell:

- In *Bobby vs. Girls (Accidentally)*, Bobby's best-friendship with Holly is set at risk if they can't move past their identities as a boy vs. a girl.
- In *Graceling*, Katsa's life is always at stake, since she's constantly fighting; her love with Po and Po's life is at stake, once he begins to matter to her; and the villain ultimately threatens the entire security of the Middluns, which matters as it further affects Katsa's life and happiness.
- *The Hunger Games* similarly sets Katniss's life at stake, and her relationship with Peeta as she gets to know him.
- *Marcelo* actually switches stakes on the reader in the course of the book. At the beginning, Arturo tells him that if he succeeds at the law firm in the course of the summer, he'll have the right to choose which school he wants to attend for his senior

year — that he can still get what he wants, which is to attend the safe haven of Paterson. But as Marcelo interacts with the real world, and especially with Ixtel, his values change, and it becomes more important to him to get justice for her than it is to attend Paterson.

Stakes need to be proportional to the size of the action that follows. *The Hunger Games* is filled with gore, suffering, fights to the death: If Katniss was going through all that to win fifty bucks, we'd have no respect for her or for any of it. But because she's fighting for her *life*, that's big enough to justify our investment.

One of the most common problems in slush manuscripts that I review is that writers have such a terrific Action Plot premise in mind — the protagonist discovers a gateway to another dimension! The protagonist's father killed himself and she's dealing with the aftermath! — that they rush to set that up in the first chapter and don't spend equal or more time setting up the character. But if I don't care about or feel involved with the character, I won't care about the plot.

This is an extremely tricky balance, I know. But I mentioned above the fact that you have to do a lot of forgetting as an author; and really, if you have a great plot in mind, you should start writing the book *as if that plot didn't exist*, telling us only about the characters to whom the plot will happen and the world in which it happens. Because, after all, the *character* does not know that that plot exists until it happens to her, or until she makes it happen; and then the development of the plot will then feel far more natural, because it (or her reaction to it) will come out of her character.

(N.B.: The single most difficult chapter to write in any novel is the first one. If you struggle with it, just put something out there and get yourself beyond it as quickly as possible, and go back and rewrite it once you've written the rest of the book.)

Exercise: Pick one of the characters you spent some time developing in the character talk above, or the main character of your WIP, either way. Suppose that character found a hundred dollars on the street in front of their home, paperclipped to an address and a picture of a terrified-looking beagle puppy. What would your character do? Think about their compulsion, or their Desire if that's different, and then think about how you can dramatize those things so that compulsion or desire drives the scene without your ever identifying them outright.

So now it's time for the second view of plot — the structural one. In this view, most plots follow a model called Freytag's Triangle that you might have learned about in school, as it's what we hardcore literary theorists call S.O.A.: Straight Outta Aristotle (and specifically his *Poetics*).

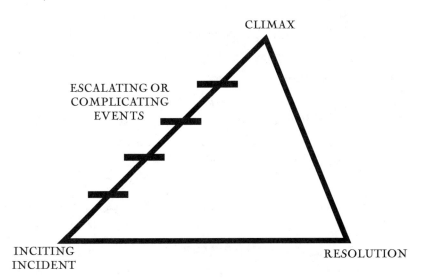

In the Triangle, there are four key events that must be dramatized for the reader:

+ Inciting Incident: an event that starts the Conflict, Mystery or Lack or makes it personal for your protagonist.

o This was step #2 in the character-based view of plot: The arrival of the thing that is going to challenge your character.

• At least two (and usually many more) Escalating or Complicating Events: things that raise the stakes, change the course of the story, or change the rules of engagement.

o In the character-based view of plot, these are the places your protagonist has to make choices: when he learns a new piece of information — like that his mother is an alien cyborg; or when your heroine gets into a fight with the bully and defeats him, but that invokes the wrath of the bully's father.

• A Climax: the summation of the Action Plot.

o In the character-based view of plot, this is the place where the character either wins or loses, OR where the emotional change finally connects. Sometimes these will be the same event; sometimes they'll be separate events (i.e., you'll have two separate Climaxes for your Action and Emotional Plots). A strong climax often involves a decision of some kind, or is the ultimate consequence of all the decisions made up to that point.

• A Resolution showing how things have changed.

When I said above that these four kinds of events must be "dramatized," I mean that you must say not just "Gina and Lisa went to the mall, and while there they got into a huge fight, and Lisa felt awful afterward." Instead you must show that entire trip to the mall, with emphasis not so much upon what stores they went into or what they bought, but upon the small personal interactions that built into this huge fight; and then show how Lisa acted and thought when she was back at home. You must find the objective correlatives for their feelings — the events that will cause their fight, their anger, and their emotions — and show those things to us, so we can feel them too.

I sometimes say that editing is the art of putting information in order. In nonfiction, you're putting the factual information in order so that it adds up to a cohesive argument. In fiction, you're putting the emotional information in order so it adds up to a cohesive emotional journey for the character. Think about every word in your book as a piece of information — you're supplying facts about the protagonist, his or her circumstances and environment, the other characters, where they're all going, what they're feeling, etc. etc. You do not want to supply any more information than the reader needs, and neither do you want to supply any *less*. You want to supply only what's relevant and necessary.

So, **Questions 8, 9, 10,** and **11**: What are the Inciting Incident, Escalating Events, Climax, and Resolution of your novel? Are all of those events dramatized? Do they build appropriately in emotional intensity, so that each Escalating Event is bigger than the last, and the Climax is the biggest of them all?

If you have subplots as well as a central plot in your book, then you might have several Freytag's Triangle structures going on here, where each individual storyline will have its own Inciting Incident and so forth. The challenge then is integrating all of those plots elegantly and getting them to play together, so each Escalating or Complicating Event might serve several purposes, or all the Climaxes happen at the same time. If this structure resonates with you, I would suggest drawing the events of your central Action and Emotional Plots out on one triangle; then use a different colored pen or pencil for each subplot, and draw those events in over the Action & Emotional Plot triangle. Are there places the Escalating or Complicating Events might connect and support each other, or serve multiple plots?

Now, within this Freytag's Triangle structure, there are three main types of plot that you can use by themselves or in combination to lead your character on to your point:

+ Conflict: One character vs. another character, or one character vs. herself

- o In the Basic Book, if the boy and girl got into a fight over the ball, that would be a Conflict plot.
- ✦ Mystery: a story where the characters need a piece of information
    - o If the cat hid the ball and the boy and girl were looking for it, that would be a Mystery plot
- ✦ Lack: a story where a character needs something to be complete and live a full life
    - o If the boy had no friends and really needed love in his life, and then he adopted the cat, that's a Lack plot.
    - o I sometimes think about renaming this the Love plot because that's almost always what the character lacks — there is some sort of emotional connection that needs to be made, in the form of friendship or a family or a romantic relationship, or in developing his or her own self-confidence or self-esteem.

Question #12: Which categories best describe your central Action and Emotional Plots?

Quite often more than one category will seem appropriate here, as you can view the same storyline from multiple angles. For instance, suppose you have a plot where your protagonist wants to learn the name of his father, but his mother won't tell him. That's a Conflict plot, as it shows the son vs. the mother; a Mystery plot, as the son wants the information of his father's name; and a Lack plot, as the son lacks his father's name and influence. If you find these formulations useful, how you choose to categorize the plot will make a big difference in the overall structure of the book, because it changes the character's primary drive in the book: to defeat an enemy? To find a piece of information? To fulfill an emotional need? So think hard about how you'd define the story for yourself and which kind of story you're most interested in telling. (How the kind of plot changes the structure will be discussed in more depth later.)

And of course, beyond the definition problem, most novels have more than one of these plots, or they combine them in interesting ways. For instance, let's take that example I offered where the boy adopted the cat. That's a sweet story just as it is (and a very good Emotional Plot in particular). But suppose that cat belonged to the girl and she didn't want to give him up. Then you have a Conflict plot on top of the Lack plot, and you would need to resolve both of those strands for the novel to be satisfying. Each additional plot adds an additional layer of interest and complication, and every relationship in a book can be its own plot as it contributes to the protagonist's growth. But all of the plots should ultimately add something to the Point — what the protagonist learns and how he learns it, if you've got a thematic point going, or doing something else to involve the reader in your emotional point.

Our example books each show these crossing-over points nicely. *Graceling* features a very satisfying Lack plot, as Katsa falls in love with Po, who appreciates her gifts, as well as a Conflict plot (Katsa vs. her ultimate enemy, whose name I'm trying not to spoil) with an ongoing Mystery inside it, as Katsa and Po must deduce both the identity of that enemy and his powers. *Bobby vs. Girls (Accidentally)* broadcasts its Conflict plot within its very title, but it's the Lack of Bobby's relationship with Holly and the suffering which follows that give it depth. *The Hunger Games* is nothing but Conflict — Katniss vs. the Capitol and all the other competitors. (I don't think its love story quite qualifies as a Lack here, as Katniss doesn't particularly seem to *need* Peeta on any emotional level at the beginning, and other than the help he provides her in the Games, it often seems she could do without him and the complications he creates in her life.)

Marcelo is framed first as a Conflict Plot — Marcelo vs. Arturo on the question of where Marcelo will work for the summer and then attend school in the fall. Then, through the action resulting from that Conflict, it turns into a Mystery accompanied by a Lack, as Marcelo must track down the girl in this picture he's found, and as he experiences feelings he's never had before in getting to know Jasmine, who helps him in the Mystery and complicates the Conflict.

One interesting thing about this book: When I acquired it, there was no Mystery plot. Marcelo found a picture in a box of a girl with half of her face torn off. As it's described: "Half of her face is intact but the other side is missing. The skin on the deformed side is withered and scarred, as if the cheek and jaw had been carved away with a dull knife. There is a mouth with lips that end halfway, an ear that seems about to fall off." In the first draft, that picture was attached to a letter from the girl's lawyer, describing what happened to her: She was in a car accident and the windshield exploded all over her. The maker of the windshield is a client of the law firm. They would like fifty thousand dollars for her surgery. The rest of the book consisted of an excellent moral dilemma, as Marcelo wrestled with choosing between his loyalty to his father and his connection to this girl, and then figured out how to get the money and get it to her. Watching him figure out what to do was certainly interesting! But Marcelo didn't have very much to do himself, other than talking to other people about his decision. And if one of the qualities of an interesting character is that they do things, as discussed previously, then Marcelo needed to *do* more, take more action, than just making a decision and talking here.

So Francisco created a Mystery plot to give Marcelo more to do. If you're trying to create action or difficulty for a character, try taking something away from him, either in the course of the action or by making him never have it in the first place. Francisco went with the latter method here and eliminated all mention of the lawyer's letter requesting the fifty thousand dollars. Now Marcelo just found the picture of the girl, which established the Mysteries of who she was, what had happened to her, and why her picture was in a box in the law firm. In order to answer those questions, he had to use clues within the picture to track her down. That means we readers saw him taking action to solve the problem, before he got to the point where he had to make a decision; and because he took action that we ourselves were involved in, the search, and the finding of the girl, meant more both to him and to us.

During the editorial process, Francisco also decided to strengthen the Lack plot here, showing how Marcelo gets to know Jasmine in the mailroom. To explain why this was important, let's say the boy in the Basic Book is named Joe, and the girl is Emily. It is incredibly easy for an author just to say, after they meet for the first time, "Joe and Emily spent a lot of time together, and pretty soon, they became friends." That's especially tempting if you have a larger, more exciting Action Plot you need to get on to — that Joe and Emily, having met, are going to time-travel together or something. But for that friendship to matter to me as a reader — for me to be a third party in the relationship, which is essentially what I want to be — I need to see *how* Joe and Emily become friends. What does he say to her that captures her (and my) interest? What does she say that keeps the conversation going? What do they like to do together? How do they connect, and why should I connect with them? Those things need to be dramatized for the reader as fully as the first time they step through that time-travel portal. In order to make that happen in *Marcelo*, Francisco wrote, I think, three new chapters that focused on Jasmine and Marcelo, all filled with great dialogue and challenges for Marcelo as he navigated his first "real world" relationship.

Even within a big, exciting Conflict or Mystery, relationships are often the most important kind of plots within your novel, because they show most directly the emotional content of the book — how the protagonist affects and is affected by other people. Relationships make it important to readers that our protagonist wins a conflict or find the answer: Other people value him, and so we readers should as well.

Clarifying what kind of plot you have can be tremendously useful to you as a writer, because it provides a certain form in which each of your key structural events happen. To demonstrate, I'm going to go through each of these of these three big plots and talk about these four types of key events within them, because events resonate differently within each one.

CONFLICT

+ **Inciting Incident:** the event that makes the conflict personal for your protagonist and establishes the antagonistic sides.
    o In *Harry Potter and the Sorcerer's Stone*, the Inciting Incident is Voldemort killing Harry's parents.
+ **Escalating or Complicating Events:**
    o The moment the antagonist hurts your protagonist further.
    o The news that the antagonist has acquired a new weapon or ally.
    o The protagonist's discovery of a new weapon or ally.
    o The protagonist's committing an act of extreme stupidity or genius.
    o The revelation of a bit of backstory that changes everything the protagonist thought.
        § All of those things happen within the HP series between Harry and Voldemort.
+ **Climax:** The two antagonists come face-to-face and finally settle their differences.
    o In Book One, Harry and Voldemort have a duel of wits over the Sorcerer's Stone; in Book Seven, they have the duel of wands that settles their Conflict forever.
+ **Resolution:** What happens to the winner? And loser? How have everyone's lives changed?

MYSTERY

+ **Inciting Incident:** Mystery Plots tend to have two Inciting Incidents:

o First, the mysterious event itself (the murder, disappearance, stealing of the magical object, whatever), which can take place before the book begins.

o And then, equally important, the event that gets your protagonist involved in the Mystery. This latter event must have some sort of stakes for your protagonist — some reason it's important to him personally that this Mystery be solved.

> o In *Harry Potter and the Chamber of Secrets*, the central Mystery is, "Who is the Heir of Slytherin?" The involving Inciting Incident in that plot happens when Harry hears a voice saying "*Rip . . . tear . . . kill . . .*", which leads him to a horrible scene with the words "THE CHAMBER OF SECRETS HAS BEEN OPENED. ENEMIES OF THE HEIR, BEWARE" scrawled on the wall. And as Harry is very quickly accused of being that Heir himself, both the protagonist's involvement and the stakes are established tout suite.

• **Escalating or Complicating Events:**

o The discovery of clues in the mystery.

o An event that raises the stakes (for instance, in a murder mystery, the discovery of another body, so we don't just have a killer motivated by hatred of one person — it's a serial thing; or, if it were a typical noir, the gumshoe's falling in love with the femme fatale — it's no longer just a matter of money).

o Again, backstory. Almost all of a traditional mystery is discovering what has happened before the novel began — the events that led to the first Inciting Incident above — and reacting to events that take place offstage, like that second murder.

§ Again, all of these things take place in *Chamber of Secrets*: Harry discovers he can speak Parseltongue, which raises the personal stakes; receives Tom Riddle's diary and some wrong leads therein; and finally works out the identity of the real Heir.

+ **Climax:** The revelation of this piece of information everyone has been seeking: the murderer's identity, the location of the missing jewels.

+ **Resolution:** Is the wrongdoer punished? How have everyone's lives changed?

LACK

+ **Inciting Incident:** An event showing us the lack in the protagonist's life — the negative space — again, whether the protagonist is aware of it or not.

  o The most common thing that's lacked is love. So, back in *Sorcerer's Stone*, all that description in Chapter 2 about Harry living under the stairs, and having to do housework and wear old clothes, is J. K. Rowling setting up the lack of affection, connection, and care that Harry gets from the Dursleys.

+ **Escalating or Complicating Events:** These differ from the other two categories in that these are events that show progress towards the lack being resolved, along with the occasional complication.

  o If the thing that is lacked is specifically romantic love, then this could be first meeting the romantic object, followed by a conversation, followed by a first date, followed by a second date.

  o Or a terrific first date followed by a bit of gossip about the newly beloved that casts doubt on the happiness.

- o Or a terrific first date followed by the reentry of the love object's ex.
- o And so on and so forth.
+ **Climax:** The lack being fulfilled by some outward sign of emotional commitment or the lacked object coming into the protagonist's possession at last.
    - o In children's fiction, the orphan might get formally adopted by a new family, or make permanent the makeshift family assembled in the course of the book.
    - o In romantic fiction, there might be a kiss, or an "I love you," or a proposal.
+ **Resolution:** Do they live happily ever after? How have everyone's lives changed?

Again, good plots often have more than one of these types of plot going on at the same time, so an Inciting Incident from your Lack plot may be followed by an Escalating Event from your Mystery plot — or, even better, those two things might be in the same scene. One useful way to keep track of all of your plots is to make a chart or spreadsheet listing the chapter or even scene numbers on the side and each plot strand running across the top. Then fill in the plot-strand events in each chapter in which they appear. That lets you see how each plotline develops in the course of the book, and points at which you might be able to make an event serve more than one plotline.

And not to be a broken record on this point, but: These large events must be dramatized. If this event is making a difference in your plot, then we readers need to see it happen (or see how it impinges your protagonist when it happens). There is very little narration in our four example books here. There's some, of course, leading into a scene, or when the characters are doing the same thing over and over again for a period of time. But they are mostly pure drama, as nearly every chapter in all four books is a sustained scene, or short scenes on a similar theme. And as a result, we readers feel like we are seeing this world mostly uninterrupted, and in coherent, smooth pieces: It feels real. More than that, because we readers are seeing events for ourselves, we get to develop our own opinions on the action — we're not being told. Thus we become active players in the drama, and that in turn sustains our interest in the story and the plot.

How do these two views of plot relate to each other? Well, I suggest you use the character-based view to write your first draft. Discover a character and what he wants, and then simply "Follow him around all day," as Ray Bradbury put it. Force him to make choices, and repeat that until you come to the end. Then go back and look at the structural model. Can you identify the kind of plot do you have? Does the event that starts that plot off — your Inciting Incident — happen in the first two chapters? Does that plot build consistently over time? Does the Climax pay off the kind of plot you have for the protagonist, or is it the peak of another character's journey or a different plot instead? Is there a Resolution? If the answer to any of these questions is "No," then you may need to make some revisions.

Finally, if you internalize this structure of Freytag's Triangle, you can use it to structure not only your novels but your individual scenes, because each scene has its own small plot. Here's one of my favorite chapters from *Marcelo in the Real World*:

Chapter 3

I get out of the car and head for the back door. I see Arturo in the backyard grilling steaks. I hoped to enter the house without him seeing me. I am not ready for the discussion that I know will take place and I need more time to anticipate his questions and memorize my replies. But Aurora yells at him from the back door.

"Sorry we're late. We got stuck in traffic."

He answers her without turning around. "I didn't see any dinner cooking, so I thought I'd grill something."

"I'll make the salad," Aurora tells him, and goes in the house.

I am about to go in when Arturo speaks. "Marcelo, can I talk to you?"

I walk as slowly as I can. Arturo is stabbing the red meat with a giant fork.

"Not done yet," he says. He closes the black lid to the grill and sits on one of the white iron chairs. "Sit down for a minute." He pulls out a chair. "How was Dr. Malone?"

"He was well." I'm still standing. I'm looking at the red needle of the thermometer attached to the grill. It is moving past three hundred degrees.

"Marcelo," I hear him call. He is holding a goblet half-filled with ruby-colored wine. I know Arturo is not fond of my visits to Dr. Malone's office. He believes the tests imply there is something wrong with me, which he does not think is the case. "So, what did the good doctor do to you this time?"

"The brain was scanned while Marcelo listened to music."

"Try saying that again."

"*My* brain was scanned while *I* listened to music." I remind myself not to refer to myself in the third person. Also, I must remember not to call him Arturo.

"Thank you. Is that right? Real music or the kind you alone can hear?"

Talking about the Internal Music, I have learned, makes Arturo nervous. I attempt to change the subject. "After Dr. Malone we went to see the newborn pony at Paterson."

"That's good. But you didn't answer my question."

There is no chance of ever changing the subject with Arturo. "Real music," I answer. It is not a lie. The IM is as real as any other kind.

"How long will these visits go for?"

"They last about an hour."

"No, that's not what I meant. I mean, how much longer are these experiments or observations going to go on?" Before I can answer, he says, "I have a proposition that I want to discuss with you."

I feel my chest begin to tighten. "I am not going to Oak Ridge High." I can hear my voice tremble as I say this.

Arturo's face turns serious. I brace myself. I know how Arturo can switch from father to lawyer in an instant. The face of Arturo the father does not come out as often for me as it does for my sister, Yolanda. I get more of Arturo the lawyer: his eyes unblinking and fixed on my face, the volume of his voice modulated with complete control. He becomes a person who will lose his composure only if he wishes to.

"Here's what I would like to propose." I expect him to pause because he is speaking faster than he usually does. But he goes on speaking as fast as he speaks to Yolanda. "I want you to work at the law firm this summer."

This is a total surprise. It takes me a while to find words, any words. When I do, I say: "I have a summer job at Paterson."

"You'll help in the mailroom." He doesn't hear or chooses not to hear what I say.

"I have a job already," I repeat.

"Sit down, please." He points to the chair. I sit.

He moves forward on his chair so that our knees are almost touching. He lowers his voice. He is a father now. "Son, I want you to have a job where you interact with people, where you have to figure out new things by yourself. What do you do at Paterson that teaches you what you don't already know?"

"I will be learning to train the ponies."

"But this is the stage of your life when you need to be working with people."

"Why?"

"It is an experience you haven't had, really. At Paterson you are in a protected environment. The kids who go there are not . . . normal. Most of them will be the way they are all their lives. You, on the other hand, have the ability to grow and adapt. Even your Dr. Malone thinks this is the case. He's said so since the very first time we saw him. All these years, it wasn't really necessary for you to go to Paterson. You don't really belong there. I know you realize this yourself. There's nothing wrong with you. You just move at a different speed than other kids your age. But in order for you to grow and not get stuck, you need to be in a normal environment. It is time. Here is what I propose: If you work at the law firm this summer, then at the end of the summer, *you* decide whether you want to spend your senior year at Paterson or at Oak Ridge High."

Now he pauses. He knows I will need time to sort this out. One summer at the law firm versus a whole year at Paterson. I miss out on Fritzy's early months, but I still get to train him next year. Arturo interrupts my thoughts. "There's just one thing." I see him pick up the glass of wine and raise to his lips. This time his words come out very slow. "You can do what you want in the fall . . ." He waits for my eyes to meet his eyes and then he continues. "But this summer you must follow all the rules of the . . . real world. "

"The real world," I say out loud. It is one of Arturo's favorite phrases.

"Yes, that's right. The real world."

As vague and broad as this term is, I have a sense of what it means and of the difficulties that it entails. Following the rules of the real world means, for example, engaging in small talk with other people. It means refraining from talking about my special interest. It means looking people in the eye and shaking hands. It means doing things 'on the hoof,' as we say at Paterson, which means doing things that have not been scheduled in advance. It may mean walking or going to places I am not familiar with, city streets full of noise and confusion. Even though I am trying to look calm, a wave of terror comes over me as I imagine walking the streets of Boston by myself.

Arturo smiles as if he knows what is going through my mind. "Don't worry," he says soothingly, "we'll go slow at first. The real world is not going to hurt you."

There is a question floating inside of me but I can't find the words for it just yet. I open and clench my fists as I wait for the question to formulate itself. Finally, it arrives. I say to Arturo, "At the end of the summer, will Marcelo, will I decide where I want to spend my senior year . . . regardless?"

"Regardless? I don't follow you."

"You said that if I follow the rules of the real world this summer, I will get to decide where I go next year. Who will decide whether I followed the rules? I am not aware of all the rules of the real world. They are innumerable, as far as I have been able to determine."

"Ahh." It is Arturo the father who is speaking now. "Well, look. The corporate world has its rules. The law firm has its rules. The mailroom has its rules. The legal system has its rules. The real world as a whole has its rules. The rules deal with behaviors and the way to do things in order to be successful. To be successful is to accomplish the task that has been assigned to us or which we have assigned to ourselves. You will need to adapt to the environment governed by these rules as best you can. At Paterson, the environment adapts to you. If you need more time to finish a test, you get it. In the mailroom, a package will need to go out by a certain time or else. As to who will determine what, it seems to me that for this exercise to have any meaning, there must be something at stake. If you go through the motions and just show up every day and not try, then no, you will not have the ability to decide where you spend next year because you will not have followed the rules of the real world. It seems to me that at the end of the summer, we will both know with absolute certainty whether you succeeded or not. But, if for some reason we disagree, it seems to me that the ultimate decision should be mine. I am the father and you are the son. I will be your boss and you will be the employee. Does that make sense?"

I nod that it does. I never lie. But I do now. There is something about what Arturo just said that does not make sense.

Arturo is waiting to see if there are further questions. He knows it takes me a while to process information. I do have one final question.

"How will Marcelo be successful in the mailroom?" I would like to have a diagram or picture of what this means so that I can prepare for it.

"Each assignment given to you will have its built-in definition of success. You have a right to ask for instructions from anyone in the law firm who gives you an assignment. Success will be based on your ability to follow those instructions. I know this is very vague and you would like more clarity. You have to trust me. You are not going to be asked to perform tasks that are beyond your abilities. Do you trust me? I have always been fair, haven't I?"

This time I don't know how the word "trust" is being used. But "fair" I understand. "Yes," I say. It is true. Arturo has always been fair.

"Good," he says. "I will be honest with you. I am hoping that after this summer, you will choose to go to Oak Ridge High. There is a life out there that is healthy and normal that you need to be a part of. So, is it a deal?"

"There are some things I cannot do even if I wanted to," I say.

"Like what?"

"There are so many things Marcelo still has difficulties with. I cannot walk by myself in a strange place without a map. I get flustered when I am asked to do more than one thing at once. People say words I do not understand or their facial expressions are incomprehensible. They expect responses from me I cannot give."

"Maybe the reason you can't do those things is not because you are not able to, but because you have not been in an environment that challenges you to do them. Jasmine, the girl who runs the mailroom, will show you the ropes. I've talked to her about you. She'll go easy on you at first. But going slow doesn't mean you won't need to expand beyond your comfort zone."

I am thinking that next fall, I will be able to work full-time at Paterson training Fritzy and the other ponies. I can visit the ponies on the weekends this summer. Arturo is basically asking me to pretend that I am normal, according to his definition, for three months. This is an impossible task, as far as I can tell, especially since it is very difficult for me to feel that I am *not* normal. Why can't others think and see the world the way I see it? But after three months, it will be over, and I can be who I am.

"Think about it. Let me know first thing in the morning."

"All right," I say. "I will think about it." I start to walk towards my tree house. Namu, who has been lying at my feet all the time, walks by my side.

"You are getting too old to live in a tree house," I hear Arturo say behind me.

I pretend his words do not reach me.

Can you see Freytag's Triangle working within this scene?

+ **The Inciting Incident:** Arturo calls Marcelo over.
+ **Escalating and Complicating Events:** This scene is almost entirely dialogue and narration, obviously, but if you track the "beats" in it — that is, nuggets of dialogue on a particular subject and in a particular emotional register — you'll see that those beats escalate and complicate the tension in this scene over time.
    o Small talk: Most of p. 241
        § They talk about what they did during the day.
    o The Proposal and Stakes: p. 242-244
        § Arturo proposes that Marcelo work at the law firm and that, if he does it successfully, Marcelo can choose his school in the fall if he wants.
        § The rules of this world; the definition of success
+ **Climax:** Arturo asks, "Is it a deal?" on p. 245, and Marcelo does not answer
    o This is the Climax because it pulls all of the preceding dialogue into a sharp clear point: Here is where the decision needs to be made, here's what it's all been building up to.

+ **Resolution:** Processing and winding down, rest of p. 245-246
  o That paragraph that starts "I am thinking that next fall" shows that even though his formal answer is up in the air, Marcelo has accepted the terms here, more or less, and is now figuring out what he'll do next.
  o The scene ends on what I think of as a fermata — a musical term that indicates "a pause of unspecified length on a note or rest." In novels, it's a final line that resonates with or reflects upon the emotional experience we've just had in the preceding text, distilling and sustaining that tone as a fermata does. Scenes and chapters should pretty much always end on either a cliffhanger or a fermata: either a line that drives the reader forward, or one that holds the emotional tone in the reader's mind, or both.

It's always interesting and useful to divide your scenes up into beats and see how each beat leads to the next. Does each beat flow logically from the previous subject under discussion? Does it flow emotionally — can you see how the characters move from one emotional state to another? Are the transitions smooth? Are all of the beats unique and non-repetitive with each other? If the answer to any of those questions was no, can you rearrange the beats or create new transitions to achieve a better flow?

The Climax of a scene should be its emotional point: the moment of highest tension, in which something in the novel changes decisively. Often it's the moment at which the protagonist makes a decision, or wins a conflict, or learns a piece of information, or finally kisses their crush. If a scene *doesn't* have a point like this, I would seriously question its place in the book. Indeed, one easy way to test the structure of your book is to find the climactic lines of every scene in your novel and write them out in a list. You should then be able to read through that list and reconstruct the novel, more or less. If there are any Climaxes that are redundant with each other, then perhaps you don't need one of those two scenes; if a Climax doesn't represent an advance in tension or emotion, maybe that scene isn't necessary.

What the Triangle signifies, the most important thing about all this altogether, is that the scene feels emotionally complete and satisfying: We have been taken on a complete emotional journey with these characters in the course of this scene. And you can do this with pretty much every scene in *Marcelo* — go through and identify the Inciting Incident, Escalating or Complicating beats, Climax, and what has changed, leading into the next scene. The same would hold true with every other book we've featured here.

A final **Exercise:** Take that incident you wrote earlier based on p. 229, with the character who found a hundred dollars clipped to the picture of the puppy, and bring in the other character from the character exercise on p. 207-208. Then write this scene three ways, trying to use Freytag's Triangle throughout:

- o First, a Conflict involving your two characters. It could be a new scene involving the hundred dollars, it could be just after it, whatever you like.
- o Then write a scene setting up a Mystery involving your two characters, or the mystery being solved.
- o Finally, write a scene showing a Lack, or a lack being addressed.

The great English mystery novelist Dick Francis said, "If you get the form of things right, every peril can be tamed." The questions throughout this talk have been designed to help you find the underlying form of your story and strengthen it so it best serves your Point. Here they are all together:

1. Does a change of some kind happen in the course of your book?
2. Who is the protagonist — who changes in your WIP?

3. What is your Action Plot — your protagonist's change in circum-stances from the beginning to the end of the novel?

4. And your Emotional Plot — how does he himself change?

5. Where do the changes for your protagonist begin?

6. What is your character's flaw/compulsion that keeps getting him into trouble in the plot?

7. What are the stakes — your character's thing to be gained or lost?

8. Identify the Inciting Incident . . .

9. . . . the Escalating or Complicating Events . . .

10. . . . Climax . . .

11. . . . and Resolution of your novel.

12. Of Conflict, Mystery, and Lack, which categories best describe your central Action and Emotional Plot? How do #8-11 reflect that?

QUARTET:
Voice

At the beginning of the talks here, I quoted one of my very favorite sayings about art anywhere: "All art is where you put the camera," said by playwright, novelist, screenwriter, and director David Mamet. The metaphor is about the movies, clearly: that if I make a "camera" with my hands and look through it, then pan slowly across the room, the world narrows to what I can see through that space. Should I decide to verbalize what I'm seeing, that could become the narration of a novel. Here's a description of my apartment on the Sunday morning I'm writing this:

> The gray light pushed at the red-striped curtains and finally muscled through, exhausted. It fell weakly upon the table in the center of the living room, strewn with books, magazines, two cups of sparkling water that had lost all its sparkle, and an iPhone; it reached out to the stiff green chairs huddled together in one corner, and the paisley couch that ruled the room with its sure, solid squareness.

I could stop and zoom in:

> The couch was not young, and its misshapen back cushions, scarred upholstery, and occasional staining testified to a long biography of owners spilling objects, drinks, food, and themselves onto it with great force. But it was well-loved for its length, its comfort (no couch ever made a better visitor's bed), and that peach-and-scarlet, seafoam-and-black paisley

that somehow absorbed all the colors of this disparate room
and united them in harmony.

And then zoom out again:

> But the light moved on toward the kitchen, and even — did it
> dare? — the archway into the hall, lined with bookshelves on
> the way to the bedroom in back.

The story would change with my angle on the room. If I were writing
a story from the point of view of a cat sitting on the floor at my feet, my
camera would be about three feet below my position on the couch now,
so I would be looking at the same scene, but what I could experience
would be the legs of the table and chairs, the shoes scattered around, the
scent of and cracks in the wooden floor. Or I could be telling this story
from where I am now, but in extreme zoom, so that every small action
seems huge. Suppose the camera was so tight on this imaginary cat that
the scene reads like this:

> The cat's nose twitched. It looked away from the shoe
> disdainfully. Twitch. Twitch. Tail flick. Twitch. It sneezed,
> then untucked its front paws from its chest to sit upright,
> glancing violently from side to side to be sure its breach of
> decorum hadn't been observed by a fellow elite. It yawned
> to show how little that opinion would matter, anyway, then
> tucked those front paws back in, returning to its horizontal
> contemplation of dust motes drifting in the light. Tail flicks:
> one. Two. Three. Ear twitch now. Blink.

Of course, if the cat were narrating this scene, or narrating the actions
of its own face in the mirror, it would most likely pick up on different

details and describe itself completely differently, based on its own feline interests and vocabulary and sentence rhythms. Or suppose I took the perspective of a fly buzzing the space:

> I buzzzzzzzzzzzzzzzz. Green! Yum! Cloth. No! Green! Better! Fuzz! Food? No food. Wood buzz wood buzz wood buzz WATER! Shine flat shine flat red fuzz feel, feel. Crumb. Yum! Crumby crumb crumb.

This draws on a lot of the same details as in the first example above, but it does it in a much more compact form, and with very different ideas of what's important within the scene — in this case, the texture of the chairs and the availability of crumbs upon them. It also moves at a much higher speed than the leisurely narration of the first example, with shorter sentences; many fewer verbs, descriptors, and details; and less punctuation (and much punchier punctuation when it's there), all of which creates an emotional atmosphere of high frenzy.

So in every case here, I've been describing the same room — but it's completely different depending on first, where I put the camera; then, how it moves through the action, at what speed and depth of detail. And ultimately those choices determine the kind of story I end up telling: a calm, domestic, Sunday sort of story about a paisley couch and a lazy cat, or a frenetic rushing story about a fly's fight for survival.

The camera in film equals the narrative voice in written fiction — the way we move through the reality of your novel. There's a wonderful David Foster Wallace speech (available online at http://moreintel-ligentlife.com/story/david-foster-wallace-in-his-own-words) in which he tells a story about two young fish hanging out on the street corner. An older fish swims by and says, "How's the water, boys?" And one of the young fish turns to the other and says, "What's water?" When I talk about voice, I am thinking of not just a novel's point of view, but its emotional atmosphere, its rhythms and flow, its narrator's thought patterns — all of the aspects of writing that create the water through which your reader moves in following the characters and story.

This is made more complicated still by the uniquely and directly emotional nature of the narrative voice. The reader is affected by the characters when they come to care about them, and affected by the plot after they care about the characters and get involved with the action; but the sounds and rhythms of a voice create an emotional effect in and of itself. I often cite Hemingway vs. Jane Austen here:

[1] "Give me bacon and eggs," said the other man. He was about the same size as Al. Their faces were different, but they were dressed like twins. Both wore overcoats too tight for them. They sat leaning forward, their elbows on the counter.

[2] The evil of the actual disparity in their ages (and Mr. Woodhouse had not married early) was much increased by his constitution and habits; for having been a valetudinarian all his life, without activity of mind or body, he was a much older man in ways than in years; and though everywhere beloved for the friendliness of his heart and his amiable temper, his talents could not have recommended him at any time.

That Austen passage is from her novel *Emma*, about a Regency-era upper-class woman who lives in elegance and makes a lot of mistakes in figuring out who she is and where she should be. And the very length and vocabulary of that sentence imply leisure, education, ampleness, relaxation. . . . Just the mere fact that it's *one single sentence* tells us it's from a time when people had time to talk like that! The Hemingway, meanwhile, is from his short story called "The Killers," about sudden death striking in an unexpected place. So having short sentences, short words even, nothing too fancy, gives an overall feeling of *tightness* and tension, which in turn contributes to the suspenseful atmosphere. Whether these authors were blessed by natural narrative voices suitable to their subject matter, or they were drawn to such subjects because of the inborn and learned rhythms of their thought, we'll never know; but either way, their voices created the perfect atmosphere and pace for the stories they had to tell.

So if you know your points, as we've been discussing all this time, and you know you need your novel to move at a specific sort of speed or take a specific attitude in both its language and its plot events to achieve those points, then you can construct a voice to help you achieve those ends. For the purposes of this talk, I'm going to look at four key elements of voice:

- The degree of involvement of the cinematographer (the person behind the camera) with the story
    o That is, the Person
- The temporal distance between the storytelling and the events of the action
    o The Tense (not something that exists in film, as all films are present tense, except in flashbacks or flashforwards *from* the present tense)
- The rhythm and grace with which the camera moves
    o What we'll call the Prosody
- And the ways in which this voice reveals the consciousness behind it
    o What we'll call the Personality — and then we'll talk about five aspects of *that*.

Movies and television derive their power partly from the fact that their cameras provide seemingly uninterrupted flows of reality. Of course we know they're very interrupted — there are cuts and special effects and behind-the-scenes manipulation all over the place. But a good show or movie, when you're watching it, feels like something that actually happened, a reality that you're visiting for the first time. You're caught up in the emotional flow of what you're seeing in front of you, and all the images come together to take you to — guess what — the emotional and thematic points of the film.

And that is more or less what a voice should approximate — that steady flow of images and their accompanying feelings. Indeed, I would say the most important responsibility of a narrative voice is to give connective flow to the facts the story reveals. This flow can take many forms — logical, temporal, emotional — but whatever it is, it must lead the reader steadily through the story, except for the times when the author *intends* some sort of break in the flow in order to achieve a specific effect. Your enemy as a writer here is anything that reminds the reader they're reading a book, that these words coming into their brain aren't real, that interrupts the movement of the camera against your intent. I'll identify some of these things as Enemies by name in the course of our discussion of these four elements of voice.

And the first of these elements is the PERSON in which you write. This is probably the single most important choice you make in your storytelling — whether you limit the camera's point of view to one person, who is a witness to or a participant in the events of the book, or you use an omniscient narrator, who can fly over the events and alight anywhere.

With first person, the reader is inside the narrator's head, looking out through his eyes. This means that we have an immediate and intimate connection with this character — immediate access to all of his thoughts; an immediate, you-are-there presence in the action. It is terrifically intense, because there is no escape from this point of view, and everything that happens to the character happens to us, the readers, as well. As I said way back in the character talk, making your protagonist the viewpoint character — and even more the first-person POV character — is a great way to connect readers with said character, because they have to depend on him or her for everything that happens.

However: That will only happen if readers find this narrator likeable or compelling in some way. If the narrator is really annoying, that greatly increases the chance that the reader will put the book down. (If I stop reading a book, nine times out of ten it's because I dislike something about the narrative voice.) And readers also need to find the narrator believable as who he claims to be. Lisa Yee's first four books were all written in the first-person point of view, and so was *Bobby vs. Girls (Accidentally)*, originally. Here's an excerpt from that first draft:

[3] "What's this?" Annie eyes the lumps on her plate.

"Pancakes," Dad says, proudly. "I made them from scratch."

I glance warily around the kitchen. It looks like something exploded. There's even a pancake slowly sliding down the refrigerator door.

Recently, my father's become a stay-at-home dad. He doesn't want Mom to know, but things like cooking and cleaning confuse him. I've caught him staring at the vacuum cleaner like it was something that fell out of the sky.

"I love pancakes!" Casey squeals. To prove her point, she flings one at me. I try to catch it but miss.

"Stop it, Casey," Annie grumps as she peels the pancake off her helmet.

"Sock," I point out.

"What?" Annie scowls, then sighs. "Oh, thanks." She pulls a sock off of her jersey. Dad's biggest battle used to be the opposing football team. Now it's static cling.

"Take off your helmet, Annie," Mom orders. She closes her eyes and savors her first sip of coffee.

"But it's for protection," Annie protests.

Mom's eyes flutter open and for a flash she looks surprised to see us. She sets her mug down. "Don't be silly, Annie. There's nothing dangerous about breakfast."

My sister and I look at the lumps on our plates then exchange glances.

Arthur and I edit Lisa together, and when we read this, we loved all the characters: the spunky older sister and princess-obsessed younger sister, the dad who's a football player turned househusband. But we actually had a hard time with Bobby, who's supposed to be a nine-year-old boy. Why? Because he was apparently the kind of boy who would say "I glance warily around the kitchen" and "Dad's biggest battle used to be the opposing football team. Now it's static cling." That voice is very precise; it uses adverbs like "warily" I wouldn't expect the average nine-year-old boy to use in his everyday mental processes; and it makes observations, like the one about the battle with static cling, that I wouldn't expect a nine-year-old boy to think. (There's only one thought I expect the average nine-year-old boy to have about static cling, and that's "Cool!") As a result of this precision and advanced vocabulary and thinking, Bobby comes off as a little fussy and adult — not really someone I want to spend time with, especially if *I'm* the average nine-year-old boy we envisioned as the ideal reader here. Essentially, we readers were seeing the novelist's voice rather than the main character's voice, and that was distancing us from all of the action, because it was hard to believe in and connect with the main character.

So we talked about this with Lisa, and she had two choices to solve this problem. One, she could rethink everything Bobby says, and recalibrate all his observations to be more authentically those of a nine-year-old boy; or two, she could put it in third person. Lisa is really, really good at first-person voices — her Millicent Min is still one of my favorite narrators of all time — but in this case, she decided to go with option two.

[4] The Ellis-Chans were already eating when Bobby slid into his seat. "What are those?" Annie asked, pointing to the flat brown blobs on her plate.

"Pancakes," Mr. Ellis-Chan said proudly. He was wearing a new blue apron. It still had its price tag on. "I made them from scratch."

Bobby glanced warily around the kitchen. It looked like something had exploded. Dirty pots and pans were everywhere. A pancake slowly slid down the refrigerator door.

"I loooove pancakes!" Casey squealed as she flung one across the table. Bobby tried to catch it, but missed.

"Stop it!" Annie grumbled. She peeled the pancake off her football helmet.

"Sock," said Bobby as he poked at a pancake with his fork. It was hard.

"What?"

Bobby pointed to her shoulder. "Sock."

Annie sighed. "Oh, thanks." The sock made crackling noises as she removed it from her jersey. Their dad's biggest battle used to be the opposing football team. Now it was static cling.

"Take off your helmet, Annie," her mother said. Mrs. Ellis-Chan was wearing her peach-colored business suit. Bobby thought she looked like the pretty dentist in that commercial where people sang about clean teeth. Mrs. Ellis-Chan closed her eyes as she took her first sip of coffee.

"I need to wear my helmet!" Annie protested. "It's for protection,"

Mrs. Ellis-Chan's eyes fluttered open, and for a moment

she seemed startled to see everyone. "Don't be silly, Annie. There's nothing dangerous about breakfast."

Bobby and his sister exchanged glances.

Clearly, this took a little rejiggering — it wasn't as simple as just changing all the "I"s to "He"s. But you can see that even though a lot of the language is the same, the whole thing works much better. In first person, a narrator is under three kinds of pressure: (1) to tell the story; (2) to be believable and compelling as the voice of that particular character; and (3) to bring a personality and richness to the story beyond mere factual narration, as no interesting human being telling his own story ever reported merely the facts. In the first excerpt, the "static cling" lines actually fulfilled the third kind of pressure, as they showed a lot of personality — but that personality conflicted with the second kind of pressure, the believability, for reasons already discussed. In third person, that second pressure is removed, so that observation about static cling comes off as funny rather than fussy or overly critical. Likewise, the "warily" works here because it's so unexpected — this is an average American suburban kitchen; what could be dangerous enough to cause wariness? We soon find out it's Mr. Ellis-Chan's cooking, and thus Bobby's wariness becomes not only justified but hilarious.

These two *Bobby* examples also demonstrate some of the limits of both POVs. For instance, in both of them, you cannot go into anyone else's head. Look again at that line toward the end of [3]: "She closes her eyes and savors her first sip of coffee." How does Bobby know that his mom's savoring her sip of coffee? Maybe she's closing her eyes and fantasizing about being on a desert island. Maybe she's wishing she were still in bed and all her kids were far, far away. Bobby can guess, but he can't know. That little slip out of Bobby's perspective and emotions into his mom's is what I call head-jumping, and it is an Enemy. It's not an Enemy unique to first person — it can happen in limited third person, too, if you're mostly in the POV of one particular character and then suddenly we hear something that's going on in another character's mind or heart. It can be okay in third person if it's done intentionally and with some consistency: In *Operation Yes* by Sara Lewis Holmes, Sara underlines the theme of community in the book by slipping into the heads of nearly everyone in the sixth grade class at the center of the book . . . and not just once, but several times, which signals to the reader that it is an intentional strategy rather than a beginner's mistake. But such head-jumping is never okay in first person; you have to recast the head-jumping as something that the main character can see from the outside. And you can see here that once *Bobby* went into third person, Lisa simply took out that bit about savoring, and the "surprised to see everyone" showed the reader that Mom had mentally exited the room for a minute there, without the narrator having to jump into her head.

Another great Enemy is infodumping. "Infodumping" is where the writer needs to supply a piece of information to the reader for plot purposes, and so it's included, whether the character could believably know that and say it at this time or not. (It is also a great danger in situations where an author has done a lot of research and wants to work it all in.) In the first-person *Bobby* excerpt, that paragraph about his dad is infodumping. Actually, it's really not that egregious; it's a bit of narration that follows naturally out of the action that Bobby's witnessing. And this was the first chapter of the book in the first draft, and readers will accept a little infodump at the beginning of a novel as it helps them get oriented within this fictional world. But it is something to watch out for, especially if there isn't any action to prompt that piece of information, or if you have a LOT of information you need to convey to the reader.

A related Enemy is "elbow-jogging" — infodumping in miniature, with tiny details included here and there outside the natural flow of the voice and action. (The term comes from the marvelous critic Anthony Lane, who defined "elbow-joggers" as "nervy, worrisome authors who can't stop shoving us along with jabs of information and opinion that we don't yet require" in his genius *New Yorker* review of *The Da Vinci Code*.) As an example, here's a sentence I made up for the first line of a book: "Ten-year-old Ginny Mulroney skipped along the flagstone path to her grandmother's house." The "ten-year-old" there is a bit of reportage, slipped in because the author wants the reader to know that Ginny is ten years old, not because the reader needs to know that straightaway. (The reader can probably live in suspense for a while about that.) An improvement would be to have the character's age revealed through what she says to her grandmother, if there's some way to work it in naturally that she's ten years old; or better yet, it could never be directly stated at all (unless it affects the plot in some way), and we readers will recognize her age in her behavior and the details of her life.

Doing a first-person voice is like writing a picture book in rhyme: You should do it only if you do it very, very well. Of the three kinds of pressure placed on the narrative voice above, #2 and #3 are by far the most important; everything else — all your informational and plotting needs — has to work within the bounds of the character's believability and personality. And if you have more than one first-person narrator within a book, then each voice has to be distinct from each other one in all the personality aspects we'll discuss below: word choices, sentence rhythms, thought patterns.

Someone asked me once if all YA novels had to be in first person. The answer is no, obviously — *Graceling* and *The Last Summer of the Death Warriors* and many other books prove it. YA and first person tend to work well together because first person has a lot of emotional intensity and it is very self-focused, obviously, and those qualities also tend to describe teenagers, God love 'em. Still, there is no "have-to" about it, and I would much, much rather have a believable third-person novel than an unbelievable-as-a-teenager first-person voice.

Contrast all this with third person, where we watch these characters from the outside. The variety of this voice that most often appears in children's and YA fiction is third-person limited omniscient, where the narration mostly follows one character and often dips into her thoughts:

> [5] It was darker outside now than it was in her dining room. She saw him, suddenly, in the reflection of the window. He was leaning back against the table, as she had pictured him before. His face, his shoulders, his arms sagged. Everything about him sagged. He was unhappy. He was looking down at his feet, but as she watched him he raised his eyes, and met hers in the glass. She felt the tears again, suddenly, and she grasped at something to say.

The great English writer Evelyn Waugh defined the three elements necessary to a writer's style as "lucidity, elegance, individuality." For a third-person narrator, the first two are by far the most important, as a third-person narrator is under only one kind of pressure: to tell the story clearly and smoothly, maximizing the reader's emotional involvement and payoff (assuming emotional involvement is something the author intends). With that said, even a third-person voice will show some individuality, which will emerge naturally from those same factors that show personality in first person. I chose *Graceling* as an example book here not only because I adored the characters, but because it has a wonderfully eccentric third-person narrative voice full of deliberate stutters and repetitions like "his face, his shoulders, his arms" and the heavy use of "sagged." The second *Bobby* excerpt above showed its individuality in that "warily" and its quick cut to Bobby and Annie's glance in response to their mother's statement. When I look at a manuscript in third person, I look for lucidity and elegance first and foremost; but a consistent, original individuality like these is always an additional pleasure.

(In passing, this excerpt is doing a zoom like I did on my sofa earlier — do you see it? It starts out with Katsa looking at Po, zooms into a description of his physical state, identifies his emotional state, and, when he raises his eyes to look at her, it zooms out again to what she's thinking and feeling as a result of what she saw in the zoom.)

Third person also allows you to adopt multiple points of view, should your story require it, without creating multiple distinct first-person voices. This is especially common and useful in fantasy, where you may want readers to be able to see something happening that your protagonist doesn't yet know about, the better to create suspense for his or her eventual discovery of that event; or you may just want to provide a fuller view of the world for your reader, outside the limits of what your protagonist sees and knows. *Harry Potter and the Sorcerer's Stone* opens with an omniscient narrator observing the Dursleys (who were "proud to say they were perfectly normal, thank you very much"); moves into Mr. Dursley's perspective, as he watches various people in capes celebrating some unknown event; then shifts back to the omniscient narrator to observe Professors McGonagall and Dumbledore, and Harry's arrival at the house. In Chapter 2, the omniscient narrator introduces us to Harry and in slow degrees slips us inside his head, where we will stay for the rest of the book. Still, J. K. Rowling's use of multiple third-person perspectives in the first chapter established her freedom to move from character to character as needed throughout the series, and thus allowed her to leave Harry's perspective when her story required it later on.

There is one other person available to writers: second person, where the reader is addressed as "you." That direct address creates a peculiar intimacy, and also divide, between reader and book, since, in true second person, the "you" becomes the protagonist, experiencing all the action described, while of course the actual "you" of the reader is merely reading a book. Very few novels try to sustain that uncomfortable dichotomy over the course of a whole book, though *If on a winter's night a traveler* by Italo Calvino does it brilliantly. A fair number of novels *do* feature a first-person narrator addressing another character as "you," either in writing or in speech — *Cut* by Patricia McCormick and *The Rules of Engagement* by Nancy Werlin, for instance — and those can be very powerful for the right story; but they still remain first-person books.

So which person is right for your book? Well — first of all, can you do first person well, as a believable teen or child voice? One way to test this: Give an excerpt to an honest, smart friend; ask them to read it and pay attention just to the language, not to the content, so much as that's possible; and then ask them to describe the speaker for you. (Better yet, give it to an actual person of the putative protagonist's age.) If your reader can identify the age of and connect with the protagonist, then the odds are good you're doing something right. If it's not coming through (and you may wish to try several readers here), then perhaps you should stick with third person.

Second, if you can do either first or third person well, consider what points you're trying to achieve. How close do we need to be to the action to feel the emotional point? Will it be more powerful if we're inside the head of the person experiencing the events, or more powerful if we see them from the outside? Sometimes it's better if we have some distance from the character, if they're going through something awful or hard to express in words. But then sometimes the power of the book comes from forcing readers to be somewhere they don't want to be — the serial-killer narrator in *Darkly Dreaming Dexter*, the pedophile of *Lolita*, the degradation of *Flowers in the Attic*. Which effect do you want to have? Whose story is this? Is it one person's, or many people's? Are you limiting yourself and what you can show too much if you stay with only one narrator? Ask yourself these questions, figure out the answers, and then decide the best way to go.

The second aspect of narrative voice we'll discuss here is TENSE. All fiction is written in the declarative mood in past or present tense. In present tense, the action is happening *now*, which gives it special intensity, immediacy, and a sense that anything can happen at any time, as events aren't yet fixed and complete in the past. Both *Marcelo* and *The*

Hunger Games use first-person present tense, which, in its combination of an intimate perspective and that feeling of constant anticipation, probably offers the greatest emotional intensity that a reader can experience. Third person, present tense is an interesting beast where you have the tension of the action happening in the present moment, but we readers must watch our protagonist's reactions to it from the outside. . . . It's very good for setting us on edge, because we have incomplete information about our protagonist as well as the sense of threat:

> [6] She throws down her cigarette and mashes it on the sidewalk, kicking it over with a pile of a dozen others. She breathes out one last, smoke-filled breath and almost smiles. There is still a little pretense left. She slips a peppermint into her mouth and lifts the latch of the gate. It groans, low and heavy, whispering Don't go in, don't go in.

This is from *The House on Lorelei Street,* by Mary Pearson — the story of a teenage girl who's living a very hand-to-mouth, tough existence. Present tense works here for the same reason it works so well in *The Hunger Games:* The jangliness provides a sense of constant readiness, that danger could strike at any moment.

With past tense: The action has been completed at some point in the past, so events are fixed, settled, certain. Past tense is very common for fantasy, like *Graceling,* where there's already so much unfamiliar material in the world and the magic that setting the reader on edge in the tense feels almost a little unkind. Or look at examples [1] and [2] above from *Bobby vs. Girls.* The person isn't the only thing that changed there — the tense did as well. I think that past tense would have been the right choice for Lisa to make even if the book had stayed in first person, because this is essentially a reassuring story about a well-known world, not a world where we want the reader to be held in a state of uncomfortable suspense.

So, again, which one is right for *your* book? Think about your emotional point — the state you want readers to be in as they experience your book. If it's a state of (relative) comfort or relaxation, try past tense. If it's a state of nervousness or unease, try present tense.

Exercise: Take one of the scenes you've written in the course of these talks, from either the Basic Book or your Work-in-Progress, and rewrite it in a different person and different tense.

Tense is ultimately all about time: the temporal distance between the occurrence of the action and the time at which this story is being told. PROSODY, the aspect of voice we'll discuss next, is likewise a temporal measure. The dictionary definition of "prosody" is "the study of metrical structure of verse," which involves metric feet, syllables, stresses, and all those good things. I'm borrowing the term to refer to the rhythm of fiction: specifically, the rhythm in which information is introduced into and narrated within a story. Unlike poetic prosody, there is no highly scientific system here, nor very strict forms; but there are some general patterns that are very useful for writers to know, and those patterns are what we're going to look at here.

Remember how we were talking about beats in a scene in the plot talk? There are beats in a sentence as well, as basically every phrase or new nugget of information is a beat unto itself. In good prose, there should be a recognizable line of connection between those beats, should you stop to sit back and analyze them. As an example, let's go back to that sentence from *Emma* quoted earlier:

[1] The evil of the actual disparity in their ages [1a] (and Mr. Woodhouse had not married early) [2] was much increased by his constitution and habits; [3] for having been a valetudinarian all his life, [4] without activity of mind or body, [5] he was a much older man in ways than in years; [6] and though everywhere beloved for the friendliness of his

heart and his amiable temper, [7] his talents could not have recommended him at any time.

Every phrase in this sentence is directly linked to the next, as we can see if we break out the individual beats:

1. There is a kind of evil (meaning danger, trouble, cause for concern) in how many years these two people (Emma and her father) are separate in age.
   a. Aside: Mr. Woodhouse had married at a late age
2. That evil was increased by his nature and behavior.
3. Explanation of that nature and behavior: He's been a valetudinarian — what we modern readers would call a hypochondriac — for a long time.
4. Which is further explained by the next phrase: He hasn't seen or done very much, so he has little to think about besides himself,
5. And thus he acts much older than he is chronologically.
6. And while he is a nice guy,
7. He is not the sharpest tool in the shed.
   a. This again reinforces the idea of the evil Mr. Woodhouse presents, because Emma is a pretty talented young woman, in the vernacular of Austen's age, and she SHOULD hang out with people who are her equals.

When I edit, I spend a lot of time thinking about this kind of sentence linkage — how one thought flows into another — because that's ultimately how one emotion flows into another, and as we said at the beginning, the narrative voice's most important responsibility is providing a consistent emotional flow. If this sort of thought-flow is something you struggle with, think first of all about the topic-sentence model of paragraph construction. (This is another thing you likely learned about in school.) A topic sentence is the first sentence of a paragraph, which sets forth its main idea or hypothesis, and while it's mostly talked about in nonfiction or expositional writing, it's a wonderful structure for description and narration as well, because it makes each paragraph function almost like an argument.

Look at p. 243 of the *Marcelo* excerpt, the last paragraph on that page. It starts with a topic sentence setting forth its premise: "As vague and broad as [the term "the real world"] is, I have a sense of what it means and of the difficulties that it entails." Then it backs it up with evidence that supports the point it's making — Showing what it's already Told, in Show-not-Tell terms:

> Following the rules of the real world means, for example, engaging in small talk with other people. It means refraining from talking about my special interest. It means looking people in the eye and shaking hands. It means doing things "on the hoof," as we say at Paterson, which means doing things that have not been scheduled in advance. It may mean walking or going to places I am not familiar with, city streets full of noise and confusion.

Then the paragraph concludes in a way that moves the story forward: "Even though I am trying to look calm, a wave of terror comes over me as I imagine walking the streets of Boston by myself." That "a wave of terror comes over me" reanchors the reader in the present action, rather than Marcelo's thoughts, and readies us to hear Arturo's next line.

Once you have a number of paragraphs properly assembled, you can link them up and turn them into a scene. The *Marcelo* chapter begins with the line, "I get out of the car and head for the back door." I think of sentences like these as "establishing shots" — another term stolen from the movies, meaning "an opening shot that sets up the environment of a show or scene." (If you ever watch *Seinfeld*, those quick shots of the diner from the outside before a scene featuring the characters inside were textbook establishing shots.) Establishing shots within a text serve as more or less a topic sentence for the scene, quickly setting up where we are temporally and geographically: Marcelo was in the car with his mother in the previous scene, so we readers can deduce that they're now at home, some brief period of time after that scene ended; and with that information in hand, we're ready to see the action of a new scene.

From a plot perspective, the rhythms of a scene should generally follow the Freytag's Triangle structure described in the previous talk, with beats of dialogue or action building toward a Climax that demonstrates a change in the overall Action or Emotional Plot. From a narrative voice perspective, it's important to keep an eye on the scene's balance among Atemporal, Immediate, and Internal narration. Atemporal narration describes things that take place outside of the present narrative time: backstory and description. Immediate narration describes things that happen in the present narrative time: action and dialogue. And Internal narration shows what our viewpoint character is thinking in reaction to both of the other kinds of narration. To demonstrate, here's a passage from the first chapter of *Bobby vs. Girls (Accidentally)*, where I've marked the Immediate narration in bold and the Internal narration with an underscore:

[7] The whole town of Rancho Rosetta, California, turned out for the annual Labor Day Fiesta at Wild Acres. **Bobby could hear a rock band playing in the distance as the riders exited Monstroso, laughing and giving each other high fives. Some people got right back in line to go on again. Bobby shook his head.** <u>The only ride worth going on over and over was the bumper cars. He also loved the Circus Train, but that was a little kid ride.</u>

The first line here is an Atemporal establishing shot, explaining where these characters are in place and time, but standing a little outside that time itself, as it sets up the general situation more than addressing that particular moment in the narrative. In contrast, the Immediate lines show the action that's taking place at that very moment, as Bobby and his family stand outside the entrance to Monstroso (a roller coaster), hear a rock band, and observe some of the riders getting back on. Bobby shakes his head in response to that decision by the riders, and by readerly convention, we understand that the lines that follow that are his thoughts — the Internal narration. ("He also loved the Circus Train" might also be Atemporal, as that love is ongoing, not an act of love in the immediate moment; but as the thought is apparently inspired by "The only ride worth going on . . . ," it can be considered an extension of his Internal narration.)

In any case, what is important about all of this is not what specific type of narration each sentence falls into, but how the three kinds of narration flow together to move the reader through the action and your viewpoint character's thoughts. I think of Atemporal and Immediate narration as moviemaking, essentially. When you dramatize a scene, you're trying to make it come to life for the reader — using the description of what your protagonist sees, the action of what she does or witnesses, and the dialogue she has with other characters to make the scene unfold fully in the reader's mind. And the more vivid and realistic the moviemaking, the more powerfully the reader is hooked into the scene — feeling the emotion from those objects, in objective correlative terms.

Description provides what the camera would show us if this book became a movie, a picture being worth a thousand words and all that. It is entirely dependent on eyelines: Only once our viewpoint character is looking at something can you describe what he sees. And as a rule of thumb, we should get all of the important description of something the first time our viewpoint character sees it. Suppose said character is meeting a new girl named Mina: "She was short, even though her boots had four-inch heels, and her brown eyes sparkled beneath garish green and gold eyeshadow." We shouldn't go through an entire four or five paragraphs of action with Mina and then get more details in passing, like "She was wearing a blue fringe dress," unless there's some reason our viewpoint character wouldn't have noticed that dress the first time he saw her (when he *did* notice a detail like the height of her heels). The character would take in all major aspects of Mina's appearance when he looks at her for the first time, so that's when we should hear it.

Meanwhile, the Internal narration offers the one kind of drama that books can do and movies can't: It shows us directly how the character interprets, and how the reader *might* interpret, the action taking place. As such, it should always have some direct hook in the Atemporal or Immediate narration — there should be a "thought line," just like an eyeline above, running from whatever the character just saw or experienced to what he's about to think. I divide Internal narration into the categories of Commentary and Reflection (which I also call Processing). Commentary is the character's immediate internal response to events; Reflection is the character pulling together various bits of information to arrive at a new conclusion, which will usually push the story forward in setting up his next course of action.

Consider the *Marcelo* excerpt again, p. 241: "There is no chance of ever changing the subject with Arturo," or further down "This is a total surprise." These are both examples of Commentary, helping to guide the reader through the minefield of this conversation by showing Marcelo's reactions moment by moment. Or p. 243: "Now he pauses. He knows I will need time to sort this out. One summer at the law firm versus a whole year at Paterson. I miss out on Fritzy's early months, but I still get to train him next year." That is Marcelo Reflecting, starting to figure out what this proposal means for him. The end of the chapter also provides some Reflection, as he generally accepts his father's proposal and starts to think about its implications for his summer. Internal narration, and especially Reflection, help the reader know what is important in and what the character is taking away from everything presented by the other kinds of narration. It confirms the emotions raised by the objective correlative of the action, and signals where we're going from here.

With that said, Internal narration is a tool that should be used carefully and sparingly, because it can quickly become telling and redundant and slow the action down. If it's obvious to the reader from the Immediate narration what the viewpoint character is feeling or doing, for goodness's sake, don't add Internal narration on top of it! It can be especially dangerous in dialogue scenes, where you might be tempted to add a line of Commentary or description after every line of dialogue — what the other person's face looks like, how each one reacts. In that case, please remember that dialogue takes place in real time as well as Immediate narrative time, so if there's Commentary after every line of dialogue, that means there is more or less a pause after every line of dialogue in how the reader hears the conversation. And this can make the conversation very lumpy and awkward and lacking all flow, if the reader has to pause after every spoken line to digest additional thoughts about it. Stay with the dialogue instead, and work the Commentary in around it only if it's truly necessary.

Indeed, it's very much worth remembering that ALL Internal and Atemporal narration takes place within the time established by the Immediate narration, as well as in real time; and the most important thing for the book is to keep the Immediate narration going and make that scene complete. If you have one or two beats of dialogue and action in Scene X, and then your narrator is inspired by something in those beats to indulge in a four-page Flashback Y or offer six paragraphs of opinions on Subject Z, your reader will wonder first, what was happening in Scene X while the narrator was thinking all this; then, when we'll get back to that scene; and then how Flashback Y or Subject Z really relate to Scene X, considering so much more real time — page time, reading time — is being spent on them compared to Scene X. As a writer, you'll need to both complete Scene X at some point (perhaps your narrator was just staring into space with Scene X going on around him while those four pages of Immediate time passed?) and justify all of that page time with some narrative payoffs for the flashback or opinions.

And Scene X will only be completed when something has changed from both an Action Plot and an Emotional Plot perspective. That is, something should have happened within the scene to advance the plot, and we readers should have been taken through the emotional change that would accompany that, to come to a new emotional state of excitement (if you end the scene in the midst of high narrative tension) or a feeling of at least temporary resolution or suspension (if you end with a fermata, as discussed on p. 247).

One of my primary rules in editing is, as much as you possibly can, *Stay with the scene.* Stay with the Immediate narration: Don't stop it in the middle for an infodump of Atemporal or Internal narration. Stay with the flow of thought: Every reference or bit of Commentary or Reflection must be clearly linked with a preceding thought or action. And most of all, stay with the emotion: Don't throw in a hilarious two-paragraph digression in the middle of a really tense horror sequence, have references that make the reader stop to think in the grip of what should be an action scene, or do anything else to distract the reader from the drama of your story and its accompanying feelings.

So once you've completed a scene according to Freytag's Triangle standards, go over it one more time and look at the balance among the three kinds of narration. Do you have an establishing shot, if necessary? Is every description triggered by an eyeline, and every bit of Commentary or Reflection by a thought line? Is all of the Internal narration necessary and useful? Is the scene complete from an Immediate narration standpoint, and is any Atemporal or Internal narration sufficiently balanced and justified by the action of the scene?

Exercise: Choose a dialogue-heavy scene from your WIP. Delete all of the Commentary and Reflection and save it as a new document.

Work on another scene for some time, then return and reread the revised scene. Can you permanently cut some of that Internal narration?

The last element of voice I'll discuss here is PERSONALITY — the "individuality" in Evelyn Waugh's style formula of "lucidity, elegance, individuality." This is by far the most important aspect of voice, because every writer will use the same elements of Person, Tense, and Prosody — there are only so many to choose from; but Personality is like a writer's fingerprint: utterly unique to that writer and generally unduplicable by anyone else. However, it is also the least conscious aspect of creating a voice, *and* the least controllable, as it is much more difficult (for me, anyway) to change the rhythms of my sentence structures or come up with original imagery appropriate for a particular character's brain than it is to switch tenses or fix thought lines. While no rubric could hope to encompass all of the aspects of voice, I'm going to highlight four key elements listed in Nancy Dean's excellent book *Voice Lessons*, as well as one element of my own; and if you struggle with creating an original or lively personality for your voice, I hope this breakdown might help you identify individual elements you can improve.

DICTION

Diction is word choice — a devilishly interesting and difficult set of choices indeed, as the vocabulary of the narration and the characters' dialogue provide not just the overt content of the information, but the subliminal content of who these people are based on their language. Consider these twelve words that all mean "blue":

• navy	• periwinkle	• cobalt
• lapis lazuli	• cerulean	• indigo
• sapphire	• azure	• sky
• slate	• turquoise	• ultramarine

Clearly these are not all the same color, and some would be more right than others for describing whatever blue a narrator might see. But if I myself was just looking at a plain, classic blue with a companion, and said companion chose to call it "lapis lazuli," I'd know I was dealing with a pretty educated guy who would expect me to be pretty well educated as well. (Or perhaps, he's a bit of a showoff; or perhaps he just likes being accurate; or perhaps, all of the above.) Likewise, in a book, that one word would characterize him to the reader for the rest of the narrative (along with many other factors of context and camera positioning, of course), and his use of it would need to ring true with all the other factors of who he is. If he was a ten-year-old boy who just emigrated to the United States from Vietnam, for instance, and he was still learning to speak English, his busting out "lapis lazuli" without some narrative explanation of how he picked up the term would ring extremely false to me as a reader. Diction always needs to be consistent with all the other elements of character.

In writing children's and YA fiction, this question of diction is further complicated by the fact that the target audience might not be familiar with all the words you might like to use. In this case, the rule of thumb is to go with the simplest possible word that is still accurate to your narrator. Picture books are both generally read by adults to children, *and* illustrated, so if you used "azure" to describe a sky, the four-year-old child reader could still discern from the pictures that you meant "blue." However, as an editor, I'd want to be sure that "azure" is in keeping with the overall narrative tone (which I would then expect to be rather old-fashioned or highfalutin'), and that "azure" was the single most accurate word for the situation . . . that we absolutely couldn't just go with "blue." In the early reader genre, the simplest possible word takes precedence over even accuracy, as the goal is to build beginning readers' confidence and familiarity with common words, not to frustrate or confuse them with difficult language. In middle-grade and YA novels, the diction should be cued to the age of your narrator and/or protagonist, which will also likely reflect the age of your intended reader. If you're concerned about vocabulary levels, the *Children's Writer's Word Book*, available from Writers' Digest Books, offers lists of words keyed to reading levels.

All of this brings me to another Enemy here: overactivity or over-specificity. I know that most writing books teach you to use strong, active verbs and specific, highly accurate adjectives and nouns over weak parts of speech, and this is also a good rule of thumb. But it is not the be-all and end-all of writing, and quite often I see manuscripts whose writers are clearly trying too hard to live up to this dictum and not allowing their natural voice to come through, so the language ends up getting in the way of the action. For instance, on one writing website, I found a writing adviser telling writers:

> Instead of saying, "The linebacker tackled the running back," say, "The linebacker torpedoed the running back," or say, "The linebacker flattened the running back." Vivid verbs appeal to the reader's senses and help make sentences more memorable. (A little alliteration doesn't hurt, either.)

Again, this is indeed true (except for the part about the alliteration, which should be used sparingly). But if those vivid verbs aren't in line with the rest of the narration, they're going to knock the reader out of the book by obviously being writerly verbs rather than easy-to-read ones — the writer calling attention to the language, when the reader wants transparency. For example:

> [8] The linebacker torpedoed the running back. Then he pummeled the ground with his meaty paws, rocketed up, and caterwauled, "WHO'S THE HEAD HONCHO? WHO'S THE HEAD HONCHO?" Chortling with jubilation, he tarantellaed around the pouting prone player.

This is vivid, all right. But it's also rather bizarre, and there is so much readerly effort involved in deciphering and picturing those specific actions that I feel rather exhausted reading just that paragraph — I can't imagine reading two hundred pages of it! Contrast that with:

> [9] The linebacker tackled the running back. Then he pounded the ground with his fists, leaped up, and shouted, "WHO'S THE BOSS? WHO'S THE BOSS?" He danced around the running back, laughing with glee.

We could certainly debate some of the choices in both of these examples (which I made up): "HEAD HONCHO" is actually really nice in contrast to "BOSS" — it's a great little hint of that linebacker's character. But overall, [9] is much easier and more pleasant to read, and I would *much* rather spend time with this second narrator than the first. In all your writing, whether in first person or third, don't worry too, too much about using active, strong words; worry about using the most natural and accurate ones for the voice you're writing in, and the activity should take care of itself.

To think about: Are your characters' dictions each distinctive to who they are? Are you overusing strong words? Underusing them? If the latter, could you amp up selected words to make the diction of your book more distinctive?

SYNTAX

Syntax is the sentence structure of your narrator's speech, its rhythms, repetitions, patterns, and variances in length. As discussed in the Austen vs. Hemingway examples ([1] and [2]) at the beginning of this talk, the *sounds* of your sentences and words in and of themselves can have a direct emotional effect on the reader; thinking about syntax means thinking about how those sounds (rhythms especially) can be manipulated to serve your informational and emotional ends. Consider the first paragraph of the *Marcelo* excerpt quoted in the previous section:

> [10] I get out of the car and head for the back door. I see Arturo in the backyard grilling steaks. I hoped to enter the house without him seeing me. I am not ready for the discussion that I know will take place and I need more time to anticipate his questions and memorize my replies. But Aurora yells at him from the back door.

Some things to notice about the sentence structures here:

Many sentences start with I. Think of all the different ways Francisco Stork could have chosen to phrase the information in that second sentence: "I see Arturo in the backyard grilling steaks." "Arturo is in the backyard, grilling steaks." "Arturo is grilling steaks in the backyard." "Arturo grills steaks in the backyard." The "I see" isn't essential to the information of the sentence at all. But including it, and then the repeated use of "I" as the subject of most of the other sentences in that paragraph, puts the emphasis on Marcelo and his action of seeing — the fact that everything is filtered through him. People on the autistic spectrum often have a hard time understanding or empathizing with the perspectives of other people so they see everything through the lens of themselves and their needs. Thus this authorial choice and emphasis subtly reemphasizes Marcelo's unique perspective here.

Very plain, straightforward sentence structures, with few commas, pauses, or interior clauses. Again, this emphasizes Marcelo's straightforwardness, his reliance on and appreciation of solidity and truth (which will soon be tested by the real world).

Very plain, straightforward thoughts, with more or less one thought per sentence. These are the facts, and again, Marcelo loves facts, things he can trust, in a world where people are often confusing.

So just that one paragraph allows us to construct a profile of Marcelo as a personality. Contrast that to this excerpt from *The Hunger Games*:

[11] I won't close my eyes. The comment about Rue has filled me with fury, enough fury I think to die with some dignity. As my last act of defiance, I will stare her down as long as I can see, which will probably not be an extended period of time, but I will stare her down, I will not cry out, I will die, in my own small way, undefeated. . . .

I brace myself for the agony that's sure to follow. But as I feel the tip open the first cut at my lip, some great force yanks Clove from my body and then she's screaming. I'm too stunned at first, too unable to process what has happened. Has Peeta somehow come to my rescue? Have the Gamemakers sent in some wild animal to add to the fun? Has a hovercraft inexplicably plucked her into the air?

But when I push myself up on my numb arms, I see it's none of the above. Clove is dangling a foot off the ground, imprisoned in Thresh's arms. I let out a gasp, seeing him like that, towering over me, holding Clove like a rag doll. I remember him as big, but he seems more massive, more powerful than I even recall. If anything, he seems to have gained weight in the arena. He flips Clove around and flings her onto the ground.

While there are obviously a lot of differences between these two excerpts — the existence of emotional reactions, details, and figurative language in the latter, for instance — notice especially how each one picks up and carries emotional weight within its sentences. In *Marcelo*, again, these straightforward sentences add up over time to create an overall impression of strong feelings hidden by flat affect. In *The Hunger Games*, each sentence is structured with a significant action or its emotional weight landing towards the end of the sentence. Consider:

- "I will stare her down, I will not cry out, I will die, in my own small way, undefeated."

+ "Has Peeta somehow come to my rescue? Have the Gamemakers sent in some wild animal to add to the fun? Has a hovercraft inexplicably plucked her into the air?"

    o Series of repeating elements, and especially series of questions, acquire weight as they go along, and the last one should always be the biggest or most emotional thought.

+ "But as I feel the tip open the first cut at my lip, some great force yanks Clove from my body and then she's screaming."

+ "But when I push myself up on my numb arms, I see it's none of the above."

    o The dependent "But" clauses shift the strength in the sentence to the independent clause; and while Suzanne Collins does put her dependent clauses second in descriptive sentences ("I remember him as big, but he seems more massive"), she almost always makes them first in action lines.

And when you have the emotional weight at the end of a sentence, readers rush to get to the end of that sentence, and then they tip naturally into the next sentence, and the sentence after that, and the sentence after that. So the massive success of this book isn't just down to the fact that Suzanne Collins had a terrifically high-stakes plot and an instantly sympathetic protagonist; she also knew how to make her sentence structures work for her overall point.

One more example here:

[12] I'm coming off this plane, and I'll tell you why that is later, and landing at London airport and I'm looking around for a middle-aged kind of woman who I've seen in pictures, who's my Aunt Penn. The photographs are out of date, but she looked like the type who would wear a big necklace and flat shoes, and maybe some kind of narrow dress in black or gray. But I'm just guessing since the pictures only showed her face.

These are the opening lines of a YA novel called *How I Live Now* by Meg Rosoff, which I was unable to finish reading because the voice drove me crazy. Really what made me nuts was the irregularity of the sentence rhythms — the fact that commas and subjects aren't used consistently; our narrator Daisy follows a bunch of "and" clauses with that abrupt "who's my aunt Penn"; the fact that she's going from general ("middle-aged kind of woman") to ultra-zoom ("big necklace and flat shoes") in the space of two clauses; and — what's most interesting to me here — the variances in sentence length. In the *Marcelo* excerpt at [10], four out of those five sentences had between eleven and thirteen syllables. In the *Hunger Games* excerpt, nearly all the sentences are in the high teens or the twenties syllablewise. That establishes what I think of as a prosodic "breathing pattern" — a loose, characteristic rhythm of thoughts and rest between thoughts. Here the first sentence has ninety-three syllables. The second has seventy-two. The third has thirteen. That is a lot of variance, and that creates a jangliness and restlessness even beyond the high tension of first-person present: The reader can't settle into knowing anything about this narrator, even how long her breaths are, because the voice could switch it up at any time.

I personally couldn't stand this — it felt like energy without consistent direction to me, and I love consistent direction. But in actuality, this was the exact right voice for the book: This story is about a girl visiting her cousin in a time of war, and the jangly rhythm of the sentences reflects the uncertainty and sudden changes in her life. And this won the Printz Award in 2004. It really worked for some people, just not for me.

I want to go back to the [5] example from *Graceling* quoted on p. 262 to say one more thing about sentence length. We saw there that the narrator was doing a zoom on Po as Katsa looked at him. If we look at it from a sentence-length perspective, we notice that when the zoom happens, the sentences get shorter. The shortest sentence in that excerpt is: "He was unhappy." Where a long sentence might bury the point in verbiage, a short sentence, especially in contrast to other, longer sentences, makes the point hit the reader hard (as this does here). Likewise, in the chapter where Katsa finally confronts her enemy, the sentences suddenly become very short and clipped, reflecting the tension she is under. Kristin Cashore herself summarized this principle on her blog:"If you're describing a place or an emotion or anything that is simple and peaceful, your writing should be simple and peaceful. Match your style of writing to the feeling you wish the reader to feel" (http://kristincashore.blogspot.com/2010/07/writing-lesson-about-trees.html).

Finally, syntax, like diction, can be a powerful tool for character-ization of non-viewpoint characters as well. Suppose that Marcelo, Katniss, and Daisy all gathered in a room together, and their conversa-tion was recorded by a third-person narrator. Each line each one spoke could only be spoken by him or her in that conversation — no one would ever mistake a Daisy line for a Marcelo one — and the reader could slowly begin to put together the personalities of these three very disparate characters from their dialogue alone. And this is the goal in all dialogue scenes: Because no two people ever have the exact same syntax and diction, your characters should each speak with their own unique rhythms and words, identifiable as that character even if a line is removed from context. Perhaps your character also has key phrases he repeats or returns to, like Arturo's fondness for talking about "the real world"; or particular habits of speech, like Bobby's best friend Chess, who loves using big words like "indubitably"; or key ideas, like Katniss's (understandable) obsession with physical threats and food sources during the Hunger Games (though this latter perhaps fits better within Imagination, as discussed below). Such identifying habits reinforce the patterns established by the syntax and diction and other vocal details of characterization.

To think about: How does your average sentence structure and sentence length reflect your narrator's personality? Are there any places in your book where the syntax doesn't match the overall emotional tone? How can you bring the two into better harmony?

TONE

Tone, in Nancy Dean's words, is "the expression of the author/speaker/narrator's attitude toward his or her listeners, audience, or subject matter." Emotionally, it establishes the energy level and atmosphere of the story. In the *How I Live Now* excerpt quoted above, the tone is excitable — rushing here and gushing there and very casual and confident in its relation to the reader ("I'll tell you why that is later"). Indeed, the narrator Daisy there is aware that she *has* an audience, with that "you," and so that consciously shapes her telling. In the *Marcelo* and *Hunger Games* excerpts, in contrast, our narrators seem more to be reporting this for the universe as the action goes along than writing this at a specific time or specifically for a reader. Thus the emotions and energy level of the story grow more out of the events and the characters' reactions to them than any preestablished tone in the voice. *Bobby* likewise takes a more reportorial view, but there are small touches throughout — like the "static cling" line in [4], with its wry commentary upon Mr. Ellis-Chan's travails — that make the tone more affectionate overall. Your narrator's attitude toward the action and characters will very much shape the reader's attitude towards them in turn (pending the reader's relationship with the narrator itself), so be sure that tone serves your overall points.

To think about: How does your narrator feel about the action s/he is recording here? If there is a specific emotional tinge to it — like the *How I Live Now* excerpt — how would you describe that?

Exercise: Choose one of the Basic Book scenes or a scene from your WIP and keep all the same action and dialogue, but try a dramatic change in your narrator's tone. If your book has been more reportorial or delicate, write it from the perspective of an extremely sarcastic thirteen-year-old; if it's already tough as nails, put it in the tone of the kindest old gentleman you know. The contrast might not ultimately be useful for the book, but it will stretch your writing muscles, at the least.

IMAGINATION

The first two times I gave a talk on voice at writers' conferences, I included an exercise in which I performed a series of random actions and asked the audience to write a simple sentence describing what I was doing. I staged a variation of it on my blog in February 2010 (available at http://chavelaque.blogspot.com/2010/02/silly-specification-experiment.html), where I would have narrated my actions as "Cheryl blinked twice, put her hand to her head, turned to the right, tilted back to blow a kiss, then suddenly snarled at the screen." But my commenters' takes on it included:

+ She blinks and rests her palm on the back of her head; turning away, she blows a kiss before whipping back toward me with a frightening hiss.
+ Cheryl demonstrates the importance of having fresh breath before kissing.
+ A female actress tries to convince Tim Burton that she can be in any of his movies.
+ She blinks her eyes in an abbreviated Morse code signifying the start of her automated ultimate kiss-off, which fellow editors aspire to duplicate, and fearful writers dread worse than a blank page.
+ One-woman play in which the actor silently summarizes the entire "Twilight" series.
+ Cheryl is trying to think of a writing idea, finally comes up with one, blows a kiss to the off-camera music that provided the idea, and then demonstrates the demonic personality of the main character in the story she just thought of.
+ Ms. Klein reacts after reading Lisa Yee's latest manuscript. (from Lisa Yee herself)

My original thought in including this exercise in my voice talk had been that everyone would use essentially the same words in the sentences (because, I thought, there are only so many synonyms for "blinked"), but we'd all use different diction and syntax in describing them, and it would be fascinating to hear the variance from writer to writer. And once everyone had heard all the different ways one thing could be described, we could go on and talk about the different strengths of each approach, and which one was most appropriate for which kind of story.

So I was surprised — quite foolishly, in retrospect — the first time I did the talk, when, in a roomful of ten writers, only two of them specifically described the series of actions that I completed. Instead, the other eight created narratives that provided context for those actions: that I turned into a robot (since that sequence involved "boop-booping," rather than snarling), that there was something psychedelic in the tea I sipped. This sort of defeated the point of the exercise as I'd envisioned it, since all eight writers were in different narrative universes, each one equally valid but none of them particularly comparable. But that ended up being interesting in another way, for what it revealed about their individual imaginations and how they'd spin a world out of a scene.

When I did the exercise on my blog, quite a few people identified me as an editor and created narratives that involve my responding to manuscripts — which made perfect sense, of course, as most of my readers know me solely as an editor, and as such, my responding-to-manuscripts function might loom large in their brains. Many responses mentioned vampires, which is also understandable; I wonder if ten years ago, when the fanged ones weren't so omnipresent in pop culture, more would have described my final snarl as a wildcat's or a rabid dog's instead. A couple of people mentioned princesses, which I imagine reflects the children's literature world in which most of my readers live; writers for adults aren't usually so close to fairy tales. I intended this exercise to show the diction and syntax aspects of voice; instead, it highlighted which narrative directions an individual writer's brain might naturally run, and how he or she would apply those directions to a set of facts.

I am calling this natural directional inclination of a writer's brain as it plays out in the voice its Imagination, though I intend it less to apply to the book as a whole (what plot events or characters you can imagine, say) than to the interplay between the voice and its content. The imagination of a voice sets the range of subjects, images, diction, kinds of and examples of figurative language, and references that that voice can include. If you're writing a first-person voice with a six-year-old narrator, it is the limits of what that six-year-old could know — that he likely couldn't refer to "Titian hair," say, in describing a redheaded friend, or liken his first-grade teacher to Norman Bates in *Psycho* (unless, of course, you had a very particular six-year-old with very lax and/or overly cultured parents, which you'd have to show in the story to explain how he could make such references). But this six-year-old might also make some fresh new metaphor about something he's just discovering — the veins in leaves, say, or the swoop of a roller coaster — because those items would be wholly new to him in a way they wouldn't be new to an adult. (Look at the excerpt from *The Slightly True Story of Cedar B. Hartley* on p. 15 for examples of lovely child-world-centric similes.) A football-obsessed third-person limited-omniscient narrator might think of life in terms of a game, with quarters and downs and the goal line, and that might be reflected in the way she tells her story. The imagination of a Christian novel will include God and Jesus as authority figures, while a secular novel might think of them as totems; the imagination of a fantasy or adventure novel will be wider than that of a realistic domestic novel, because it can include magic, or dragons, or explosions, or secret government programs. To pretentiously quote Shakespeare for a moment, imagination is what is dreamt of in a voice's philosophy, and the limits on that dreaming.

Imagination can also be seen in anti-examples, which violate that range to achieve specific (often comedic) effects. *Pride and Prejudice and*

Zombies was a huge hit off its concept alone because it opened the imagination of Jane Austen's ironic, elegant narrative voice (and the Regency social world it portrays) to brains-hungry, bloodthirsty zombies. Every week, the *Onion* takes the straightforward, almost anodyne journalistic voice and visual style of *USA Today* and widens its imagination (its definition of news, really) to include mundane subjects like a woman taking out her familial frustrations on soap scum, or ridiculous ones like the National Funk Congress's deadlock over whether the nation should get up or get down. (I vote to get down.) Suppose you applied the imagination of a paranormal romance novel to a middle-grade school drama — what would that look like?

Image systems also grow out of the overall imagination of a voice. "Image systems" is a term taken from Laurie Halse Anderson, who gave an amazing talk about them at the Kindling Words conference in 2008. They are the physical embodiment of the objective correlative — actual physical objects or ideas in the text that symbolize the character or aspects of their journey.... albeit I hate using the word "symbols" because that makes them sound pretentious and separate from the action, and your goal is to make them real and integrated with it.

For instance, if you've read Ms. Anderson's own *Speak*, you know that trees are an important image system there: The story starts in winter, when everything is dead, and so is our narrator, inside. She's taking an art class, where she's assigned to the word "tree," and as a result, she draws them, sculpts them, and carves them in class. And as the story moves from winter to spring, she herself starts to bud out and regain leaf, metaphorically speaking.

In *The Hunger Games*, birds are very important: Birds can fly out of the Hunger Games arena, and Katniss can't, so they represent a freedom and escape that is denied her. She wears a brooch with a mockingjay on it as a reminder of her home district, but mockingjays are a genetically engineered bird that the Capitol created and then lost control of — and if you sense a metaphor there, you're right. In *Marcelo*, there's a reason that we put the treehouse on the front cover: We're told that Marcelo moved into the treehouse some years before to learn to be more independent, to test his strength in a safe location. But it's now turned from a place of challenge to a place of so much safety that he's isolated from the suffering, and beauty, of the world below. By the end of the novel, he's thinking of moving back into the house to rejoin his family and the messiness of the real world; and that perfectly characterizes his journey throughout the novel as a whole.

Image systems aren't essential to a novel. But they're ways of pulling character, plot, and theme together in one neat package, subtly providing unity and coherence and taking your writing to the next level.

Exercise: Once you've completed a first draft of your novel and taken some time off from it, sit back and think about it not as a conglomeration of words, but an accumulation of images, letting them drift through your mind. What picture comes immediately to mind when you think of the book? What objects are important to your main character? What does she love or work on? What emotional journeys or other metaphors might you make concrete? Write down all of these things and see if you can find resonances between those objects or images and the larger emotional or thematic ideas of your book. Perhaps there are ways you can integrate that key image, or images or ideas associated with it, throughout the whole text. Or perhaps you'll find you want to change one of those object elements to better reflect those themes.

Exercise II: One of my favorite writers in all of life, the romance novelist Jennifer Crusie, creates collages or dioramas for every book she works on. She collects objects and images in a box or a file, then moves them around in a frame until they achieve the right balance, finding new connections, motifs, backstory, and themes along the way. I've always thought this sounded like a wonderful way to let your inner visual artist or subconscious instincts (what Ms. Crusie calls the Girls in the

Basement) roam free, and especially to discover your image systems. She's written about this at http://www.jennycrusie.com/for-writers/ essays/picture-this-collage-as-prewriting-and-inspiration with instructions, and, with visuals, http://www.jennycrusie.com/more-stuff/book-collages.

The imagination of your voice will likely emerge naturally as you discover what kind of story you're telling and the narrator who's telling it. Don't worry too much about it in the first draft, but as you're revising, keep an eye on references that may be inappropriate for the imagination of your narrator, or alternatively, ways that you can push at those limits to further integrate the voice of your book with its content.

To think about: Can you list three mental preoccupations of the narrator of your book? What are three things, in contrast, that s/he would *never* think about (or to be more accurate, would never talk about, like graphic sex or dinosaurs in a Jane Austen novel)? What sets those limits for your narrator? What images or image systems are important to the book?

DETAILS

Details are the specific small things that make a story believable and therefore real. They might be things your characters notice (and the sorts of things a character notices characterize him for us in turn); they might be gestures they do or characteristic phrases they say; they might be the small sensual touches that make a setting come to life in the reader's mind. In the *Bobby* excerpt at [4], the pancake sliding slowly down the refrigerator door instantly sets up the air of cheerful domestic chaos that prevails in the Ellis-Chan household. In the *Hunger Games* excerpt at [11], Katniss's determination not to shut her eyes tells us everything we need to know about her fierceness and bravery. And in the *Marcelo* chapter quoted on p. 242, the lines following "I know how Arturo can switch from father to lawyer in an instant" provide many of the details that make those characters and their relationship real: They imply Marcelo's awareness of the way that people on the autism spectrum are generally treated; reinforce the distance with which Arturo sometimes treats his not-quite-of-the-real-world son (a distance we will see further here); and establish a whole history of this distance for these characters, which underlies the tension we see in the action of this scene.

Perhaps most importantly, all of these details echo what I as a reader know or can surmise from my real life outside of books: that pancakes aren't supposed to be on refrigerator doors, so the fact that one *is* there equals trouble; that force of will is sometimes the last weapon we have in the face of an enemy; the way that everyone (myself included) can change identities based on what we're saying or to whom we're speaking. And from all of that reality comes believability — that I can believe that, at the moment I'm reading that book, somewhere out in Southern California, Mr. Ellis-Chan's pancakes are going horribly wrong; in some hopefully far future version of America, Katniss is determined to watch her own coming death; and somewhere up in the Boston area, Marcelo and his father really had this discussion in their backyard. Getting a reader to believe in your fictional world is one of the holy grails of fiction, so details like these are immensely powerful in advancing that end.

(With that said, as with any element here, it's important not to go overboard on the details; when describing something, keep in mind the principles discussed in the Prosody section above about balancing Immediate, Atemporal, and Internal narration, then choose just a few important details, and make them count.)

To think about: Can you find at least three revealing details in each scene in your book?

If all of the Enemies I listed earlier are avoided and all of these aspects of voice are used well, so this is a voice I believe in, with sentence rhythms I appreciate, and grace in balancing its Atemporal, Immediate, and Internal narration, and so forth, then the voice moves from having just Personality into Authority for me. Authority is the feeling that I am in good hands, that I can trust the person who's telling me the story. I trust someone when I know they are telling me the honest truth, reality as they see it, and that truth they're telling resonates with the reality I know about human behavior and physical laws. And it comes from the surety that these are the right words, in a distinctive order, saying something interesting, and that they'll likely keep being interesting the whole book long. That surety gives the book a special energy, a straightforwardness, so I know I can relax into the story and trust the narrator to take me somewhere good.

Authority is probably the most important quality I look for in a narrative voice because it's the summation of so much else — reality, competence, interestingness; I'll read a whole book with a good Authoritative narrator even if I find the story flagging, just because I like spending time with him or her. And if you ever hear an editor say that they're looking for a really distinctive voice, truly what we mean is that we want a voice with Authority to grab us and carry us along.

So, with all of this established, we now have a formula where

$$\text{Voice} = \text{Person} + \text{Tense} + \text{Prosody} \\ + (\text{Diction} + \text{Syntax} + \text{Tone} + \text{Imagination} + \text{Details})$$

And for the last time: Each one of those things should be chosen to serve your thematic and emotional points. Of course, the fact that you'll probably discover said points as you write the book, using whatever voice might come to you at the beginning, means that some revision may be required afterward . . . and revising a voice is a huge pain, I admit, because in some cases, like changes of Person or Tense, it can require a second look at every line in the book. But once you get the right voice for the book — the right place to put the camera to bring out your characters, plot, and point at their fullest strength — everything else will lock into place. If the idea for your next book starts with a character or a plot concept, and not so much a voice that speaks to you from the beyond (as some writers are fortunate enough to experience), you might spend some time playing with different combinations of elements in the formula above, to find the voice that's most comfortable for you and right for the project altogether before you move forward.

That brings us to the end of this quartet of talks. I sometimes think of a good book as being like a car, where its four wheels each stand for character, plot, voice, and your points. One of those four probably will be the dominant wheel — the thing that first excited you about this book, and the ultimate reason this story is being told. But the closer you can get to all of the wheels being in balance, working together, moving in the same direction, the farther and faster your book can go.

Ultimately, your book will show you the strategies you need to write it as you write it. Experiment with things. Play with things. There is no one right way to write a book — only the way that works for you. My author Sara Lewis Holmes swears (and I've heard many other authors say this too) that the answer to any narrative problem is already in the manuscript. That is, when you get stuck, maybe put your book away for a few days, and then go back and reread with fresh eyes. What details do you notice that you can expand on? What character traits might be elucidated further or could resonate unexpectedly in a certain scene or in combination with a different character? What image systems are already spinning away? What plot developments do you love? The seeds are already there. Have faith in them, feed them, and let them grow.

TWENTY-FIVE
REVISION TECHNIQUES

I wrote the original version of this talk for the Southern Breeze SCBWI in February of 2010. This revised (ha) text draws on nearly all the talks from earlier in this book.

Vision

When I talk to writers about how they revise, I sometimes think the key syllable they hear there is "vise" — as in a large set of pincers that will slowly crush their spirits, their souls, and the life out of their work. But the word "revise" actually comes from the Latin *revisare* or *revidare*: literally, "to visit again" or "to see again." And I believe the revision process should indeed start with *seeing again*: taking a step back to recharge your creative batteries on the project, moving your brain away from solving the practical problems of getting your hero to the climax or perfecting that last phrase, toward the larger questions of what this book is and what you want it to be. Here I suggest some techniques through which writers can hopefully consider their work with fresh eyes, and then revise, if not in comfort, then at least with less of a sense of impending death by simple machine.

1. Know how you work best. Some authors would utterly loathe "taking time off from the project," as advised in point #2; they thrive on momentum and the energy of creation and need to dive right into a revision. That's GREAT! Not all of the techniques suggested here will work for everyone, and if you already know your revision style, please ignore all the ones that don't work for you.

2. Take time off from the project. Give yourself a minimum of two days and a maximum of two months away from the book, and try to think about something else in that time. Go on vacation; read an adult book you've been anticipating; if you can't stand being away from the computer, try writing something in a completely different genre or mode from the manuscript you just completed. The point is, you want to have some time to defamiliarize yourself with the work so you can read it with fresh eyes, as ultimately a reader will, and consider its strengths and weaknesses, as said reader might.

3. **Before you look at the manuscript again, write a letter to a sympathetic friend saying:**
> a. **What you wanted to do with the book, and/or wanted the book to do**
> b. **What the story is, briefly**
> c. **What the book is "about" in a larger sense**
> d. **What you love about it**
> e. **What you suspect needs some work**

The identity of this "sympathetic friend" isn't important, and you don't have to actually pass the letter on to him or her (though it can be very useful, especially if s/he is willing to read the manuscript as well and discuss it with you). The point of this exercise is just to set out your vision for the book for someone who would be interested in your writing and its aims. I often ask my writers to complete this task for me before I dive into the editing, and it's often tremendously useful in elucidating what the writer wants to do with the book and what directions we should explore in the editing.

4. **Compressing 3(b), write the story in one sentence.** For more on this, see p. 84 in "The Art of Detection" earlier in this book.

5. **Expanding off 3(b), write the flap copy.** See p. 85 in "The Art of Detection."

6. **Fun stuff:**
> a. **Make a collage.** See the second Exercise on p. 288.
> b. **Make a playlist.** Go to your iTunes (or whatever music software you use) and assemble a playlist (a) reflecting

the emotional journey of your protagonist, or (b) with a theme song for each main character, or (c) with a song for the dominant emotion of each chapter or scene. Listening to these songs might help you key back into the emotion you intend for that scene during revision, or turn up new connections as you figure out why you chose that song for that character or point in time.

c. **Look at your word frequency using http://www. writewords.org.uk/word count.asp.** Paste the entire text of your manuscript into the text box there, hit "submit," and look at the results. Once you eliminate pronouns, prepositions, conjunctions, articles, and proper nouns from the list, are there any surprises in your top one hundred or so words? Those might show a hidden theme, image, or idea lurking in your text that you can expand on in the revision.

Examination

Here we set aside all the vision work we did above for the moment and take a hard look at the manuscript as it stands. Note that many of the exercises in #10-15 are redundant with each other, and deliberately so: Some writers are energized by working on character, some by plotting, some by pacing, so I wanted to provide methods that appealed to each constituency. However, if you actually performed all of them on the same novel, I would suspect you of putting off the hard work of diving into actual revisions in favor of the (comparatively) more fun work of highlighting and making charts. . . . Remember these sorts of examination techniques are a means to an end, not the end itself.

7. **Change the font, then print out and reread the entire manuscript on the page before making any revisions.** I really want to emphasize "on the page" here. Books read differently on computer screens than they do on paper, and as a majority of your readers (at present) will be reading

on paper, it's important that you have that same experience in reading your work.

8. As you read, take notes on both the good and bad stuff. Resist the urge to start revising the actual writing right now; your goal at this stage is to see how the big stuff you envisioned in #3 above — the ideas, the story, what it's all about — accords with what is actually on the page. Record new ideas, large plot points you want to revisit, things that need work. Do not fail to write down things you love and pat yourself on the back for things you did well.

9. Identify the turning points in both your Action and Emotional Plots. These are the major, major Escalating or Complicating Events that change the direction of the action or your protagonist's approach to it.

10. Picture book writers: Put your text into a thirty-two-page framework and/or thumbnails or a dummy. See p. 149 of "Words, Wisdom, Art, and Heart."

11. Novelists: Book map (outline) the action of the book chapter by chapter / scene by scene. See p. 88-89 of "The Art of Detection" and Anita Nolan's excellent essay at http://www.anitanolan.com/theend.html.

12. On your bookmap (or multiple copies of the bookmap):

    a. Highlight the events of each Action Plot or subplot in a different color. This is especially useful if you're juggling a lot of small relationship plots, as in many middle-grade novels, or large Action Plots, as in high fantasy. Does the color for the thorough-line of your main plot appear in every chapter? Do any colors disappear for a long period of time, or clump up where they should be more evenly distributed?

    b. Underline the key events of your Emotional Plot. What specific events cause your character's change or growth?

When you read through just those underlined events, can you see an arc connecting them?

13. Chart Plotting: Three Methods

    a. **Make a chart listing each significant character, his or her identity at the outset, his or her desire or goal at the outset (conscious or unconscious), the perceived reward for the goal, the obstacles in the way, the action he or she takes to achieve the goal, and the actual results and how the reader feels about them.** Like the Plot Checklist below, this is an easy way to map out what actually happens in your book and identify where you might be lacking stakes (the reward), motivations (the goal), complications (obstacles and action), or conclusions (results).

    b. **Make a table with each plot or subplot in the columns on top and the chapter numbers in the rows down the side. Write in what happens in each plot in every chapter.** #12a is probably more useful for character-driven novels; this one is more useful for heavily plotted novels, as it helps you get a visual read on the questions asked in #11a above.

    c. **Try Spreadsheet Plotting.** The writer and writing coach Darcy Pattison explains this technique on her website at http://www.darcypattison.com/revision/spreadsheet-plotting/ It is very much like a combination of Anita Nolan's vision of bookmaps and #12b.

14. **Try Darcy Pattison's Shrunken Manuscript technique.** In this method, you single-space the text of your book and set it in very small type, so the manuscript is only about thirty pages altogether, and then highlight the strongest chapters (or anything else you want to track) for a visual map of your book. You can see instructions for it at http://www.darcypattison.com/revision/shrunken-manuscript/.

15. Run the Plot Checklist. See p. 93-94 and http://www.cherylklein.com/plotchecklist.html.

16. Make a Mini Map. For each spread or scene, write a one-sentence summary of the action and then identify its climax/point. If you can't identify a point in a scene, note that for later: You may need to revise the scene to make that point more evident, or you might be able to cut the scene altogether. If the same point is made in multiple scenes, consider deleting one of them. Ultimately, you should be able to read through just this list and have a fairly accurate arc of your book. If a logical or emotional point seems to be missing from that list, then you may need to add a new scene; if a point seems to be out of order, you might need to rejigger the order of the action.

17. List the first ten things each significant character says or does. See p. 84 of "The Art of Detection."

18. Take a second look at what you created for steps #3-6 above and compare the results to what you discovered in exercises #8-16. Based on this analysis, **compile a To-Do list of things you want to accomplish in a revision.** This To-Do list will prove extremely useful in keeping track of your larger goals as you work through the minutiae of revising.

Action

Here we sit down to apply everything we discovered above to the manuscript itself.

19. Remember you don't have to do everything at once, but all spot changes should resonate in the whole. If you're a person who works best by starting with the first word of Chapter One and revising holistically from there, more power to you. Other writers may want to take it "bird by bird," to use Anne Lamott's lovely phrase, and address one item on the To-Do list at a time. As in #1, go with what works best for you.

Remember that the ultimate goal of revising is not to complete every item on the To-Do list, but to have a stronger manuscript when you're done, one that integrates all the elements of fiction into a satisfying whole. To that end, keep an eye on how each spot revision affects the entire novel, and be sure to give yourself time away from the manuscript occasionally so you can reread the revisions with fresh eyes and see how the new elements are growing into the original framework.

20. Set a deadline for completing each stage of revision, and a reward for each one. It is very, very easy to get bogged down in the weeds of a revision, so give yourself an end date for completing a new draft or a certain number of pages or items on the To-Do list (just before a vacation is always good). Better still, tell a friend or writing partner about this deadline and ask them to keep you responsible to it — either that they'll check in with you occasionally about your progress, or they'll take the manuscript away from you on that date so you can't fiddle with it any further, forcing you on to the next stage in the revision or submission process. Do be kind to yourself in the course of the revision, and even generous after you reach your goal: Writing is hard work, and you deserve recognition and relaxation for completing that work.

21. Work large to small. Prioritize your To-Do list from #18 so you take care of the most wide-reaching stuff first. It is no good getting the dialogue pitch-perfect in a scene at one stage if you discover you need to delete the scene later.

22. Once you're reasonably satisfied you have the big stuff where it needs to be:

> a. **Cut as many adverbs, telling uses of the word "feel" or "felt," non-"said" dialogue tags, and unhelpful "babies" as you possibly can.** By "unhelpful 'babies,'" I'm referring to the famous writing dictum "Kill your babies" — that is, "eliminate anything you love and are especially proud of." I think this aphorism often needs to be taken with a grain of salt, as I've heard writers say things like "I really love this. That means I should cut it, right?" No: Babies should

die only if they're getting in the way of your larger points or ends. If they serve those ends, please let them live, as the odds are good then that your readers will love them too.

b. **Check the balance among Atemporal, Immediate, and Internal narration, especially in dialogue scenes.** See p. 269-274.

c. **Highlight each character's dialogue in a different color, then read through each color in turn.** Does each character speak in a distinctive voice, register, or language? Do any two characters sound too much like each other, or like the narrative voice?

d. **Look at establishing shots, topic sentences, and conclusions.** Establishing shots are discussed on p. 268 and topic sentences and conclusions on p. 267 and 268.

e. **Check the first line of the book for its hook, and the last lines of every scene and chapter for emotional resonance.** See notes on scene-ending fermatas on p. 247.

23. **Read the book aloud.** If you're a picture-book writer, you absolutely MUST read the text aloud every single time you complete a new draft; and for novelists, there's no better way to discover repetitions or feel the actual pacing of a scene. It's even more useful to have someone read your work to you; writing partners might perform this service for each other, you can record your own voice and then play it back, or you can find applications online that will convert your text to speech, which leaves you free to read along on the page and take notes about what you're hearing.

24. **Keep a copy of everything.** Save every complete new draft in a new file, and then save that file to a USB drive or e-mail it to a free online e-mail account set up especially for this purpose, so you always have backup of all the work you've completed. You can do this every day if you're especially concerned about losing your files.

25. Don't let the perfect be the enemy of the good. The truth is, once you complete this revision and reread it, you may need to make further revisions after that; and once you submit the manuscript to your writing group, agent, or editor, *they* will likely ask you to make more revisions still. Thus, trying to get it "perfect" is ultimately a waste of time. Take the manuscript as far as you can; celebrate your accomplishment in finishing the draft; and let it find its way.

ON THE EDITOR-AUTHOR
RELATIONSHIP

March 11, 2008

In January, Jon asked:

> *Anyway, I have a request that maybe you'd consider someday [and, no,
> it's not that you read my book :)] I would very much like to hear your
> thoughts on the author/editor relationship. Where are the boundaries?
> What is the best strategy to build a good relationship with your editor?
> How does an editor best serve an author, and likewise? I know you're
> posting the stories behind some of your books, and you linked to that
> Raymond Carver article . . . so I'd also be interested to hear your perspec-
> tive on this. I think sometimes people don't appreciate what editors bring
> to the table, in terms of their sheer contribution to a finished novel, and
> sometimes authors get hurt/pushy/angry/insulted/wounded by their
> interactions with editors, whom they see as controlling their very futures.
> But the best editor/author relationships result in magic . . .*

In "Finding a Publisher and Falling in Love," I wrote that if I like
a manuscript and its author, we'll "get married: That is, we'll sign a
contract for the manuscript, edit it and publish it, and hopefully have
lots of beautiful books together." The metaphor works in the context of
that talk, which is all about how the submissions process is like dating,
but something about it has always made me vaguely uneasy. It is that,
unlike a marriage, and especially unlike parenthood, my authors and
I are not equal partners and contributors to the relationship. *They* are
the people setting up an imaginary house in the world, they're the ones
conceiving and birthing these ideas; I'm the interior decorator who steps
in to help with the draperies, or the kindergarten teacher teaching the

kid to tie her shoes. From an artistic perspective (the artistic part being my favorite part of my job), my work doesn't exist without the work these authors do, and the "marriage" metaphor made me uncomfortable just because it didn't acknowledge that essential disparity.

But just recently I hit on what I think is the proper relationship metaphor for my work with my lovely authors, and it actually grew out of some fun conversations with several of those authors, particularly Olugbemisola Rhuday-Perkovich and Lisa Yee. They both came to Scholastic to discuss their novels sometime in the last two months; we went out to lunch, and then we came back to the office to get down to work, dissecting the plot structures (lord, how I love plot structure), talking about backstories and future courses of action for all the characters, rehashing our favorite moments and scenes. I love, love, love afternoons like this, even more than plot structure, because it feels basically like gossiping about our mutual friends, the characters — and better yet, the friends *have to do what we say.*

Then, based upon that thought about gossip, it came to me: This is exactly the way I relate to my friends when we discuss our love lives. We go through the overall narrative. We zoom in on moments that seem telling and what they could mean to the full story. We debate the consequences of various possible courses of action, we try to come to a conclusion about what action should be taken next — and then, of course, we can't wait to hear about the results. Every single friendship and conversation is different, based upon our shared history, my knowledge of my friend's past relationship history (and my friend's knowledge of mine), where we each are emotionally when we're talking, and our mutual knowledge of how honest we can be. Through all our discussions, I try to listen carefully for what my friends really want, what they really feel, and reflect that back to them; and I advise them based upon my own experience, both personal and learned. But any decisions are, in the end, my friends' and not mine to make.

And so it goes with editorial-authorial relationships. Every single one is different, and it is my job, as a good friend and editor, to adapt to what the author and the book needs, not to go imposing my vision on them. I ask lots of questions to try to suss out what the author wants the book to be, if that isn't clear to me, or to help them formulate a vision themselves; I try to listen carefully to what both book and author are saying — as they're sometimes different things, and then I need to help them try to resolve that discrepancy. I offer advice based on my personal reaction to events in the book; my knowledge of How Books Work, encompassing everything from characterizations to pacing to structure to sentence flow; and my long, long experience as a reader and my ever-growing experience as an editor. Just like my personal friend-ships, I tailor the manner in which this advice is given to each individual author, based upon our history together, the comfort level of our rela-tionship, and my understanding of what will speak best and deepest to that author, and most to what he or she is trying to do. Finally, I try to be as honest as I can about the book and what it needs, but to do so in a way that will make the author feel energized and excited about making the revisions, not depressed and beaten down.

Because, again, all the decisions are the authors' to make in the end: I am just a friend to them and their books, not the one living those lives. I do hope very much that they take my advice, because I try to make it good advice, with both their best interests and the interests of their readers at heart. (Another way I think of my job is as the readers' advo-cate: "Could I have more detail about what he's thinking, please?" "Could you show us this scene?" "This paragraph of description doesn't really seem relevant — could we cut this to pick up the pace?") If the authors *don't* take that advice, I really hope they have a good reason for it, and that we can talk that out. . . . Sometimes I haven't been listening prop-erly, or the author didn't understand my meaning properly, and then it's a matter of resolving the miscommunication; and sometimes I just have to accept the author and I don't see eye-to-eye. But at the end of the day, it is my authors' names on the books, not mine, their happy endings to pursue. My job is only to speed them on their way.

So, Jon, to answer your questions about boundaries and suchlike: I think both sides are wise to learn as much as possible about each other's tastes and visions before making a commitment to publish a book together. *Can* you be friends? Do you have a shared sense of fictional values, and what the right values are for this project — what needs work, what direction the book should take? And then both sides have the responsibility to bring their best to the manuscript, emotionally, mentally, everything; to be as honest and clear as we can be, and as grown-up and unselfish as well in accepting those honest judgments and working to fix the problems.

I am still learning — both how to edit and how to work with authors. Every book teaches me something new. I am grateful every day for this job and the marvelous authors I work with; and grateful, too, that they put up with my endless kibitzing about structure and detail. Like all my friends, sometimes they listen to me and sometimes they roll their eyes. But they know (I hope they know, anyway) that it's done in a spirit of love for them and their books and the truths they tell; and those truths are the most important thing for all of us to convey.

Thus endeth my testament.

Please visit

http://www.cherylklein.com/moresight.html

for links to additional talks and blog posts on writing,

more recommended reading,

and Cheryl's Highly Idiosyncratic

Guide to Punctuation.

RECOMMENDED READING:
Craft & Publishing

Some books I've found useful and instructive:

Theory

• *The Poetics* by Aristotle – Probably the most important piece of literary criticism ever, and the theoretical basis for Freytag's Triangle and many of the plot ideas in this book.

• *The Wave in the Mind* by Ursula K. LeGuin – This woman couldn't write an unintelligent, unlovely word if she tried.

• *The Sound on the Page* by Ben Yagoda – A fascinating discussion of voice as it's practiced by many writers across all genres.

• *Writing Changes Everything* collected by Deborah Brodie – An anthology of quotations about the writing, revising, editing, and publication processes.

Practice

• *Bird by Bird: Some Instructions on Writing and Life* by Anne Lamott – For inspiration, getting started, philosophy, and reassurance, and also the humor and pleasure of her voice.

• *Characters and Viewpoint* by Orson Scott Card – This is the single best book on writing fiction I think I have ever read — a terrifically lucid and useful guide to figuring out the type of story you're writing, crafting characters with depth and individuality, and creating the right voice to reveal it all.

• *On Writing* by Stephen King – The second half features a terrific discussion of the tools in a fiction writer's toolbox and how they can best be put to use.

• *The Elements of Style* by William Strunk and E. B. White – Still the definitive guide to writing elegant, concise prose. Maira Kalman's illustrated edition of it is a joy.

• *The Forest for the Trees: An Editor's Advice to Writers* by Betsy Lerner – A former editor and present agent offers a commonsense guide through the publication process.

• *The Fiction Editor, the Novel, and the Novelist* by Thomas McCormack – A highly technical but very insightful handbook for editing fiction, returning always to the basic principles of "who is this character, what do they want, how is that shown in the action," by a former editor-in-chief of St. Martin's Press.

• *Making Shapely Fiction* by Jerome Stern – A pleasantly readable and practical reference on the shapes of various kinds of stories, as well as common literary terms, forms, and situations.

• *The Artful Edit: On the Practice of Editing Yourself* by Susan Bell – A fascinating history of editing, in particular the editorial process of *The Great Gatsby*, with many useful tips for applying larger editorial principles to your own work.

Children's/YA Specific

• *Dear Genius: The Letters of Ursula Nordstrom* by Ursula Nordstrom, edited by Leonard Marcus – Ursula Nordstrom edited *Where the Wild Things Are*, *Charlotte's Web*, and *Harriet the Spy*, among hundreds of other terrific books, and her letters to her writers are brilliant, insightful, educational, and just huge fun.

• *Dreams and Wishes* by Susan Cooper – A wonderful collection of essays and lectures on children's literature, especially fantasy.

• *Writing with Pictures* by Uri Shulevitz – An absolutely essential book for aspiring creators of picture books.

• *Picture This: How Pictures Work* by Molly Bang – A succinct and stylish guide to the hows and whys of composing an image, especially for illustration.

• *Children's Writer's Word Book* by Alijandra Mogliner – A useful reference for finding the right vocabulary words and story concepts at each age/reading level.

• *The Complete Idiot's Guide to Publishing Children's Books* by Harold Underdown – A smart and thorough overview of the entire writing, submitting, and publishing process, written by one of the nicest guys in the biz.

• *The Children's Writers and Illustrators Market* edited by Alice Pope – A submissions guide for nearly all children's publishers, accompanied by useful essays from a wide range of writers and editors.

INDEX TO ALL MATERIAL
BY *SUBJECT*

ACKNOWLEDGEMENTS
AND THANKS

I owe enormous debts to the following people:

Arthur A. Levine, for a great initial opportunity and a marvelous editorial education; Zehava Cohn, who taught me about emotional completeness and the dangers of too many "that"s; James Monohan, for narrative brainstorming, emotional reassurance, and overall support; my lovely friends Melissa Anelli, Kathryne Beebe, Emily Clement, Donna Freitas, Rachel Griffiths, Jill Santopolo, and Ted Salk, who listened and cheered at various points in the process; April's friend Matt, for telling me about Kickstarter at a random summer picnic in Prospect Park; my parents, Alan and Becky Klein, and sister and brother-in-law, Melissa and Joe Jackson; all of the SCBWI and other conference coordinators who have given me the chance to speak over the years, and inspired me to investigate these subjects in depth; the child_lit listserv, for the same; the good people of Kindling Words East in 2008 and the Vermont College Novel Writers' Retreat in 2009, particularly Laurie Halse Anderson, Kathi Appelt, and Elise Broach; Caroline Meckler for *Voice Lessons*; Loy Markley of Raymore-Peculiar High School and Susan Jaret McKinstry, Vern Bailey, Owen Jenkins, and Connie Walker of Carleton College, for encouraging my writing and teaching me about narrative and moral development and plot structure; my dear writers and illustrators, every one of whom has educated me in the crafts of editing and writing, and especially the three kind enough to grant permission for their original material to be used in this book—Olugbemisola Rhuday-Perkovich, Francisco X. Stork, and Lisa Yee; Whitney Lyle, for excellent design and putting up with all my changes (including this one); my blog readers and commenters, who let me know I'm not speaking into the void; and anyone who ever wrote to thank me for material posted on my website, which encouraged me to keep thinking and working on these topics.

This book is dedicated to the memory of my maternal grandparents: my grandfather, Philip Sadler, who instilled in me a love of children's literature and an enormous respect for writers and illustrators; and my grandmother, Carol Sadler, with whom I spent many wonderful weekends doing nothing but reading. They are both very much missed.

Finally, this book would not exist without the generous donations and encouragement of the people who participated in the Kickstarter fundraising process, including:

Genetta Adair

Christine Bernardi

Jen Cohen

Karen Cushman

Samantha Ethier

Elizabeth Parker Garcia

Kiki Hamilton

Dave H.

Greg Holch

Sara Lewis Holmes

Glenn Johnson

Ena Jones

Carol and John Klein

Rebecca Klein

Elizabeth Langston

Sarah Darer Littman

James Monohan

Edna Cabcabin Moran

Natalie

Debbie Ridpath Ohi

Anne Speirs

Francisco X. Stork

Joan Stradling

Cindy Swanson

Pamela Witte

Sarah Y

My very great thanks to you all.

ABOUT THE AUTHOR

Cheryl B. Klein is the senior editor at Arthur A. Levine Books, an imprint of Scholastic Inc. Among the books she has edited or co-edited are *A Curse Dark as Gold* by Elizabeth C. Bunce, winner of the inaugural William C. Morris YA Debut Award; *Marcelo in the Real World* by Francisco X. Stork, winner of the Schneider Family Book Award for Teens; *Millicent Min, Girl Genius,* by Lisa Yee, winner of the Sid Fleischman Award for Humor; *Moribito: Guardian of the Spirit* by Nahoko Uehashi, translated by Cathy Hirano, winner of the Mildred L. Batchelder Award for Translation; *Moribito II: Guardian of the Darkness,* winner of a Batchelder Honor Award; and *The Snow Day* by Komako Sakai, a *New York Times* Best Illustrated Book. Cheryl has worked on translations from six different languages, and she also served as the continuity editor on the last two books of the Harry Potter series by J. K. Rowling.

Since 2005, she has maintained a blog about writing, life, books, and nonsense at http://chavelaque.blogspot.com, and a website for writers at http://www.cherylklein.com. The site was named one of Writers' Digest's 101 Best Websites for Writers in 2010. For a complete list of books she has edited, please see her website at http://www.cherylklein.com/books.html.